Rooted in Belonging

Critical Place-Based Learning in Early Childhood and Elementary Teacher Education

Melissa Sherfinski *with* Sharon Hayes

Foreword by Christopher P. Brown

TEACHERS COLLEGE PRESS
TEACHERS COLLEGE | COLUMBIA UNIVERSITY
NEW YORK AND LONDON

Published by Teachers College Press,® 1234 Amsterdam Avenue, New York, NY 10027

Copyright © 2023 by Teachers College, Columbia University

Front cover design by Holly Grundon / BHG Graphics. Photo by PeopleImages / iStock by Getty Images.

All rights reserved. No part of this publication may be reproduced or transmitted in any form or by any means, electronic or mechanical, including photocopy, or any information storage and retrieval system, without permission from the publisher. For reprint permission and other subsidiary rights requests, please contact Teachers College Press, Rights Dept.: tcpressrights@tc.columbia.edu

Library of Congress Cataloging-in-Publication Data

Names: Sherfinski, Melissa, author.
Title: Rooted in belonging : critical place-based learning in early childhood and elementary teacher education / Melissa Sherfinski with Sharon Hayes ; Foreword by Christopher P. Brown.
Description: New York, NY : Teachers College Press, [2023] | Series: Early childhood education series | Includes bibliographical references and index.
Identifiers: LCCN 2022047032 (print) | LCCN 2022047033 (ebook) | ISBN 9780807768235 (hardcover) | ISBN 9780807768228 (paperback) | ISBN 9780807781661 (epub)
Subjects: LCSH: Early childhood teachers—Training of. | Elementary school teachers—Training of. | Portfolios in education. | Inquiry-based learning.
Classification: LCC LB2157.A3 S54 2023 (print) | LCC LB2157.A3 (ebook) | DDC 370.71/1—dc23/eng/20221110
LC record available at https://lccn.loc.gov/2022047032
LC ebook record available at https://lccn.loc.gov/2022047033

ISBN 978-0-8077-6822-8 (paper)
ISBN 978-0-8077-6823-5 (hardcover)
ISBN 978-0-8077-8166-1 (ebook)

Printed on acid-free paper
Manufactured in the United States of America

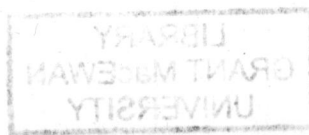

Contents

Foreword *Christopher P. Brown*	ix
Acknowledgments	xiii
Introduction	1
"The Bubble"	2
Place-Based Education and Its Potential	4
A Dynamic Charge for Teacher Education	5
Chapter Summaries	5
1. The Need for Place-Based Teacher Education	7
Contexts for the Book	7
Three Challenges Connecting the Places	9
Why We Need Place-Based Teacher Education	11
Neoliberal Challenges to Place-Based Teacher Education	13
Reclaiming Accountability	16
Challenges of Reclaiming Accountability	18
Questions for Reflection and Discussion	20
What's Next?	20
2. Theoretical Framework	21
The Nature of Meaning-Making	21
Three Approaches to Place-Based Education	22
Humanizing Place-Based Education in School Classrooms	23
Place-Based Teacher Education	29

	Negotiation: Sensing and Resisting Neoliberal Policies	32
	Questions for Reflection and Discussion	37
	What's Next?	37
3.	**The Narrative Portfolio Project**	**38**
	Context of the Teacher Education Program	38
	The Narrative Portfolio as a Counter-Narrative to Failure	44
	Questions for Reflection and Discussion	56
	What's Next?	56
4.	**Resisting Neoliberalism Through Place-Based Narrative Portfolio Work**	**57**
	Getting Lost in Places	58
	Vignette 1. Critical Reflection on Place	61
	Vignette 2. Dialogism With Place in Mind	65
	Vignette 3. Transforming I-It to I-You	71
	Vignette 4. Diffraction: Bending Around Barriers	75
	Conclusion	80
	Questions for Reflection and Discussion	81
	What's Next?	81
5.	**Pairing Our Place-Based Approach With Racial Justice**	**82**
	Antiracist Education	83
	COVID-19 and Antiracist Teaching	87
	Place-Based Education Post-Graduation	99
	Conclusion	105
	Questions for Reflection and Discussion	106
	What's Next?	106
6.	**Practice and Policy Implications**	**107**
	Teacher Education Program Assessment in the "Cluster"	108
	Transforming Teacher Education Assessment	112

Contents

The Change Process	114
Suggestions for Practice	118
Conclusion	123
Questions for Reflection and Discussion	123
What's Next?	123

Appendix A. Methodology: Capturing Meanings of Place-Based Education and Assessment — 125

Background for the Study	125
Method	125

Appendix B. Lenses of Teacher Education and Revised "10 Characteristics of the Novice Teacher" for PDS Mentors and Faculty Professional Development — 133

Appendix C. A Portrait of Becoming — 137

Our Places	138
Learners and Teachers	139
Beginning the Year: Looking and Seeing as an Ethnographer	139
Exploring the Literature: Disrupting the Commonplaces	140
Our Journey	141
Our Learning	141
A Reflective Pause With an Eye to the Future	142
Final Thoughts	143

Appendix D. Destiny's Book Club: *Stamped* by Reynolds & Kendi (2020) (Abbreviated Version) — 145

References — 147

Index — 163

About the Authors — 175

Foreword

The fields of teaching and teacher education across the globe have been and continue to be in a state of crisis (Brown et al., 2021). Teachers are leaving the field in large numbers and fewer students are enrolling in teacher education programs. While the COVID-19 pandemic exacerbated this exodus, it is mostly the result of neoliberal reforms that seek to privatize public education and teacher education (see, e.g., Dunn et al., 2017) while reinforcing a settler-colonial White framing of governance and racial capital (Nxumalo, 2021; Tuck & Yang, 2012).

This is why *Rooted in Belonging: Critical Place-Based Learning in Early Childhood and Elementary Teacher Education* by Dr. Melissa Sherfinski is so important. In it, Melissa provides a detailed examination into her path (not *the* path) forward so that both preservice teachers and teacher educators can begin to resist policymakers' neoliberal reforms and chart their own courses forward.

Throughout this book, Melissa provides detailed insight into how she has sought to pop what she terms the neoliberal bubble of conventional teaching and teacher education, where teaching is framed by ideas of accumulation, Whiteness, settler colonialism, and racial capital, by implementing a place-based teacher education program. For Melissa, place-based teacher education, which roots instruction in the place in which it occurs rather than in a standardized vision of teaching and learning, seeks to empower preservice teachers to view their engagement as professionals within their school communities as a part of the larger democratic project of working toward racial and economic justice.

Melissa's book is so important because it exemplifies Cochran-Smith's (1991) argument that "teaching is fundamentally a political activity in which every teacher plays a part" (p. 280). Essentially, Melissa and her colleagues strive to create a teacher education program that places the principle of teaching as a political act at its core, creating the space for preservice teachers to recognize the impact of policymakers' neoliberal reforms on the schooling process while they learn how to engage in instructional practices that can create democratic learning communities (Brown et al., 2022).

In saying this, I recognize that Melissa's work takes place in the primarily White, rural, conservative communities of West Virginia, which creates the opportunity for some readers to dismiss its impact easily. I hope this is not you. The lives and histories that exist in West Virginia contain many of the same challenges and schooling experiences that I have experienced as an early childhood teacher and teacher educator in Maryland, New Mexico, Tennessee, Virginia, Wisconsin, and Wyoming. My point is that the worlds Melissa examines, which exist in communities of Whiteness, racial capital, and settler colonialism, demonstrate that change is possible even in the face of what appears neverending neoliberal reform.

By providing a counterexample of teacher education, Melissa illustrates how she and her colleagues enacted a version of place-based teacher education that sought to empower preservice teachers with the knowledge and skills needed to address local social justice issues through research and leadership. In doing so, Melissa recognizes the limitations of her identities, positionalities, and connections to the contexts in which she inhabits and the ideas she puts forward. Still, her work demonstrates how teacher educators can assist preservice teachers in coming to understand and recognize their interconnectivity with the natural world. She offers illustrations of how these teachers-in-training included such insight into their teaching. In doing so, Melissa provides real-life examples of how these preservice teachers strove to incorporate rather than erase people among whom they live during their field placements. Each of these instances provides touchstones for teacher educators, teachers, and teachers-in-training to consider how they might alter their practices to address the political and personal issues that exist within the places that they live.

What I also appreciate about this book is that Melissa also sought to reclaim issues of accountability within her program through a narrative portfolio project that asks preservice teachers to use the placed-based tools in their local school communities. These powerful assessment experiences have the potential to inform the next generation of teachers of alternatives that exist in contrast to standardized testing. Melissa's work on this and other issues in her teacher education program demonstrates what teacher educators can do to support the next generation of early childhood and elementary school teachers.

I hope that by reading this book you will see new spaces within your own work where you can resist, refuse, and reform policymakers' continued neoliberal onslaught on teaching and teacher education.

—Christopher P. Brown, PhD

REFERENCES

Brown, C. P., Barry, D., & Ku, D. (2021). Refusing policymakers' manufactured crisis: Countering conceptions of school readiness. In G. S. Cannella & T. A. Kinard (Eds.), *Childhoods and more just worlds: An international handbook* (pp. 103–119). Myers Education Press.

EARLY CHILDHOOD EDUCATION SERIES
NANCY FILE & CHRISTOPHER P. BROWN, EDITORS
ADVISORY BOARD: Jie-Qi Chen, Cristina Gillanders, Jacqueline Jones,
Kristen M. Kemple, Candace R. Kuby, John Nimmo,
Amy Noelle Parks, Michelle Salazar Pérez, Andrew J. Stremmel, Valora Washington

Rooted in Belonging:
Critical Place-Based Learning in Early Childhood and Elementary Teacher Education
MELISSA SHERFINSKI WITH SHARON HAYES

Transforming Early Years Policy in the U.S.:
A Call to Action
MARK K. NAGASAWA, LACEY PETERS,
MARIANNE N. BLOCH, & BETH BLUE SWADENER, EDS.

Music Therapy With Preschool Children on the Autism Spectrum: Moments of Meeting
GEOFF BARNES

On Being and Well-Being in Infant/Toddler Care and Education: Life Stories From Baby Rooms
MARY BENSON MCMULLEN

Principals as Early Learning Leaders: Effectively Supporting Our Youngest Learners
JULIE NICHOLSON, HELEN MANIATES, SERENE YEE, THOMAS WILLIAMS JR., VERONICA UFOEGBUNE, & RAUL ERAZO-CHAVEZ

Resisting the Kinder-Race:
Restoring Joy to Early Learning
CHRISTOPHER P. BROWN

Reshaping Universal Preschool:
Critical Perspectives on Power and Policy
LUCINDA GRACE HEIMER & ANN ELIZABETH RAMMINGER, WITH KATHERINE K. DELANEY, SARAH GALANTER-GUZIEWSKI, LACEY PETERS, & KRISTIN WHYTE

Pre-K Stories: Playing with Authorship and Integrating Curriculum in Early Childhood
DANA FRANTZ BENTLEY & MARIANA SOUTO-MANNING

Ready or Not: Early Care and Education's Leadership Choices—12 Years Later, 2nd Ed.
STACIE G. GOFFIN & VALORA WASHINGTON

Teaching STEM in the Preschool Classroom:
Exploring Big Ideas with 3- to 5-Year-Olds
ALISSA A. LANGE, KIMBERLY BRENNEMAN, & HAGIT MANO

High-Quality Early Learning for a Changing World:
What Educators Need to Know and Do
BEVERLY FALK

Guiding Principles for the New Early Childhood Professional: Building on Strength and Competence
VALORA WASHINGTON & BRENDA GADSON

Leading for Change in Early Care and Education:
Cultivating Leadership from Within
ANNE L. DOUGLASS

When Pre-K Comes to School: Policy, Partnerships, and the Early Childhood Education Workforce
BETHANY WILINSKI

Young Investigators: The Project Approach in the Early Years, 3rd Ed.
JUDY HARRIS HELM & LILIAN G. KATZ

Continuity in Children's Worlds: Choices and Consequences for Early Childhood Settings
MELISSA M. JOZWIAK, BETSY J. CAHILL, & RACHEL THEILHEIMER

The Early Intervention Guidebook for Families and Professionals: Partnering for Success, 2nd Ed.
BONNIE KEILTY

STEM Learning with Young Children:
Inquiry Teaching with Ramps and Pathways
SHELLY COUNSELL ET AL.

Courageous Leadership in Early Childhood Education: Taking a Stand for Social Justice
SUSI LONG, MARIANA SOUTO-MANNING, & VIVIAN MARIA VASQUEZ, EDS.

Teaching Kindergarten: Learner-Centered Classrooms for the 21st Century
JULIE DIAMOND, BETSY GROB, & FRETTA REITZES, EDS.

The New Early Childhood Professional:
A Step-by-Step Guide to Overcoming Goliath
VALORA WASHINGTON, BRENDA GADSON, & KATHRYN L. AMEL

Teaching and Learning in a Diverse World, 4th Ed.
PATRICIA G. RAMSEY

In the Spirit of the Studio: Learning from the *Atelier* of Reggio Emilia, 2nd Ed.
LELLA GANDINI ET AL., EDS.

Leading Anti-Bias Early Childhood Programs:
A Guide for Change
LOUISE DERMAN-SPARKS, DEBBIE LEEKEENAN, & JOHN NIMMO

To look for other titles in this series, visit www.tcpress.com

continued

Early Childhood Education Series, *continued*

Exploring Mathematics Through Play in the Early Childhood Classroom
AMY NOELLE PARKS

Becoming Young Thinkers
JUDY HARRIS HELM

The Early Years Matter
MARILOU HYSON & HEATHER BIGGAR TOMLINSON

Thinking Critically About Environments for Young Children
LISA P. KUH, ED.

Standing Up for Something Every Day
BEATRICE S. FENNIMORE

FirstSchool
SHARON RITCHIE & LAURA GUTMANN, EDS.

Early Childhood Education for a New Era
STACIE G. GOFFIN

Everyday Artists
DANA FRANTZ BENTLEY

Multicultural Teaching in the Early Childhood Classroom
MARIANA SOUTO-MANNING

Inclusion in the Early Childhood Classroom
SUSAN L. RECCHIA & YOON-JOO LEE

Moral Classrooms, Moral Children, 2nd Ed.
RHETA DEVRIES & BETTY ZAN

Defending Childhood
BEVERLY FALK, ED.

Starting with Their Strengths
DEBORAH C. LICKEY & DENISE J. POWERS

The Play's the Thing
ELIZABETH JONES & GRETCHEN REYNOLDS

Twelve Best Practices for Early Childhood Education
ANN LEWIN-BENHAM

Big Science for Growing Minds
JACQUELINE GRENNON BROOKS

What If All the Kids Are White? 2nd Ed.
LOUISE DERMAN-SPARKS & PATRICIA G. RAMSEY

Seen and Heard
ELLEN LYNN HALL & JENNIFER KOFKIN RUDKIN

Connecting Emergent Curriculum and Standards in the Early Childhood Classroom
SYDNEY L. SCHWARTZ & SHERRY M. COPELAND

Infants and Toddlers at Work
ANN LEWIN-BENHAM

The View from the Little Chair in the Corner
CINDY RZASA BESS

Culture and Child Development in Early Childhood Programs
CAROLLEE HOWES

Educating and Caring for Very Young Children, 2nd Ed.
DORIS BERGEN ET AL.

Beginning School
RICHARD M. CLIFFORD & GISELE M. CRAWFORD, EDS.

Emergent Curriculum in the Primary Classroom
CAROL ANNE WIEN, ED.

Enthusiastic and Engaged Learners
MARILOU HYSON

Powerful Children
ANN LEWIN-BENHAM

The Early Care and Education Teaching Workforce at the Fulcrum
SHARON LYNN KAGAN ET AL.

Supervision in Early Childhood Education, 3rd Ed.
JOSEPH J. CARUSO WITH M. TEMPLE FAWCETT

Guiding Children's Behavior
EILEEN S. FLICKER & JANET ANDRON HOFFMAN

The War Play Dilemma, 2nd Ed.
DIANE E. LEVIN & NANCY CARLSSON-PAIGE

Possible Schools
ANN LEWIN-BENHAM

Everyday Goodbyes
NANCY BALABAN

Playing to Get Smart
ELIZABETH JONES & RENATTA M. COOPER

The Emotional Development of Young Children, 2nd Ed.
MARILOU HYSON

Young Children Continue to Reinvent Arithmetic—2nd Grade, 2nd Ed.
CONSTANCE KAMII

Bringing Learning to Life
LOUISE BOYD CADWELL

A Matter of Trust
CAROLLEE HOWES & SHARON RITCHIE

Bambini
LELLA GANDINI & CAROLYN POPE EDWARDS, EDS.

Young Children Reinvent Arithmetic, 2nd Ed.
CONSTANCE KAMII

Bringing Reggio Emilia Home
LOUISE BOYD CADWELL

Brown, C. P., Ku, D., Barry, D., & Puckett, K. (2022). Examining preservice teachers' conceptions of teaching to consider the impact of policymakers' neoliberal reforms on their sensemaking of their new profession. *Journal of Teacher Education.* https://doi.org/10.1177%2F00224871221105803

Cochran-Smith, M. (1991). Learning to teach against the grain. *Harvard Educational Review, 61*(3), 279–311.

Dunn, A. H., Farver, S., Guenther, A., & Wexler, L. J. (2017). Activism through attrition?: An exploration of viral resignation letters and the teachers who wrote them. *Teaching and Teacher Education, 64,* 280–290.

Nxumalo, F. (2021). Disrupting anti-Blackness in early childhood qualitative inquiry: Thinking with Black refusal and Black futurity. *Qualitative Inquiry, 27*(10), 1191–1199.

Tuck, E., & Yang, K. W. (2012). Decolonization is not a metaphor. *Decolonization: Indigeneity, Education & Society, 1*(1), 1–40.

Acknowledgments

I would not be writing this book right now without the openness to change of my immediate family, Kevin, Will and Anna, and Emma and John Connor. My love for and pride in each of you is beyond what words can say.

My mom and stepfather, Beth and Greg Reed, and dad, Cary Frank, have given so much to me that I am grateful for, as have my siblings, Jennica, Heather, Andreya, Robin, and John. I also recognize the love and support of my in-laws, Sherry and Pete Sherfinski, Todd and Tabita, and Julie. As a proud auntie, I would be remiss not to acknowledge Zach, Alex, Hunter, Caryana, Mia, Ava, Sam, Siena, Leah, Cary, and Ivan.

I deeply appreciate my education from the University of Wisconsin–Madison. Almost every day of my career, I have remembered critical lessons learned during my years as an undergraduate, master's, and especially doctoral student. I want to particularly recognize Beth Graue, who gave me rare opportunities to help with the SAGE project, which greatly expanded my lens on elementary education. I also thank Alice Udvari-Solner, who spent much time and careful effort teaching and modeling for me how to work with preservice teachers.

I would like to acknowledge Marlys Sloup, my Madison, Wisconsin, elementary teaching mentor for many years, and Jill Hayes, who was the kindergarten teacher of my two children. Jill opened up the wonders of the early childhood teaching world to me when I volunteered in her classroom, and inspired me to embrace early childhood education as a career.

There would not be this book without the talented and thoughtful preservice teachers centered in it. The preservice teachers in this book worked hard to become better teachers for children, families, and communities. I am fortunate that so many former preservice teachers from the 5-Year Teacher Education Program were willing to share their stories of place-based education and assessment with honesty.

My departmental colleague, Sharon Hayes, welcomed me into the 5-Year Teacher Education program in 2011. I am so glad she was willing to share a place-based teaching journey together. Sharon, as well as Aimee Morewood and Sam Stack, read and gave great feedback on various chapters of the book. Working and writing with Audra Slocum over the years has elevated my abilities to theorize this data. My department chairs, Nathan Sorber and

Sam Stack, have been very supportive and generous, and I really appreciate their belief in me. Also, I appreciate my many additional departmental colleagues, who would do anything for our students.

Cheng-hsien Wu helped create our narrative portfolio shell, and Charline Barnes-Rowland teamed with Sharon and me to pilot the first narrative portfolio cycle. Most colleagues, along with some of our mentor teachers and doctoral students, have participated in narrative portfolio work in the form of reviews and feedback over the 7-year period discussed in this book. These individuals have helped the preservice teachers develop their thinking and they have aided Sharon and me to improve the process.

Michael Hanlin is a talented local teacher, mentor, 5-Year program graduate and adjunct professor in the program. He was a helpful editor, contributing greatly to the quality of this text. I would also like to recognize Wen Juan Mo (Helen) and Sandra Ayivor, who proofread the references for the draft of the book.

Outside of my institution, Min Yu and Amber Brown provided insightful feedback on various chapters that helped me frame local stories for a national audience. I also recognize Alexa Schindel, who inspired me to start thinking more critically about place-based education early in my career.

The Rockstar Writing Bootcamp group from the AERA Early Education & Child Development Special Interest Group, including Jennifer Baumgartner, Michelle Bauml, Amber Brown, Ji Hon Kim, Sohyun Meacham, Tomoko Wakabayashi, and Christine Wang, was a source of support and encouragement during my writing process.

I do not possess enough gratitude for the series editors. Chris Brown has mentored me through several projects, including this book. Chris has been incredibly generous with sharing his expertise in the policy and politics of early childhood and elementary education, reading chapters, and pushing me to make a stronger and clearer argument. I also am appreciative of Nancy File, whose knowledge of early childhood curriculum has inspired my thinking and writing, for her willingness to discuss my work, and for her mentorship and support during my career. At TCP, I am grateful to Sarah Jubar, who helped create a super title and gave me excellent, detailed feedback that has enhanced the structure and quality of the book, and to Sarah Biondello, for her enthusiasm and support of my work from its beginning stages. Furthermore, I appreciate the entire TCP team, including Nancy Mandel and Lori Tate, who provided wonderful editorial support.

All of this said, the argument, sentiment, and any mistakes made in this text are fully my own.

Rooted in Belonging

Introduction

Most of the 30 or so students I supervised during 2 years of my doctoral program at the University of Wisconsin–Madison were White women in their early 20s, but I did have one student in her 50s. Tammy (a pseudonym, as are names of people, other than my colleague Sharon Hayes, and institutions throughout the text), was White as well; she had been a childcare provider and now, with her own children grown, was fulfilling her dream of earning her bachelor's degree. (Please note, I chose to capitalize White throughout this book as "White" is not neutral but a race, and Whiteness functions in the schools and communities described [Appiah, 2020]).

I am a Midwest-born White woman; Tammy was the first person I had met from West Virginia. As it happens, my life experiences had not brought me into close contact with anyone from West Virginia, and I found that I held a handful of stereotypes: lush green mountains, coal mining, and a vague notion of "hillbilly" culture from growing up watching *The Beverly Hillbillies* on television. The program provided caricatures of a family from the Ozark Mountains who struck it rich when they found oil on their land, then moved to a mansion in Beverly Hills, California, and experienced culture shock as they started a new life. In *The Beverly Hillbillies*, comedy came at the expense of mountain people who were portrayed as simple and stupid. Tammy, on the contrary, was creative, loving, full of life, and shared amazing ideas for using drama, crafts, songs, and nature in her work with children. Her character and intelligence defied the hillbilly stereotype, and our shared interest in early childhood and our shared experience as White mothers drew us together.

Everything I observed suggested to me that Tammy would be an excellent teacher. The principal at the school where Tammy was placed to student teach kindergarten perceived something else, though, and asked that she be removed, claiming that she was not "with it" enough to keep up with the students. "Our students already face enough challenges—they need their adults to have it fully together," the principal said.

While Tammy's mentor teacher and I disagreed with the principal (I observed that she was a solid preservice teacher who treated students equitably), some distinctive language markers, her dress, and her age differentiated her from the other student teachers. Tammy ultimately moved to a smaller school across town. I could not help wondering if regional and cultural differences related to accent, vocabulary, mannerisms, and ways of relating with the children did not come into play in this decision, which seemed based on implicit bias rather than evidence of problematic behaviors.

Later that year I received a job offer for an elementary and early childhood teacher educator position at Mayville University (a pseudonym) in West Virginia. Tammy acted as a cultural translator, advising me about the community and state. That was 11 years ago, and I have worked in West Virginia ever since.

Present-day people often are viewed by outsiders via outdated stereotypes, yet dismissing the ways local communities influence people's lives fails to account for the complexities that globalization leaves (Zhao, 2010). One of the most enduring aspects of globalization is the persistent "bubble" that White educators in particular often resist "popping." I define the "bubble" as the discourses and practices used by adults such as educators and family members to try to protect young children from the world they perceive to be outside their communities. Creating the "bubble" around children has become more normalized as globalization results in opportunities to see and potentially engage with people who are different from oneself. It is, I think, vital that children be shown as early as possible how to escape their own bubbles. That is why helping early-childhood educators develop bubble-popping strategies is also vital. This book will propose that place-based teaching can be such a strategy.

"THE BUBBLE"

When I suggest that early childhood and elementary educators should "get out of our bubble," I have a particular notion of "bubble" in mind. The "bubble" is caused by the Western family's desire to protect their innocent children from perceived worldly problems (Duhn, 2012b). Middle-class and White parents create special environments for their "bubble-wrapped" children to protect them from what they see as a world that is frightening. Parents try to protect their children from dangers and at the same time they agree to an education that prepares the children to become "human capital" in an economic system that values them only as workers (Brantlinger, 2003).

Of course, there is a price that children and families pay when they must be complicit in the culture of fear and protection. In the developmental period of early and middle childhood, when children should unquestionably have rights to joyful play-based learning in both outdoor spaces and classrooms, the bubble can have a damaging effect. It is easy to protect young children to the point of suffocation, snuffing out their voices and choices (Sobel, 2013). Moreover, young children of color, those in poverty, and those from other marginalized groups know all too well the realities of a deeply unequal society. Children need opportunities to discuss their lived realities during early childhood and elementary education (Sherfinski et al.,

2016). Children of color and children who live in poverty disproportionately bear the burden of diminished policy and institutional contexts that tragically squeeze the vibrancy and intellectual challenge out of their daily lives from early education on (Brown, 2021).

In this context, in order to be a good teacher who supports middle-class and White children's and families' needs, the teacher may become enmeshed in rules she must enforce and find herself enacting a regime of surveillance and a plethora of rules that heightens her and the children's levels of anxiety and cautiousness (Jones, 2003). Human capital—even when the subjects are young children—must *capitalize*, it must accumulate by producing. To support a system that accumulates wealth and power by producing goods and services, children and families who have been historically and are presently marginalized by their race and class status are targeted by teachers who create particular roles for children and families that support this capitalist system (Nxumalo, 2020). "Getting out of the bubble" in order to address the contexts and effects of the bubble is an antiracist and anticlassist act that has life-altering possibilities for young children and their families.

The neoliberal business model of education, requiring ongoing behaviors to maintain the status of White and middle-class families, strongly influences teaching and teacher education. Schooling itself distracts us from, and distorts actions toward, local places (Gruenewald, 2003b). Becoming more critical about place means understanding the idea of the "bubble" so that educators can learn to use place-based education to undermine it.

Place-based education is teaching and learning rooted in belonging, participation, and contribution in the context of diversity and change (Duhn, 2012a). For example, preservice teachers in my study examined their natural environments, studied community history, and addressed local issues through action research with children, families, and others in the community (Furman & Gruenewald, 2004). The preservice teachers' work followed Gruenewald's (2003a) notion of place-based education, which involves educators consciously and deliberately extending their understandings of accountability and pedagogy outward, toward places:

> Thus extended, pedagogy becomes more relevant to the lived experience of students and teachers, and accountability is reconceptualized so that places matter to educators, students, and citizens in tangible ways. Place-conscious education, therefore, aims to work against the isolation of schooling's discourses and practices from the living world outside the increasingly placeless institution of schooling. Furthermore, it aims to enlist teachers and students in the firsthand experience of local life and in the political process of understanding and shaping what happens. (Gruenewald, 2003a, p. 620)

Accountability typically refers to the mechanism the state uses to hold educational programs and the individuals employed by them responsible for public school children's academic performance (Darling-Hammond, 2020). Place-based education resists neoliberal ideals because it recognizes that accountability pressures reinforce the assumption that achievement—whether that of a school, teacher, or child—can be measured by routinized classrooms alone and that all that matters is quantifiable and statistically comparable individuals. This quantification draws attention from the rich cultural contexts of living and the perspective of place; typical notions of accountability are problematic because they do not recognize the mediating role that schools play in the production of place through the education of individuals who inhabit local spaces and have the knowledge and skills through place-based education to transform those places (Gruenewald, 2003a).

Place-based education requires transformative learning, meaning the process by which people realize that they are actually seeing the world through a specific lens, which is not a universal perspective (Mezirow, 2000). In order to address the "bubble" and its related challenges, this book asks three main questions:

1. How might we navigate place in teacher education in a way that helps all of us get out of our "bubble," yet at the same time recognizes and respects our local communities and one another?
2. What is a shared vision worthy of these goals?
3. How might we assess learning and hold one another accountable to support a place-based vision?

PLACE-BASED EDUCATION AND ITS POTENTIAL

In this book, to answer my three questions, I highlight notions of "place" and how they influenced the teacher education program. People's learning is situated within the expectations and norms of the social and cultural contexts in which they live (Vygotsky, 1978). The beliefs and values held by members of these social and cultural contexts determine what knowledge and skills are worth learning, and shape their understandings of the best places for learning (Rogoff, 1990). This is how "the bubble" is created, so we must consider how to get out of our own bubble while recognizing and respecting our local communities.

Cultural contexts are powerful and affect how people think. For example, race and class are important constructs that shape thinking. Belief in meritocracy—that those who reap the benefits deserve them because of their hard work, and that privileges of race or class are unimportant or unreal—is an aspect of neoliberal thinking (Apple, 2006).

In my teacher education program, I addressed navigating place; creating a shared vision designed to connect more with children, families, and communities; assessing learning; and holding one another accountable through place-based education. Working with my colleague Dr. Sharon Hayes for the past decade, we developed a narrative portfolio assessment system to facilitate place-based education and action research, which was situated in the inquiry strand of teacher education that Sharon originally designed, and that is highlighted in this text. (I use the phrase "my teacher education program" for ease when I discuss my place-based practices at Mayville University during the study years 2015–2021, but I do not take singular credit for the good work done.)

Place-based education should begin from specific attributes of place rather than seeking to standardize the experiences of students from diverse places in association with globalization. To disrupt this trend of standardization that undermines the growth of our youngest learners, I studied place to increase preservice teachers' engagement with it through experiential, multidisciplinary, and intergenerational learning (Gruenewald, 2003b). Place-based curriculum can be thought of as a community-based project in which many perspectives come together, there are tensions, and the outcomes emerge rather than being prescribed (Mueller & Whyte, 2020).

Place-based education has also contributed to getting out of our bubble because a global pandemic challenged educators across the world to find new ways of engaging with children and families in new kinds of places, such as online and hybrid environments for public schooling due to outbreaks of COVID-19 and health and safety concerns. Of course, the COVID-19 pandemic will leave its mark on education into the future, yet place-based education will remain an important form of teaching and learning well beyond the present health crisis.

A DYNAMIC CHARGE FOR TEACHER EDUCATION

Ultimately, it is necessary to have a dynamic view that responds to the global context and the impacts of globalization but also addresses local places. Place-based education in this book centers on how to draw on local knowledge while showing how that knowledge can (and cannot) transfer to other places, since "learning to teach is complex, contextually specific, autobiographically grounded, and informed by sociopolitical realities . . . good teaching looks different in different settings" (Goodwin, 2010, p. 30).

CHAPTER SUMMARIES

This book offers a counternarrative to the neoliberal standardized preservice teacher development and assessment processes like the edTPA by examining how a group of teacher educators in West Virginia worked alongside their preservice teachers to redesign their teacher education program. They implemented and experienced a type of place-based approach to teacher education designed to teach preservice teachers how to address local social justice issues as teacher researchers and teacher leaders in the fields of early childhood and elementary education. By highlighting these experiences, this book illuminates for higher education professionals the affordances and challenges of this process, and it points to creative possibilities and future uses of this work in early childhood and elementary teacher education.

I set the stage in Chapter 1 by introducing the central problem of accountability being "shoved up" from P–12 into teacher education in ways that affect preservice teachers. I also describe the places that will be central in the research. I then explain that an alternative assessment form, beyond simply testing, may offer an antidote to the problems of over-testing.

In Chapter 2, I describe the main types of place-based education as well as associated teaching strategies in depth so that others working in a range of places might be inspired to create place-based education that fosters preservice teachers' growth and development as well as the learning of children, families, mentors, and teacher educators. I provide tools for readers to consider.

In Chapter 3, I illuminate the challenges of the teacher education context. I then show how I have faced the challenges by designing a narrative portfolio project with my colleague that facilitates preservice teachers' use of place-based tools of curriculum and pedagogy.

In Chapter 4, I introduce how the preservice teachers working in Appalachia used a collection of strategies to support children and families by using the narrative portfolio project as a tool for learning about place-based education.

The pandemic and Black Lives Matter brought a jolt to my teacher education program. Convinced of the need to author the narrative in a way that not only taught social justice–oriented lenses but engaged specifically antiracist ones, I explain how I began to weave together antiracist education and place-based education. This is described in Chapter 5.

In Chapter 6 I argue for the need for strategies in teaching and teacher education to speak back to the audit culture that limits engagement with place. This chapter offers strategies for creating a place-based approach to teaching and teacher education that is holistic and deeply contextual in order to create places where all of us can learn in deeper, more meaningful ways.

Finally, I present four Appendices. The first Appendix, A, captures the Research Methods used in my project. Appendix B presents a tool we used for program change and Appendices C and D contain narrative portfolio assignments.

CHAPTER 1

The Need for Place-Based Teacher Education

This book represents critical research that asks deep questions about early childhood and elementary teacher education in the rural and Appalachian context to provide a place-based example of how mainly White teacher educators and preservice teachers worked to see, resist, and disrupt commonplace notions of early childhood and elementary education. Furthermore, the study bears witness to the ways in which place-based education can disrupt neoliberal education and so offer young students a vision of a different culture in which they will be valued for who they are and effective in making change in the areas that are least likely to have rich curricula and place-based education—high poverty, culturally and linguistically diverse, and rural places (Comber, 2016).

CONTEXTS FOR THE BOOK

The main context for the book is West Virginia; secondary contexts are high poverty, culturally diverse urban and suburban settings in other states.

West Virginia's Rural Communities

West Virginia is in Appalachia; it is a small, poor, rural state greatly reliant on extractive industries now in decline. West Virginia ties with Maine and Vermont for the highest White population in the United States at about 89% (U.S. Census, 2020). Not every child in West Virginia, nor every teacher, is White, however. Small African American populations associated historically with the mining industry remain (Lewis, 2002) and, as in most of the United States, racial, ethnic, and linguistic diversity in the region has increased every year (U.S. Census, 2020). West Virginia has the fourth highest poverty rate among states at 19.1% (U.S. Census Bureau, 2018). West Virginia also has a high rate of home ownership (76.3%) that is unexpected given its poverty rate (Housing Assistance Council, 2012). From the Great Depression through the 1990s, West Virginians solidly voted for candidates affiliated with the Democratic Party; these Democratic politicians, most notably FDR, created economic relief policies to support communities suffering from intense poverty due to coal busts and related factors such as rural geography (see Stack, 2016). However, beginning in 2000 with the presidential election between candidates George W. Bush and Al Gore, West Virginians have fled the Democratic Party for the Republican Party. Democrats' centering of climate issues and criticism of the coal industry nudged out individuals already comfortable with the conservative social policy of Republicans (Schneider, 2016). Presently, West Virginia has a strong Republican majority.

Media and scholarship portray the region as a space of deficiency and its people as poor and powerless, but Appalachian people generally identify themselves as being family-oriented, neighborly, self-sufficient, and morally strong (Keefe, 2000). Natural resource extraction continues to create intense boom and bust economic cycles that shape economic well-being in many West Virginian communities (O'Leary, 2018). Corporate power also shapes educational policy, including by influencing state standards, curriculum, and assessment frameworks (Sherfinski et al., 2022).

In West Virginia, school privatization efforts are just gaining steam. In 2019, West Virginia teachers went on strike for about 3 weeks and "drew on a long state history of protest—against slavery, for mine workers' rights, and as recently as 1990 for teacher pay and benefits" (Sherfinski, Hayes, et al., 2019, p. 19). West Virginian public school teachers have had some recent history of protests and demands—in part successful—for respect, congruent with a state tradition of workers' movements particularly among miners (Slocum et al., 2018). But West Virginia's schools are now feeling the pressure toward corporatization and privatization, including charter schools, that has affected the rest of the country (McElhinny, 2022). However, the legislature's efforts to expand charter schools have started to gain success, and the first charter school in Mayville (pseudonym), West Virginia, a community our teacher education program is located in, was preparing to open in 2022, at the time of this writing.

Varied Suburban and Urban School Contexts

The secondary places in the study are two racially and culturally diverse suburban contexts and one urban site that program graduates now teach in. One is a suburban site with a high English Language Learner (ELL) population in New Jersey and the second suburban site is a public magnet school in North Carolina. The urban site is a school with an all-Black population, in Maryland. The percentage of White population in these states is 54.6% (NJ), 62.6% (NC), and 50% (MD) (U.S. Census, 2020), and rates of poverty are 9.4% (NJ), 12.9% (NC), and 9% (MD) (U.S. Census, 2020).

In urban centers and increasingly in suburban areas, racialized housing patterns, as well as busing and "choice" reforms (such as magnet schools, vouchers, and charter schools) have formed barriers to desegregation (Andre-Bechely, 2005). The examples from these places suggest how readers might transfer some of the ideas from this book to inspire and support place-based educational work in racially, culturally, and linguistically diverse places.

THREE CHALLENGES CONNECTING THE PLACES

Neoliberalism, White supremacy, and poverty are interrelated challenges in the study locations (West Virginia, the suburban districts in New Jersey and North Carolina, and a major urban district in Maryland), and indeed everywhere. I define and briefly explain each of these below.

Neoliberalism

Neoliberalism is the first key concept affecting our three locations. Neoliberalism is a market-based orientation, where children and educators are fitted into a culture of consumerism and individual libertarianism (Brown, 2009b, 2015) that is posited as an attractive alternative to public welfare (Ball, 1999). Neoliberalism positions educators, families, and children as "economically rational actor[s] who [are] constructed by and construct a reality in which democracy is no longer a political concept but is reduced to an economic one" (Apple, 2007, p. 114). Neoliberalism trades democratic relationships away for consumeristic ones (Biesta, 2009). This has clear implications for teacher education programs now positioned to maintain their own status quo to preserve the bottom line of robust numbers of teacher candidates and limited provisions to support them (Sleeter, 2017). In the neoliberal policy context, early childhood and elementary programs have a role in demonstrating what it is to teach and be accountable for meeting standards as the heart of their business models (Brown, 2015). Under standards-based education accountability frameworks, the mandate of all children obtaining a singular body of knowledge is the "pivot" for decision-making that trickles down to the curriculum, dispositions, and skills that the teachers must implement in their classrooms (Brown, 2009c).

Federal education policies have affected the education of U.S. children in poverty for many years. Since the 1960s, policymakers have shifted their ideals from social welfare to neoliberal visions of education (Brown & Barry, 2020). The 1965 Elementary and Secondary Education Act (ESEA), part of President Johnson's War on Poverty, aimed to remediate children's "deprivation" (Mueller & Whyte, 2020). It established systems targeted to children defined as "at risk;" these children were low income and often non-White. The 1965 ESEA provisions did not focus on curriculum issues, but on issues of funding, custodial care, and general readiness for school (Brown & Barry, 2020). By the 1980s, research showed that Head Start and similar programs under ESEA did not improve IQ scores over the long term, but did produce a cohort of employable future workers who would not burden the welfare system (Schweinhart & Weikart, 1980). These findings led to the articulation of human capital theory (Heckman, 2000), also called "return on investment" theory (Reynolds et al., 2002), which shifted the reasons for funding programs from breaking the cycle of poverty to saving taxpayers money.

In the public school system, ESEA ushered forth a whole wave of reforms related to standardization, academic achievement, and accountability through which children are prepared for math and reading tests (Brown & Barry, 2020). The prevalence of tests even in the early years governs the way many people think about education. The power of testing is enhanced when funding is contingent on demonstrating achievement gains in quantitative assessments that lack a place-based vocabulary (Gruenewald, 2005), or when education is viewed as an entrepreneurial, technological marketplace rather than a field for reimagining human connections (Hursh et al., 2015).

White Supremacy

A second connecting theme across places in the study is White supremacy. White supremacy is the belief that White people should dominate society (Kendi, 2019) and it persists in all our spaces, although, as Iruka and colleagues (2020) have noted, Whites generally believe that Black and White children should attend desegregated schools and live together in the same neighborhoods (Bobo, 2001). Many White people also believe that people of color are too sensitive about issues of race (Kanter et al., 2017). Implicit bias, an unconscious, structurally induced prejudice, reveals itself through discriminatory actions against people of color (Banks & Hicks, 2016). Whites may often see people of color as less than human (Costello & Hodson, 2014). Whites with these privileged and biased views tend to socialize together so their thinking becomes normalized, and their places become more racially segregated (Sinclair et al., 2014). In the realm of education policy, White supremacy works through highly racialized neoliberal notions of high-stakes testing, school choice and charters, and discipline and criminalization (Keisch & Scott, 2015).

Poverty

A third connecting theme among all of the places in the study is *poverty*, which affects all of the communities. In this research, poverty was often silenced, meaning that the material needs of children, families, and preservice teachers experiencing poverty sometimes were not seen and not addressed. The silencing of poverty is a phenomenon that is maintained by both neoliberalism and White supremacy.

Neoliberalism and White supremacy's work to silence poverty is a learning process that begins in childhood. In neoliberal society, children are taught to see the world through a consumeristic lens over time, which deflects attention from learning about structures that create poverty and inequality (Derman-Sparks & Ramsey, 2011). Consumerism affects the ways in which children engage with their worlds, for example, values often center on "getting and having" things such as toys, video games, and clothes rather than "using and enjoying" them (Derman-Sparks & Ramsey, 2011, p. 58). Children and adolescents from working poor families may believe this powerful "myth of the meritocracy" and feel confused and disturbed about their families, who work extremely hard but still may have very little income.

White supremacy also works to silence poverty because the mythical narrative of U.S. society as a meritocracy is laced with colorblind ideas that deny the race-based inequities and racism in the systems that disproportionally lock out Black and Latinx Americans, American Indians, non-English–speaking immigrants and refugees in poverty, and thus contribute to the maintenance of a White-dominant society (Beech et al., 2021). In states that have historically had higher populations of people of color, there are higher levels of poverty today; however, a lack of attention to the specific ways in which racial regimes have been created has silenced attention to the intersection of poverty and racial inequalities (Baker, 2022). Teachers—and sometimes parents—silence knowledge about such realities as poverty, racism, and social injustices past and present, and instead the focus becomes individual deficits of character, beliefs, or behaviors of children and their families that individual teachers are responsible to remediate (Schindel & Tolbert, 2017).

WHY WE NEED PLACE-BASED TEACHER EDUCATION

One main approach to pushing back against neoliberalism and White supremacy has been *place-based teacher education* (Demarest, 2015). Place-based teacher education is a tool for understanding the social contexts that structure everyday life in early childhood and elementary education. Place-based teacher education is a form of democratic professionalism that "centers students, families, and communities in teachers' work and in teacher education programs . . . [and] that offers the potential to help productively manage the tensions and contradictions that have long existed between professional educators and nondominant communities that they are supposed to serve" (Zeichner, 2020, p. 41). Critical, place-based education does not deny local culture or shield children from societal conflicts, but is relevant to children's and families' lives and can build well-being and community life when educators leverage the fact that curriculum and pedagogies are rooted in cultural narratives situated in places with histories (McLaren, 2003).

I realized that teacher educators missed understanding the social context of education in the teacher education program when we did not take the time to show life's complexities and to understand the lives of students and their families. My teacher education program begged to address diversity, social justice, and equity by responsively meeting the needs of preservice teachers, which suggested opportunities to teach about colorblindness, cultural conflict, meritocracy, deficit conceptions, and expectations for learning (Milner, 2010). This was no easy challenge.

My teacher education program was designed to produce teachers who could uplift the quality of education while being responsive to the perceived needs of a high poverty and White state. The 5-Year Teacher Education Program at Mayville University (pseudonym) had, since the 1990s, sought to put teacher educators, mentors, and preservice teachers on the same page through a framework that simplified the outcomes of teaching and teacher education into the "10 Characteristics of a Novice Teacher."

10 Characteristics of the Novice Teacher

1. Lifelong learner
2. Effective communicator
3. Professional, moral, and ethical
4. Facilitator of learning
5. In-depth knowledge of pedagogy
6. In-depth knowledge of content
7. Integrates content and pedagogy
8. Reflective practitioner
9. Respect for human diversity
10. Liberally educated

Preservice teachers were expected to create a portfolio of artifacts to show that they knew this list of characteristics and could perform work that reflected them; this turned out to be problematic. For example, the first time I conducted a "10 Characteristics" portfolio review in 2012 (which I performed as a panelist with other educators), I saw a portfolio that included video of a preservice teacher's Thanksgiving "Indian dance" as evidence for meeting Characteristic 9, Respect for Human Diversity. In the same portfolio, a photo of a note written to a parent scolding them for not helping their child with homework was submitted as evidence for meeting Characteristic 2, Effective Communicator. What struck me was that not only preservice teachers, but also educators on the review panel, believed this was good practice and a solid portfolio. For local educators, knowing the vocabulary of the 10 Characteristics did not equal having a deep understanding of teaching for diversity and social justice.

I have come to recognize that the lag in multicultural teaching in West Virginia was a symptom of broader structural problems within education—namely, neoliberalism and White supremacy—that teacher education programs around the country struggle with as well (Nieto, 2000). As more teacher educators with backgrounds in teaching for diversity and social justice and more faculty of color were subsequently hired at my university, more teacher educators have become interested in issues of diversity and social justice, and we completed a diversity audit of the program.

The audit showed a need for changing the language of assessment and instruction in the program to reflect a more critical multicultural stance addressing a broader range of issues, more kinds of educational content, and profounder needs. My colleagues and I formally started this process in 2014–2015 by instituting the narrative portfolio project as a tool for teaching, gathering, and assessing place-based ideas about teaching and learning and creating opportunities for conversations between preservice teachers, teacher educators, and mentor teachers.

Teacher educators now do a better job of supporting children by taking a stand on social justice and diversity, making social justice ubiquitous in teacher education, and promoting teaching as a lifelong journey of growth and development (Nieto, 2000). A major goal articulated by many teacher education faculty working in the 5-Year Teacher Education Program at Mayville University, through the developing mission, vision, and conceptual framework, was that all educators in this place should work together with children and families to create the conditions to foster culturally responsive teaching and critical multiculturalism and thus push back against the neoliberalism of teacher education.

NEOLIBERAL CHALLENGES TO PLACE-BASED TEACHER EDUCATION

Although the challenges to place-based teacher education are many, the most vexing ones stem directly from the neoliberal policy contexts in P–12 education and teacher education, which I describe in more detail below. I emphasize the power and possibilities of place to build understandings and networks to support current and future practices and policymaking.

P-12 Policy Context

The No Child Left Behind (NCLB) reform in the early 2000s was seminal in accelerating standards adoption in public schools (Brown, 2015). This was associated with the "accountability shove-down" of neoliberal standards logics to the early years of education in ways that could sometimes be inappropriate for young children (Hatch & Groenke, 2009). Accountability often devalues individuals—imposing common standards on all learners ignores their strengths and needs, and may jeopardize learning opportunities for children who most need extra support (Hatch, 2002).

In this scenario, teachers are technicians rather than professional decision-makers who work with tact and nuance in response to learners and their places (Mueller & File, 2020). In this shove-down, knowledge is characterized as "transmissible" from teacher to student, like a kind of object that can be passed along rather than socially constructed, and teachers' verbal and cognitive abilities as measured on tests and other sorting mechanisms are directly implicated in their abilities to deliver subject matter to students (Cochran-Smith & Lytle, 2009). In audit culture, opportunities for approaching education holistically with attention to the cognitive, social, emotional, and physical domains of teaching and learning are increasingly limited because the business organization of teacher education contributes to creating a dichotomy of "good" versus "bad" educators by positioning "good" teaching as narrow traditional, economic, and cognitive conceptions of the profession (Sherfinski, 2020). The goal of teachers fixing their students' deficits justified NCLB's rationale for a full arsenal of teacher training, recruitment, and retention incentives to create and keep teachers who are "highly qualified" (Cochran-Smith & Lytle, 2009).

Neoliberalism and Teacher Education

Neoliberal standards-based education affects not only early childhood and elementary education, but also middle and secondary education, and 2-year, 4-year, and post-baccalaureate teacher education. In recent years, there have been moves to strengthen the alignment between P-12 education and teacher preparation in particular ways aimed at producing workers to fit the needs of the globalizing economy (Groenke & Hatch, 2009). Another reason that neoliberalism has intensified in teacher education is that the federal government in the United States has placed higher education under more stringent oversight due to a surge of for-profit colleges and the associated financial aid monies for low-income students attempting to complete their educations there (Price, 2014). There has been an associated efficiency and entrepreneurial movement driving a culture of lean fiscal management with teacher education becoming more standardized and regulated (Apple, 2013).

Teacher education programs are increasingly set up in the neoliberal context to do the monumental task of continually producing more and better teachers and children with fewer and fewer resources (Sleeter, 2017). As I have explained elsewhere (Sherfinski, Hayes, et al., 2019), neoliberal policies influence early childhood and elementary teachers and teacher educators in two ways (Ball, 1999). First, in *marketization*, education is subject to a competitive business model. Marketization encourages "designer teacher" identities created in tandem with mandates of effectiveness and efficiency (Sachs, 2001). Second, *accountability* processes isolate individual educators from one another (Hargreaves, 1994). An example of an accountability process that isolates individuals from one another is performativity, in which not only teachers and teacher educators, but P–12 students and organizations such as teacher education programs and schools become products to be bought and sold. The specific assessments' performance indicators and practices are used to drive, evaluate, and compare people and organizations. Scores on tests become substitutes for quality and thus programs are valued instrumentally instead of intrinsically (Moss, 2008). "Scores become proxies for relationships and interactions; numbers belie the complexity, depth, richness, authenticity, and intimacy of quality caregiving and teaching that teachers provide" (Buzzelli, 2020, p. 170).

Indeed, in both P–12 and teacher education, teachers' caring roles may be sub-leased by others with the compartmentalized tasks of delivering psychological, social–emotional care while teachers and teacher educators handle the content expertise. The issue of who controls the field of judgment is especially crucial, as it shapes a surveillance context in which educators struggle for their souls as thinking humans and experience the resultant anger and terror toward neoliberal constraints when they realize that the goals of the project are dehumanizing yet officially required (Ball, 2003). Research has shown that educators may lose their ability to maintain a reflective, critical distance from the neoliberal practices taught in teacher education once they begin teaching in the schools without the affordances of their teacher education program (Holloway & Brass, 2018; Sherfinski, Jalalifard, et al., 2019).

Auditing has become the main organizing principle of the higher education field and its teacher education programs. My program prepares educators for auditing that uses the Council for the Accreditation of Educator Preparation (CAEP)/National Council for Accreditation of Teacher Educators (NCATE) tools; for example, the examination batteries preservice teachers must take before and during their time in the program (Sherfinski, Jalalifard, et al., 2019). In teacher education, audit culture promotes the need to validate preservice teachers' educational performances through standardized measures instead of assessing how preservice teachers act as researchers and leaders to engage holistic teaching to promote equity, diversity, and social justice in their local communities. In my teacher education program, I have become stuck in a dilemma: I feel that teacher educators spend significant time aligning all of the curriculum to standardized tests and then realigning it again each time students struggle, whether the challenges be with algebraic thinking in mathematics, economics in social studies, or "academic language" in literacy. And yet my students will be obliged to work within this testing-focused system, so I need to show them how to manage testing and accountability expectations, while opening up a more democratic and critical space. This book reflects the "both/and" orientation I have, with difficulty, arrived at. A both/and orientation in which teacher educators work mostly within the tools of accountability to reclaim a more democratic and critical space has not been easy; this book details what I have done and continue to do.

RECLAIMING ACCOUNTABILITY

Place-based teacher education has a key role in reclaiming accountability (i.e., holding stakeholders responsible for providing appropriate education for young children) that is democratically conceived and responsive to places. In their book *Reclaiming Accountability in Teacher Education,* Cochran-Smith et al. (2018) name the reauthorization of the 1998 Higher Education Act's (HEA's) Title II provisions as the most significant act influencing the current state of teacher education accountability. It stipulated mandatory reporting, linked state grants to revising certification, and provided funding for alternative certification routes. Title II's effects were intensified by No Child Left Behind (NCLB) in 2002 and by Race to the Top (RTTT) in the Obama era. All of these policies emerged at a time when intensifying global neoliberal attention to teacher quality helped define public education reform specifically as the way to address poverty and inequality in the United States. Policymakers sought to address poverty and inequality by shifting the language of public policy and accountability from "highly qualified teachers" to "highly effective teachers," whose effectiveness can be quantified and compared through their students' test scores.

Assessment Systems Impacting Teacher Education Programs

Cochran-Smith et al. (2018) chronicle the histories and effects of a cluster of neoliberal reforms that have deeply affected the work of teacher education programs in recent years. These assessment systems have been proposed by the National Council for Accreditation in Teacher Education (NCATE), the Council for Accreditation and Educator Preparation (CAEP), the Council for Teacher Quality (NCTQ), and the Educative Teacher Performance Assessment (edTPA). As the Elementary Education Special Professional Association (SPA) Leader for NCATE/CAEP for 6 years, I witnessed the challenges of preparing early childhood and elementary teachers committed to deep understandings of equity, diversity, and social justice while navigating the cluster of assessment systems.

edTPA. edTPA is a teaching assessment by Stanford Center for the Assessment of Learning and Equity (SCALE) administered by Pearson Learning, Inc. For this performance exam, preservice teachers write a set of literacy lesson plans and videotape themselves teaching from these plans. They write and submit to Pearson Learning a series of essays that serve to evaluate their young students' learning. These materials then are scored by an anonymous teacher located somewhere in the United States who has met the reliability requirements, which are standards that Pearson has devised based on their training protocol for reviewers, to ensure that the teacher can score the tests appropriately (Greenblatt & O'Hara, 2015).

My institution made the controversial decision to require edTPA as a high-stakes exam for certification and program completion in 2017. edTPA is seen as a mark of distinction by some educators and preservice teachers who see it as a pathway toward National Board Certification (Sherfinski, Hayes, et al., 2019). Some also believe the test is necessary to support the enrollments of out-of-state students, many of whom come from states where edTPA is required for certification. edTPA has even been used in West Virginia's policies promoting teacher quality for both alternative teacher certification and traditional certification pathways. Beginning in 2019, all teacher education programs in the state of West Virginia needed to provide evidence of the successful completion of a valid and reliable performance assessment instrument such as edTPA and the Praxis PPAT. Individuals enrolled in a state-approved alternative certification program after July 1, 2019 are required to pass the edTPA or Praxis PPAT prior to being eligible to receive their WV teaching certificate (West Virginia Department of Education, 2016).

Running the edTPA requires intensive labor by faculty at my institution. The exam focuses heavily on teaching "academic language" (specific language supported by the culture of power and used in curriculum, on tests, etc.). It was developed in California and with an eye to improving instruction for ELLs. Yet, in my context, preservice teachers rarely received instruction and practice in teaching ELLs, or instruction and practice in working with "academic language" in the context of the language diversity and the language bias in this region.

Praxis. While not named as part of the cluster, Praxis tests of decontextualized academic knowledge assumed necessary for teaching can be problematic in preparing preservice teachers for many reasons. For example, Praxis tests may have undue influence on shaping the content of university education programs (Cornelius & Harris, 2018). They are biased racially and culturally, and may prevent Black and Latinx preservice teachers from graduating from a university teacher education program (Bennett et al., 2006). Overall, White middle-class preservice teachers (most from out-of-state) tend to do well on the exams, but preservice teachers who are minoritized or White and working class are more likely to struggle. This is especially disturbing given that, during the period of my study, the total exam bundle and retakes normally cost each preservice teacher in excess of $1,000.

These challenges brought me to see the need for a more democratic approach to accountability that might coexist with and even break through the challenging aspects of the neoliberal audit culture. I wanted preservice teachers to understand how to create curriculum and pedagogy responsive to local communities that addresses issues of social justice and diversity in ways that were deeply contextual and place-based, and to take that thinking and transfer it to new settings if their journeys required it. I also wanted to decouple the ways accountability was viewed in the program from the preservice teachers' performance on edTPA and other exams (Cochran-Smith et al., 2018).

CHALLENGES OF RECLAIMING ACCOUNTABILITY

Equity-oriented pedagogies required that I change the content and structure of instruction by engaging students' and families' Funds of Knowledge (FoK), encouraging culturally relevant teaching, and analyzing the culture of power in schools and society with my preservice teachers (Buchanan et al., 2019). Brief definitions of these concepts are presented in the text box.

> *Funds of knowledge* (FoK): The social, economic, and productive activities of local people such as children and their families (Moll et al., 2005) that are historically contingent, emergent within relations of power, and not always distributed equitably (Mercado, 2005).
>
> *Culturally relevant teaching*: A framework promoting the engagement and success of all children, but particularly children of color, by emphasizing learning and achievement, affirming children's cultural competence, and facilitating their abilities to see and critique social and educational inequities (Ladson-Billings, 1995).
>
> *Culture of power*: The structure built by and for those who have power and their rules (i.e., those upholding White supremacy), as they affect opportunities and experiences in schools and other institutions (Delpit, 2006).

When preservice teachers are expected to be carbon copies of their mentor teachers to fulfill curriculum transmission, they may follow their mentor and thus miss opportunities for practicing in equity-oriented ways (Buchanan, 2017).

The accountability movement has a significant impact on teachers and their practices due to pacing guides and expectations that they will teach curriculum packages with fidelity and so (supposedly) enhance test performance (Apple, 2006). Teacher education programs should resist these neoliberal challenges and instead identify preservice teachers who are decision-makers (Feiman-Nemser, 2012) and are prepared to "reflectively adapt teaching practices and exercise judgment about the use of these practices at particular moments in time and in particular circumstances" (Zeichner, 2020, p. 39). To do so involves cultivating self-understandings and seeing children, families, and communities as "abundantly" capable, thus "constantly in the process of constructing meanings based on . . . lived experiences" (L. Miller as cited in Dudley-Marling, 2020, p. 55).

Partnerships between colleges or universities and local school districts are one promising way to address the challenges and create spaces for place-based education to flourish, yet there can be some issues in establishing and maintaining these. Teacher education programs have often built collaborative partnerships with public schools in order to spur experimentation, reflection, and discussion between practicing teachers, administrators, teacher educators, and preservice teachers (Yendol-Hoppey et al., 2013).

Public schools and teacher education are two very different organizations, which adds complexity to this work. An important part of facilitating collaborative partnerships between teacher education and public schools is to build clinically rich experiences for preservice and inservice teachers, which require adjustments in faculty workload assignments; some universities are unwilling to make concessions and support teacher educators to engage in this work. Clinical preparation is delegated to adjunct faculty, graduate students, clinical faculty, or turned over to P–12 schools (Murray et al., 2009). This marginalizes clinical teacher preparation within the academy.

It can be very difficult for faculty to support teacher development and engaged partnerships when the state prescribes narrow, rote curriculum and testing to which teachers are held accountable (Brown & Weber, 2016). There is also a rift between teacher educators and schools created when teacher educators and local teachers are forced to prepare preservice teachers for an expanding battery of exams, including the Praxis and edTPA, often without compensatory time (Sherfinski, Hayes, et al., 2019). The ever-increasing focus on narrow, standardized curriculum and tests at the public-school level likewise affects teachers' time to collaborate with university teacher educators around concerns that are broader and more vital to communities than a set of individual literacy lesson plans as required for the edTPA.

QUESTIONS FOR REFLECTION AND DISCUSSION

Examining Your Context
- What do you know about the place(s) served by your teacher education program?
- How has neoliberalism affected your teacher education program?
- How does neoliberalism affect your life as an educator?

Your Values and Practices
- What are the values that shape your practices?
- How are these values and practices shaped by place? How do they shape your place?
- How do you negotiate values and practices in your place?

WHAT'S NEXT?

The present chapter introduced the community in which my teacher education program is situated. It showed how the neoliberal context of teacher education presented challenges, and how our context is not totally unique, but influenced by the cluster of reforms facing teacher education more broadly. In Chapter 2, I present the theoretical framework for the book, discussing three principal approaches to place-based education. I then explain how, within the place-based approaches, I teach preservice teachers practice-based strategies to support their professional and political journeys as teachers.

CHAPTER 2

Theoretical Framework

Showing how my teacher education program created a place-based approach to teaching and teacher education requires that I define the construct, show how it plays out in classrooms, and connect these ideas and practices to teacher education. Before I proceed, it is helpful to consider how I thought about the nature of meaning-making within my early childhood and elementary teacher education program, as it guided my approach to place-based education.

THE NATURE OF MEANING-MAKING

New teachers bring knowledge from their own home and P–12 school experiences when learning to teach, and the knowledge all comes from somewhat different places (Ball & Cohen, 1999). These preconceived ideas about schooling shift and change as they learn from their young students and respond to their cultural knowledge, their social, emotional, cognitive, and physical strengths and needs, and their knowledge of their natural worlds (Brown & Mowry, 2015).

Social constructionism and social constructivism frame how teacher educators make meaning. *Social constructionism* means that meaning-making takes place in a social context; for example, when preservice teachers work with their teacher educators and mentors to create new social realities (Charmaz, 2014). *Social constructivism*, by contrast, involves an individual's own subjective interpretation of experience in the process of meaning making (Vygotsky, 1978); for example, when a preservice teacher engages in individual reflective work through journaling to make sense of their classroom experiences.

When creating place-based education, we started with our context, the "place elements," such as children's and families' Funds of Knowledge (FoK) and knowledge of community contexts. We then used an inquiry approach to studying teaching and learning practices with the aid of theoretical lenses of the field such as culturally relevant teaching (Ladson-Billings, 1995) and reaching and teaching students in poverty (Gorski, 2018) as well as several others, and a democratic assessment tool called the narrative portfolio.

Briefly, the narrative portfolio is a project that asks preservice teachers to use placed-based inquiry tools in their local school communities, and to continuously document, gather, analyze, and produce new political and pedagogical understandings. The documentation is organized and elaborated in a shared portfolio space and is revised and added to over a period of time. (Chapter 3 provides a detailed examination of the narrative portfolio.)

Preservice teachers were taught to sense, and to deal with, the challenges of neoliberal barriers to democratic education such as thin mundane curricula and mechanistic pedagogy in early childhood and elementary education—the period when learning should be its most active and joyful. Preservice teachers also learned to detect overreliance on accountability mechanisms such as standardized testing at both the early childhood/elementary school and teacher education levels. Additionally, by learning four strategies—reflection, dialogism, I-It vs. I-You relationships, and diffraction—preservice teachers grew in their abilities to address neoliberalism. The four strategies are presented below in Table 2.1 and elaborated on later in this chapter.

It was through working to construct and co-construct practices in local contexts using these strategies, lenses, and tools that more humanizing and democratic place-based practices materialized.

THREE APPROACHES TO PLACE-BASED EDUCATION

Place must be shared through socially just counternarratives that pierce the standardization of neoliberalism because place is "deeply entangled with the self, to such a degree that the self cannot exist without being in a place" (Duhn, 2012a, p. 103). Places are made and remade in complex cycles of decay and renewal, for example as boom and bust economic cycles affect the environment and community life in Appalachia. Sometimes these relations among cycles of decay and renewal are contained in a place and sometimes they stretch beyond it as other places become implicated in the changes (Massey, 1994). For example, when White Appalachian families were forced to resettle in Midwestern cities in the 1950s due to job losses, these children's and their families' complex literacy challenges emerged (Purcell-Gates, 1997). The literacy challenges faced by children of Appalachian families when they move away from their homeplaces exemplify the stretching of place-based patterns to new locations. Place holds multiple identities and links local places to distant, global ones (Massey, 1991). The linkages occur through processes of "unfolding," which simply means that places change in complex and multidimensional ways.

Places are ecologies like "nesting dolls" that exist within macro-, meso-, and micro-levels of context (Bronfenbrenner, 1992); the nested contexts are part of forces and forms that constitute *place*. The specific properties of a

Table 2.1. Four Strategies for Supporting Place-Based Learning

Strategy	Meaning
Reflection	Stepping back from the object one is thinking about, to see one's own life experience, and to change it.
Dialogism	Navigating the languages of authority and one's own understandings and beliefs in order to gain meaning to inform (in)action.
I-It vs. I-You Relationships	Forming caring "I-You" relationships among humans and just relationships with land and nature.
Diffraction	Attuning to differences and their effects in the process of knowledge creation in order to navigate around neoliberal obstacles.

place emerge through the ways in which boundaries and borders are drawn and lived within as well as reconfigured and distanced from (Deleuze & Guattari, 1988). *Place*, which is built up, cultivated, and governed by people, comes into existence through its relationship to space and nature (Duhn, 2012a). *Space* can be positioned as either confining or open to change and *nature* is positioned as wilderness, land that is dangerous and separated from humanity in many people's eyes (Duhn, 2012a).

Dynamic connections between rural and urban spaces and bidirectional movements of social life require learning about the complex interconnectivity between rural, suburban, and urban places and nuanced contemporary understandings of place (Lichter & Brown, 2011). Place-based education has three main approaches for local communities (Figure 2.1).

One approach is connecting people to the earth, which seeks to sustain the natural environment. A second approach is expanding cultural and linguistic diversity in local communities. Finally, a third approach is dealing with settler colonialism, which means the ongoing systems of power that perpetuate the oppression of indigenous peoples and cultures by exploiting resources and occupying land (Tuck & McKenzie, 2015). The exploitative processes of settler colonialism on which the United States was built, and that continue even today, include Indigenous elimination, anti-Black racism, and immigrant exploitation (Kashyap, 2020). This third approach to place-based education, which is also called critical place inquiry (Tuck & McKenzie, 2015), seeks to reclaim land rights with Indigenous communities.

HUMANIZING PLACE-BASED EDUCATION IN SCHOOL CLASSROOMS

In following social constructionism and constructivism, I wanted to understand these three place-based education approaches of sustaining nature,

Figure 2.1. Three Approaches to Place-Based Education

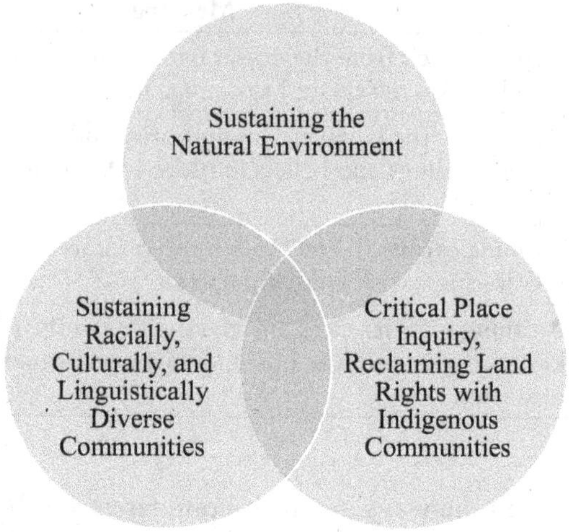

[Venn diagram with three overlapping circles labeled: "Sustaining the Natural Environment"; "Sustaining Racially, Culturally, and Linguistically Diverse Communities"; "Critical Place Inquiry, Reclaiming Land Rights with Indigenous Communities"]

Source: Author

expanding diversity, and dealing with settler colonialism as opportunities for school classrooms, and I wanted to do so in humanizing ways. Humanizing place-based education approaches recognize students' knowledge, culture, and experiences, and share power among people, including between children and teachers (Bartolome, 1994). Humanization requires educators to value the lived experiences, perspectives, and cultural knowledge that children bring with them to school, and then to use these experiences to create democratic classrooms (Freire, 1970). This humanization also has the potential to circulate outside the classroom borders, unfolding among the multiple ecologies that constitute place such as home and community. I believed that all three approaches of place-based education could be used in school classrooms. In my view, all of them are important and, in most cases, some combination of them would be locally appropriate. I myself have worked mostly with the approaches related to sustaining nature and to increasing diversity, studying them and then weaving elements of them into practices in school classrooms.

Sustaining the Natural Environment

Teachers who have the goal of sustaining the natural environment wish to support children in learning to love the earth when they are young, before they have to save it when they are older (Sobel, 2013). As put forth in the literature, the goal of sustaining the natural environment is connected to the notion that modernity, with its use of technology and videogames, is contributing to the "bubble" that separates humans from the natural world; young children today spend far less time outside than any previous generation (Mendoza & Katz, 2013). This fact holds true for diverse children and families. Sustaining the natural environment is linked to the idea that while children are ever more connected with the wider world by technology, they may miss contributing to their local places through democratic citizenship (Anderson, 2017). Finally, sustaining the natural environment critiques the neoliberal standardization of the school curriculum that requires everyone to be on the same page on the same day because the standardization hurts the attention to particularity and adaptation to local communities' needs (Sobel, 2013).

The *pedagogy of place* is a framework that emphasizes the interpenetration of school, community, and environment in contributing to sustaining the natural environment (Sobel, 2013). The idea behind the pedagogy of place is that the child's work quality deepens because of the situated nature of the learner in the community. Traditional school reform, in creating a bubble that protects the White middle class, assumes that (as Smith and Williams [1999], drawing on the work of Wendell Berry, say), "The purposes of an extractive economy [are] to dominate nature and increase the material wealth and security of our species" (p. 2). Instead, a pedagogy of place supports the natural environment because it takes up environmental sustainability, meaning *learning to live within one's means at local and global levels*.

A second principle of the pedagogy of place is *from fragmentation to systems thinking*. Fragmentation means alienation separating children from school. For example, Dewey (1902/2000), in *The School and Society*, saw the deep irony in schools separating children from their lives by not using the child's everyday experience as the basis of education. Instead, he proposed, there should be an ecological and community-based orientation toward education.

The third principle is *from here-and-now to long-ago-and-far-away*, meaning the younger the children are the closer the curriculum should connect with the immediate world, as it is present to the child. To sustain the natural environment, young children should not be studying outer space or cultures around the globe but should be rooted in their local surroundings first and then move slowly "outward" developmentally toward spaces further from home.

Sustaining Racially, Culturally, and Linguistically Diverse Communities

Teachers who have the goal of sustaining racially, culturally, and linguistically diverse communities wish to erase opportunity gaps for diverse communities (Paris & Alim, 2017). Place-based education does not always have a critical perspective, as critical thinking is often downplayed in order to focus on celebrating place. Critical pedagogy has also downplayed ecological dimensions in social injustice (McInerney et al., 2011). However, critical pedagogy and place-based education need not be mutually exclusive (Gruenewald, 2003b).

A critical perspective in place-based education requires teachers to support children in connecting local issues to global economic, social, and environmental concerns like poverty, trade, climate change, and water scarcity. Together, teachers and children question the established order, view how things look from the position of the most disadvantaged, and work for the common good instead of their individual interests (Hursh et al., 2015).

Teachers working to sustain racially, culturally, and linguistically diverse communities acknowledge the danger in focusing only on what is wrong with the world. Critical place-based educators believe this will engender feelings of hopelessness among children rather than imbuing them with a sense of agency and possibility. Hence, this work must combine "a respect for, and a critical reading of, the social institutions, histories, cultures, and environments that constitute students' lifeworlds" (McInerney et al., 2011, p. 12).

Place-based education connects to concerns for equity and culturally sustaining practices in public schools with racially, culturally, and linguistically diverse populations (Demarest, 2015). Culturally sustaining practices are those in which educators tie learning to the histories of nation-states, states, cities, neighborhoods, and histories of the racial, ethnic, and linguistic communities that they are embedded within (Alim & Paris, 2017). Place-based education involves "multiple educational traditions, inquiry, standards-based curriculum design, project- and problem-based learning, and associated best practices" (Demarest, 2015, p. 1). Therefore, place-based education that is culturally sustaining resists standardizing education and stripping it down to the narrowest of facts and skills to implement a "colorblind" approach driven by high stakes assessments, which is often seen as a solution for urban and immigrant students of color (Gutierrez, 2008) and rural White children like those in West Virginia and elsewhere (Howley & Howley, 2015). Instead, in place-based education, spaces are filled with stories from many perspectives that might be categorized as academic subject–specific, or might instead reveal hidden contexts that have been silenced, such as oppression, abuses, and genocides of groups in those spaces in the past and present (Greenwood, 2013). The goal in this work is to help students forge deeper connections to their places, by beginning with what the stories mean to them. For example, following the book *Play Lady/La Señora Juguetona* (Hoffman, 2002), in which a beloved older neighbor's trailer home is vandalized and the local children help her to recover and revitalize her home and garden, children may make multigenerational connections to the problems they and their families and communities have experienced and overcome.

Theoretical Framework

At school, teachers are constrained by mandated curriculum requirements, but there is still opportunity for place-based learning that sustains racially, culturally, and linguistically diverse communities in the selection of subject content and pedagogies. Common Core standards may be a useful tool, according to this approach, as long as teachers have "artistic license to weave them together with authentic experiences and multiple assessment strategies" (Demarest, 2015, p. xii). For example, kindergarten children living in Appalachia might create their own photo-documentation panel of their experience planting, tending, and harvesting pumpkins while researching, discussing, and acting on new knowledge about how acid mine drainage into the local river may affect local crops. This work would align with several Common Core Writing Standards (Common Core State Standards Initiative, 2022) and West Virginia Next Generation Content Standards and Objectives for Science (West Virginia Department of Education, 2022), as shown in the box below.

CCSS.ELA-LITERACY.W.K.3

Use a combination of drawing, dictating, and writing to narrate a single event or several loosely linked events, tell about the events in the order in which they occurred, and provide a reaction to what happened.

CCSS.ELA-LITERACY.W.K.6

With guidance and support from adults, explore a variety of digital tools to produce and publish writing, including in collaboration with peers.

CCSS.ELA-LITERACY.W.K.8

With guidance and support from adults, recall information from experiences or gather information from provided sources to answer a question.

S.K.GS.3

Students will use observations to describe patterns of what plants need to survive.

S.K.GS.6

Students will communicate solutions that will reduce the impact of humans on the land, water, air and/or other living things in the local environment.

The challenge of culturally sustaining place-based education is to get teachers who themselves were educated traditionally to teach in emancipatory ways (Ladson-Billings, 2009).

In assessing this form of place-based learning, students may become a part of the actual assessment approach, as they set goals and track these goals in meaningful ways, not just through rubrics that roll out at the end, but by creating their own tools with criteria that get at understanding what the projects mean to them, what they learned that they did not know before, and how they learned to work together with others (Demarest, 2015). Researchers posit that pursuing locally focused pedagogies might increase student achievement compared to traditional standardized measures (Gibbs & Howley, 2000), although this is not the ultimate point of place-based education.

Reclaiming Land Rights With Indigenous Communities

Teachers who reclaim land rights with Indigenous communities work with children and families to challenge the narrative and practices associated with the colonization of native people, land, animals, and plants. Many scholars, most of them from outside the United States, have developed crucial scholarship that sees a core to place-based education that is not Deweyan (stemming from John Dewey's scholarship on project-based learning and democratic communities from the late 19th and early 20th centuries), but that is Indigenous and has been developing for thousands of years. A main consideration of place-based scholarship that draws on Indigenous knowledge, sometimes called critical place inquiry (Tuck & McKenzie, 2015), is the importance of land in its materiality as well as its intellectual, spiritual, and emotional dimensions. Particular attention might be paid to the relationships between "the global" and "the local" to argue that the intersection between the two provides opportunities for critical engagement with education as an ethics of care (Duhn, 2012b). This care is important to disrupt the discourse of human capital common in globalization. Instead, critical place inquiry is about negotiating new ways of becoming in relation to the world while remembering the histories and stories of a place (Yazbeck & Danis, 2015). Stories should recognize the role of revitalization in culturally sustaining pedagogy and root accountability in Indigenous education sovereignty (McCarty & Lee, 2014), among other decolonizing possibilities, to push back on narratives that present Indigenous and Black communities as "damaged" (Tuck, 2009).

Colonizing approaches from the global West might focus on a belief in the strong individual and see humans as separate from and superior to nature, whereas decolonizing Indigenous beliefs might see individuals address nature appropriately and with respect in order to not disrupt the vibrancy of the universe and to maintain constructive and cooperative relationships

(Tuck & McKenzie, 2015). The ontology of place is "Land-We" (Bang et al., 2014), which is collective and centers the land in the relationship, as opposed to "I-You," which centers personhood. Both of these relationships ("Land-We" and "I-You") can be contrasted with neoliberal "I-It" relationships, which are individualistic and do not center land, but see people as data and objects to colonize.

In reading about the three approaches to place-based education, teachers may draw inspiration from one or more approaches that connect with the assets and needs of local communities. A caution to this work is that White people need to resist their desire to claim a counternarrative of oppression and/or Indigeneity for themselves when doing place-based education, and resist their urge to "save" communities that may seem different or deficient with respect to White and middle-class worldviews (Pearson, 2013; TallBear, 2019). Instead, White teachers and communities might work to create affinity spaces with affected communities and places (Michael & Conger, 2009), which I discuss more in Chapters 5 and 6.

PLACE-BASED TEACHER EDUCATION

I next describe place-based education in my teacher education program, explaining the main goal of becoming more critical about place, and talk about preservice teachers' identities in relation to neoliberal education. I then explain four main pedagogical strategies the preservice teachers learned to help sense and resist neoliberal practices in their places: reflection, dialogism, relationships, and diffraction.

Becoming More Critical About Place

A quality regime dependent on testing demands specific answers; it imposes conformity. Obsessed with its definition of quality, it will impose its framework privileging college and careers on cultures and places that choose other kinds of meaning-making (Dahlberg & Moss, 2005). Perhaps even more concerning, the neoliberal standardized "bubble" can limit, rather than enhance, the individual's search for meanings so central to place-based pedagogies (Fyfe, 2012). As a counter to this, place-based education develops knowledge of the local surroundings, including the sociopolitical context and relationships with those surroundings (Comber & Kamler, 2004; Comber et al., 2001; Schindel & Tolbert, 2017).

Examining social and geographical identities. Preservice teachers must know how their own backgrounds inform their teaching and potentially interact with their practices (Karabon, 2021). Rural and Appalachian identities may affect how preservice teachers respond to social justice pedagogies. Settler colonial notions can come into play in the form of self-indigenization, or taking on the identity of a person Indigenous to the Land (Pearson, 2013). For example, when a White rural student is "from here," they may feel that they know the place the best and that they do not necessarily need their teacher education program and particularly the perspective of a professor and classmates who are from other places (Moffa & McHenry-Sorber, 2018). Preservice teachers might also become part of the "Whitewashing" process because they are White and middle-class and it has benefitted them since they were small. They "become teachers because they liked school as students, thrived within its regimes, and return as wholehearted participants in their historical mission and procedures, thus helping to perpetuate the historical function and process of schools" (Smagorinsky, 2021, p. 30).

Preservice teachers may feel they need the academic pieces from teacher education (i.e., how to teach reading and mathematics content) but not the relational, culturally responsive and social justice–oriented pieces that situate them within a broader social context. The question of who has the right to belong and the realities of globalization collide when White locals, Indigenous people, and the larger world impinging through globalization come together and people are left to decide what to do with the dissonance. This collision presents a challenge for teacher educators because a key component of teacher education is learning to reflect on one's beliefs about other people and oneself, and to shift one's deficit perspectives to see others as valuable people who can contribute to classroom communities. When people are mired in dissonance, it can be challenging to get out of "the bubble."

In culturally sustaining communities, the practices brought to the schools by students of color and other marginalized groups support socially sensitive curriculum development (Paris & Alim, 2017). To do this, classroom teachers must have access to information about students' backgrounds (Karabon, 2021) and know how to incorporate student practices and culture into their teaching and to offer them agency (Karabon & Johnson, 2020). It was important in the teacher education program to work from a place-conscious perspective to include and support all of the preservice teachers. Place-consciousness recognizes that preservice teachers do not all come from wherever the program is located; in our West Virginia case, for example, 40% of preservice teachers come from well outside Appalachia. I needed to take the diversity of preservice teachers' experiences into account when we discussed place-based education. I did this by talking about place more abstractly in the beginning, to allow multiple entry points for preservice teachers with different relationships to the places in which they student taught. Communities of practice and critical friends groups were two types of spaces in which these discussions occurred.

Communities of practice. Communities of practice, which are groups that work together to learn knowledgeable skills (Lave & Wenger, 1991), are an important structure for place-based teacher education. Communities of practice draw on both social constructionism and social constructivism to support preservice teachers' learning. Communities of practice have three components: possessing a shared concern that provides the community with unique identity, engaging in shared activities and discussions, and developing shared practices over time (Wenger, 2002). They can be places in which preservice teachers learn about their students' families' practices through their FoK. Much of the learning processes and habituated knowledge absorbed within a community of practice involves individuals' subjectivities within social, cultural, and natural worlds. However, communities of practice may adopt a focus supporting social constructionism guided by place-based concerns. Working in communities builds understanding and empathy among stakeholders (Brown & Barry, 2020).

In my program, communities of practice were formal small group structures (usually about 10–13 students per group) that met weekly or biweekly throughout the entire 3-year-long Inquiry Strand of the program and had coursework attached that bridged school placements and learning through various perspectives. The communities of practice used Cochran-Smith and Lytle's (1999) social constructionist/constructivist framework, *inquiry as stance,* which can be defined as:

> the positions teachers and others who work together in inquiry communities take toward knowledge and its relationships to practice. We use the metaphor of stance to suggest both orientational and positional ideas, to carry allusions to the physical placing of the body as well as to intellectual activities and perspectives over time. In this sense, the metaphor is intended to capture the ways we stand, the ways we see, and the lenses we see through. Teaching is a complex activity that occurs within webs of social, historical, cultural, and political significance. (Cochran-Smith & Lytle, 1999, p. 288)

The narrative portfolio acted as a bridge between different parts of a community of practice; it opened up spaces to bring people and communities together, to learn from documentation and stories of practice, and to engage in decomposing practices, which means breaking down complex practices to see them more clearly (Grossman, 2011). If all small group members could not be together, the portfolio allowed a space for collaboration. Portfolios, shared online among group members and open for comment, made collaboration possible before sessions when group members met in person. Video clubs, face to face meetings in which preservice teachers met informally with teacher educators to discuss videos of their teaching of young children, were an added layer of the communities of practice. Communities of practice were led by teacher educators, and whenever possible the groups had the same teacher educator over time to build trust, community, and depth of understanding. A peer structure called *critical friends* was also part of the place-based community of practice organization.

Critical friends. I organized 3–6 preservice teachers, typically in the same professional development schools (PDS), into critical friends groups. This idea was inspired by the *pedagogistas* of Reggio Emilia, Italy, who act as "critical, caring friends" who form communities of practice in which "provocations to new thinking and practice" are constructed over time and in relationships (Dahlberg & Moss, 2005, p. 187). I hoped that as their relationships evolved over time, they would foster each other's capacity to undertake instructional improvement and schoolwide reform as fellow intellectuals instead of mere technicians, by learning to use place-based pedagogy to change school curriculum. Critical friends sought to increase early childhood and elementary students' learning and achievement through ongoing practice-centered collegial conversations about teaching and learning (Curry, 2008).

NEGOTIATION: SENSING AND RESISTING NEOLIBERAL POLICIES

To teach early childhood and elementary preservice teachers to engage in place-based practices that may disrupt the "bubble" of the neoliberal accountability cluster, I taught them four strategies to negotiate the context by sensing and disrupting neoliberal policies and practices: reflection, dialogism, I-You vs. I-It thinking, and diffraction (see Table 2.1). The four strategies allow preservice teachers to crystallize aspects of place to make actionable meaning. In other words, the strategies allow multiple paths for preservice teachers to identify, create, and do place-based practices. They can be used separately or combined. The strategies can be integrated organically, through inquiry, readings, assignments, and action research and discussed in communities of practice.

Now, we'll dive deeper into the four strategies.

Reflection

Reflection means taking a metaphorical mental step backwards away from the object being reflected upon in order to think about one's life experience in order to change it (Barad, 2007). The object could be data on one's teaching practice from one's teacher-researcher notebook, a video clip showing a recent lesson, etc.

The idea of teachers' reflection was first put forth by Dewey (1933) and later by Schon (1983). In reflection, beliefs must be grounded in evidence that can be examined in terms of both its truth and its ability to support one's beliefs (Dewey, 1933). In reflecting, open-mindedness is a concept that suggests all belief systems are imperfect and might be strengthened when they are confronted with contrasting beliefs (Dewey, 1933). Educators must strive to meet their teaching goals but at the same time not refrain from the questions of what is good in meeting the goals, for whom, and in what ways (Zeichner & Liston, 1996). For example, how do they as teachers affect families and communities, including racially and culturally diverse ones?

There is a difference between reflection-in-action and reflection-on-action (Schon, 1983). In this view, teachers have tacit knowledge of their own practices that should be made visible through the process of reflection. It is not reflection alone that results in transformation; it is the will to act upon those insights to make change that matters (Mezirow, 1990).

Critical reflection is thoroughly local and personal from start to finish; it is not a standardized process (Liu, 2015) and thus it is often well-suited as part of place-based education. It involves thinking about one's values and how the values and biases situated in social and power arrangements influence the processes of reflection (Brookfield, 1995). Critical self-reflection is a moral action in that there is a particular set of values that guide judgment. It has connected reflection to criticism of social norms and the need to ground political action in social change (van Manen, 1977). In critical reflective learning, teachers "step backwards" to notice the meanings and purposes of education within the broader context in which policies, politics, philosophy, and sociology matter to understandings (Ng & Tan, 2009).

> Critical reflection is a process of constantly analyzing, questioning, and critiquing established assumptions of oneself, schools, and the society about teaching and learning, and the social and political implications of schooling, and implementing changes to previous actions that have been supported by those established assumptions for the purpose of supporting student learning and a better schooling and more just society for all children. (Liu, 2015, pp. 144–145)

Unfortunately, critical reflection is becoming more difficult to engage with as neoliberalism strengthens its hold on early childhood and elementary education (Holloway & Brass, 2018). An "ethics of immanence" (Davies & Gannon, 2013) recognizes that being within something like an oppressive context or relationship can make it impossible for one to remove oneself for the purposes of critical reflection. Recognizing that identities are multicultural, gender-diffuse, class-confrontational, and inclusive would support place-based education that allows members of the community to live better with themselves, others, and their natural settings (Kincheloe et al., 1994). Teachers and teacher educators have a powerful role as both navigators of and constructors of narratives of place that have contributed to local educational cultures (Weinstein, 2007).

Critical reflection is a crucial strategy for social change, yet it does not address every challenge. In order to discern existing power relationships promoting neoliberalism in place-based contexts, I recommend a second strategy called dialogism.

Dialogism

An important way that teachers and teacher educators navigate educational discourses in local settings is through *dialogism*. Dialogism can be defined as the process of meaning-making that evolves from listening to multiple people in order to decide what is most persuasive; dialogism is affected by the social and political contexts affecting the people involved (Bakhtin, 1981). The theory of dialogism (Bakhtin, 1981) supports preservice teachers' processes of critical reflection guided by their teacher educators. Teacher educators can support preservice teachers in understanding the process of dialogism by making their own thinking related to complex issues of policy, assessment, curriculum, and pedagogy visible in communities of practice—for example, by storytelling and thinking aloud.

Preservice teachers are enmeshed in discourses reflecting political, religious, and moral positions. Their thinking—like everyone's—takes the form of internal argument between their own ideas and the authoritative discourses to which they are exposed. They weave in and out of these authoritative and individual discourses, depending on the context of who is addressed and who is answered to. They might ventriloquize policymakers' thinking (i.e., speak in the authoritative voice of policymakers) about the value of high stakes testing if the edTPA shows that they are a good teacher. However, every preservice teacher is different and shaped by their own history, identities, and experiences with local narratives of teaching and other discourses in their student teaching (Sherfinski, Hayes, et al., 2019). Unless teachers can break free from their enmeshment and hear new voices, they will go on to repeat the official language of schooling throughout their daily interactions as teachers (Brown et al., 2021). Recognizing a gap between the authoritative discourses and then separating from the power of the authoritative discourse of teaching is difficult:

> Thus in examining how [preservice teachers] author themselves in relation to policy makers' reforms, paying attention to how and whether there are moments of separation can further illustrate opportunities for [teacher educators] to support [preservice teachers] in conceptualizing how to create democratic learning experiences for their future students that speak back to policy makers' reforms so that they can author themselves as the teachers they want to be. (Brown et al., 2021, pp. 3–4)

Dialogism has the potential to be a powerful opportunity for teacher educators and their preservice teachers to leverage as they work to create more place-based learning opportunities in challenging neoliberal contexts affecting the places in this study, among many more around the United States and the world. By looking for opportunities to both model the process of dialogism and talk with preservice teachers to help them connect their awareness to action and advocacy in early childhood and elementary school classrooms, teacher educators in our program have found dialogism to be an important teaching tool.

It is also important to cultivate relationships that see individuals as equals. This is the third strategy we study in our teacher education program.

Relationships

Caring is "a relationship that contains another, the cared-for . . . the one-caring and the cared-for are reciprocally dependent" (Noddings, 2003, p. 58). Individuals are all the cared-for and the ones caring at different times in relationships, although relationships are rarely equal and symmetrical. A relationship of caring (whichever side you are on) is an "I-You" relation (Buber, 1958). For a teacher, caring is not an official role and requirement; rather, caring is love and compassion for all students. This relation resists the neoliberal context that might diminish teachers' caring roles with its emphasis on human capital investments (Buzzelli, 2020). Caring and personal connections are crucial in early childhood and elementary education because in my place, and beyond it, young children and their families might be excluded or even bullied in schools and communities for not having new clothes, for not going to church or going to the "wrong" one, for looking and speaking differently than the White and middle class newscasters on television, for having an LGBTQ+ family, or for having a parent vote for a candidate who does not fit with the local norm.

In caring relations, life is an encounter in which it takes two to come together as "we," thus overcoming the dualism between "I" and another who matters (Buber, 1958). This theory has special implications for what counts as true educational dialogue, which is carried out in I-You as opposed to I-It relations:

> For Buber, dialogue is an I-You relationship; more being than context, eschewing the negotiation of goals and experience. An I-It relationship is a relationship of things, objects, experience. . . . I-It is an alienation from being human, from encountering others as human, from becoming. There is nothing inherent in a conversation that requires an I-You relationship; indeed, we would argue that overwhelmingly conversations are I-It relationships, especially conversations in educational settings in which there is a goal that the teacher and the students are pursuing. Our argument here is that such conversations, regardless of their structure, are not dialogic. Rather, dialoguing is reflected by an I-You relationship. (Power-Carter & Bloome, 2021, p. 149)

"If dialogue is to occur in schools, it must be legitimate to discuss whatever is of intellectual interest to the students who are invited into dialogue" (Noddings, 2003, p. 183), which would include difficult place-based concerns affecting humans and the environment. Although teachers may fear crossing a line and offending families, administrators, or policymakers by supporting authentic and humanizing dialogue, in reality:

> At present, values are rarely discussed in schools. The supposition is that they are, and should be, discussed at home and church. But even if this were so, it would not be enough. Both home and religious institutions are often engaged in the deliberate inculcation of particular values, and these are sometimes in conflict with each other. The school, ideally, is a setting in which values, beliefs, and opinions can be examined both critically and appreciatively. It is absurd to suppose that we are educating when we ignore those matters that lie at the very heart of human existence. (Noddings, 2003, pp. 183–184)

If educators take to heart the idea that the very work of education in its truest sense relies on examining "critically and appreciatively" values, beliefs, and opinions at school, then the value of place-based education becomes clearer. Place-based education requires humanizing relations, which means the need to form caring "I-You" relationships, which have the potential to expand outward toward places.

However, expansion of our critical place-based values in resistance to neoliberalism is not always easily possible. In this case, diffraction might become an important strategy for educators.

Diffraction

Places are continually made, and remade, through the politics of inclusion and exclusion that determine who does and does not have the right to belong (Duhn, 2012a). *Diffraction* is a process of paying attention to how differences occur and what the effects of those differences are, like in physics, where *diffraction* means waves of light bouncing off an object. It involves acknowledging the powerful role of the knower in knowledge production. It is an ongoing process of relating between matter (places, things, nature, people) and meaning (Barad, 2007). Educators can use diffraction as a way to "bend around" barriers that seemed otherwise impenetrable.

As a method, diffraction is attuned to differences and their effects in the process of knowledge creation—an alternative to reflection, which assumes mirroring fixed positions (Bozalek & Zembylas, 2017). Diffraction is a way of troubling dualisms like nature–culture (Haraway, 1997); whereas in reflection, dualisms are essential in categories like Black–White, student–teacher, child–adult, poor–rich, woman–man, etc. In place-based early childhood and elementary education, the neoliberal push for standardized curriculum might "split" teachers and children from opportunities for authentic engagement with nature. To bend around the barrier, educators might creatively manipulate time and space, for example by reconceptualizing the power of home and community spaces in children's learning to reposition their families' FoK as vital entry points for learning.

QUESTIONS FOR REFLECTION AND DISCUSSION

Approaches of Place-Based Education
- How might you use one or more of the three approaches to place-based education in your place (nature-sustaining, culturally sustaining, critical place inquiry/reclaiming land rights)?
- What questions do you have about approaches to place-based education, and how will you pursue them?

Strategies for Speaking Back to Neoliberalism
- Which strategies for speaking back to neoliberalism (i.e., reflection, dialogism, relationships, diffraction) are familiar? Which ones are new to you?
- How might you use the various strategies for sensing and resisting neoliberalism in your place?
- What additional strategies for sensing and resisting neoliberalism have you heard of or used in your own practice? How might you share these with others in our field?

WHAT'S NEXT?

In this chapter, I discussed social constructionism and social constructivism as epistemological orientations influencing how I see the process of meaning creation occurring in my work in teacher education. I then introduced three approaches to place-based education and specific strategies that preservice teachers might use as tools to engage in place-based education toward the goal of resisting neoliberal policies and practices. In Chapter 3, I build on these conceptual understandings by introducing the context, a narrative portfolio project in which preservice teachers asked and began to answer their own questions about place-based teaching and learning.

CHAPTER 3

The Narrative Portfolio Project

For most of my early years at the university, neoliberal teacher education was, in my opinion, failing teacher educators and their preservice teachers. Neoliberal education was also failing the local public schools when it weakened teacher education. Teacher education and local schools have many opportunities to work together to build relationships for the benefit of children, families, and communities, and for the preservice teachers who are the future of the profession. However, paths toward creating these connections can be difficult for many reasons. These include challenging power relationships, structural inequalities, geographical distance, time pressures, and resistance to engaging diversity in curriculum and teaching (Sherfinski, 2017).

    The narrative portfolio project was a way to speak back to neoliberal educational efforts that emphasized a narrower focus on academics and decontextualized learning. The project challenged power relationships by creating more democratic structures for constructing and coconstructing place-based knowledge. It pushed against structural inequalities by teaching preservice teachers to see and address racist discourses, curriculum, and policies. The narrative portfolio project created a central space to span geographical distance and diminish time pressures by using a digital portfolio approach. And it addressed the resistance to engaging diversity in curriculum and teaching by using place-based approaches and strategies, as discussed in the previous chapter. To understand how these project elements could be developed, it is important to understand the context of my teacher education program before diving into the narrative portfolio project in more depth.

CONTEXT OF THE TEACHER EDUCATION PROGRAM

The *Nation at Risk* report (National Commission on Excellence in Education, 1983), and the U.S. governors' reform initiatives promoted a decentralized system of education that emphasized the development of educational goals and naming the content and skills students are to learn, while assessing their performance (Brown & Barry, 2020). These early initiatives were precursors to an onslaught of standards-based reforms such as the Improving

American Schools Act (IASA), Reading First, No Child Left Behind (NCLB), the Common Core, and Every Student Succeeds Act (ESSA). Policymakers have framed these standards-based reforms as investments in children who are expected to succeed as repayment to the state for the initial investment of tax dollars through their employment, avoidance of social services and prison systems, and they have positioned teachers as technicians who must achieve these future aims (Brown & Barry, 2020).

Teacher education programs have had a hand in this reform work as well. In response to *A Nation at Risk*'s dire warning of America's failing schools, many universities around the United States joined The Holmes Group, a consortium started by a small group of deans at major universities who were concerned with teacher education accreditation and standards. The Holmes Group (1995) drafted a forward-thinking plan called Tomorrow's Schools of Education (TSE) to combat the supposed failure of public schools in general and progressive education in particular because "Much like the nation's automobile industry, university-based education schools long took their markets for granted—in turn, giving insufficient attention to quality, costs, and innovation" (Holmes Group, 1995, p. 5). This project is a prime example of "conservative modernization" efforts of the era, in which new business models of education joined with conservative thinking and created new opportunities and roles for individuals in the field of education (Apple, 2006).

Using the Tyler rationale as its curriculum model, the new plan focused on core academic areas of expertise. The Tyler rationale was established in 1949 as a bureaucratic rationalization of curriculum (Stremmel et al., 2020). It was about setting objectives, planning, organizing educational experience, and administering assessment to create a "fabric" that has quite a bit of control over the lives of children (Foucault, 2007; Kumashiro, 2008). Ralph Tyler, a famed scholar of curriculum evaluation and assessment who worked at the Ohio State University, the University of Chicago, and Stanford University in the early-mid 20th century, modernized the social efficiency approach of curriculum scholars such as Bobbitt by grounding himself in promoting policies and practices of collecting evidence for the evaluation of students' success (Hlebowitsh, 2005). The Holmes Group took up the opportunity to modernize through TSE, and my university and teacher education program were a part of it.

The "10 Characteristics" portfolio used under TSE followed the Tyler logic, as preservice teachers checked off the 10 program objectives. In contemporary times, the Tyler rationale has been taken up largely as "backwards design" (Wiggins & McTighe, 2005). In backwards design, the standard is positioned as the goal and teachers engineer understandings by stepping through a series of objectives forming the "fabric of habits" designed to produce learners who can absorb the standards of schooling (Stremmel et al., 2020).

The TSE project was an opportunity to create alliances that had not existed in the past. Throughout the 1990s, a private foundation contributed over five million dollars to sustain this work. At the inaugural meeting, over 250 educators from public schools and higher education gathered at a local resort to draft its foundational documents. The project's three overarching goals were to revise programs that prepare teachers and other education professionals to make these programs intellectually sound and congruent with one another; to establish public, non-charter professional development schools (PDSs) that would bridge the gap between research and practice; and to establish enduring collaborative processes, strategies, and structures. According to the Holmes Group (1995),

> The PDS is no McDonald's franchise to be set in place ready to operate simply by acquiring the proper equipment and following the rules in a manual. Sweat and tears make the PDS. It is as much a process as a place and its dynamism means that the PDS evolves constantly. (p. 79)

For the first decade, a grant from a local foundation covered the clinical portion of the program. When this funding waned, the program leaders made a three-part plan. First, a collection of mainly White and female local teachers was hired to fill clinical and teaching faculty positions. Second, the program created a "liaison" role for faculty in order to help address the expanded operations of teacher education. Third, one veteran teacher per school was chosen as the Teacher Education Coordinator (TEC). They were paid a stipend to serve as the "university's eyes and ears in the schools" and carry out a number of important functions, including the clinical supervision of preservice teachers.

Seeing the need to cultivate teachers as mentors, in 2011–2013, teacher educators worked with TECs and preservice teachers to provide professional development on reflective teaching, mentorship, and the observation cycle (pre-observation conferencing, observation, post-observation conference as well as prompts and probes toward critical reflection) to improve the quality of supervision in the program. Keeping with the structure of the program, the TECs had the responsibility to train all of the mentor teachers in their schools on this new approach to supervision.

Experiences of Preservice Teachers

The participants in this study represent seven cohorts graduating in 2015–2021, born in the years 1992–1999. This age range spans from the end of the Millennial generation to the beginning of Generation Z (Seemiller & Grace, 2019). These cohorts of preservice teachers were socialized into their own early childhood and elementary educations during the No Child Left Behind Act of 2001 (NCLB) reform era, 2002–2015, which greatly emphasized standardized testing. As "children of NCLB," preservice teachers often see the goal of schooling as completing standards and testing instead of learning (Brown, 2009a). Preservice teachers are situated in places, seeing the world through geographical, social, and cultural attributes of the place(s) they inhabit currently and have inhabited in the past because place is where they form relationships and social networks, develop a sense of community, and learn to live with others (Gruenewald, 2003b).

Assessment and Evaluation Context

Standardized testing in teacher education, and specifically the edTPA, gets personal. My 41-year-old sister died unexpectedly in the fall of 2017, just as the preservice teachers were heading into the home stretch toward submitting the first round of the edTPA examination. I found myself emailing the preservice teachers from my sister's funeral in Wisconsin about details of the exam, afraid they would miss or misunderstand a direction, which might—in addition to the bias I expected some of the preservice teachers to receive from reviewers—cause them to fail. I share this personal example to provide a glimpse of the weight edTPA carries and how preservice teachers and teacher educators might be affected.

In my experience, the preservice teachers most often harmed by standardized testing (e.g., edTPA, Praxis, etc.) were from impoverished White communities or communities of color and/or were first generation college students. Unfortunately, standardized assessment and associated accreditation contexts set up barriers that limited the development of the kinds of teachers all children and their families need. The standardized tests set misaligned performance expectations (Denton, 2013) and then force teacher education programs and schools to surveille the strictures that bind preservice teachers into particular ways of performing as teachers in line with the expectations of these ostensibly neutral measures of quality teaching (Ball, 2003; Bradbury & Roberts-Holmes, 2018). These tests reflect basic academic content knowledge and related skill acquisition (Richmond et al., 2019) in ways that set up the White and middle-class families' advantage seeking while tacitly compromising students in poverty (Brantlinger, 2003).

I have learned to do a better job educating the preservice teachers about the exams and supporting them as they learn academic language to support all learners. Nevertheless, when I interviewed recent program graduates in 2021, 11 of the 12 study participants believed that these standardized tests were not valid measures of good teaching. In their minds, the challenges of Praxis were associated with memorizing content and repeating the tests many times. edTPA was described as a "gatekeeper" that was culturally "biased" toward both students of color and Appalachian students. Both tests set first-generation students and students of color up to fail, according

Figure 3.1. Preservice teachers' experiences with Praxis and edTPA exams

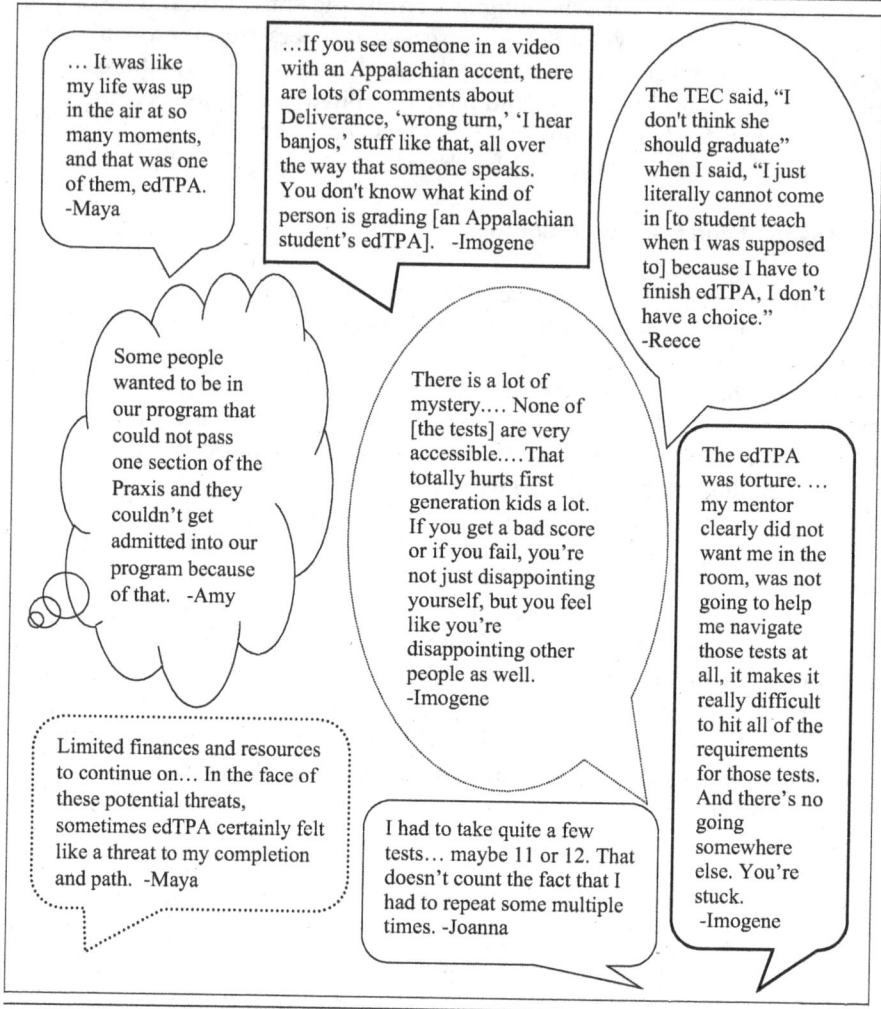

to participants, and the costs involved were prohibitive. Figure 3.1 above shows some of the feelings recent graduates expressed about these tests.

School Classrooms and Mentor Teachers

Through our past study of our teacher education program, my colleagues and I found that:

> A pervasive finding in our data was that deficit perspectives of children and families were prevalent amongst many preservice teachers... both insiders and

outsiders to rural Appalachia. The deficit perspective limited possibilities for Funds of Knowledge (FoK). (Sherfinski et al., 2021, p. 116)

This deficit perspective developed because many teachers were saturated in a view of children, families, and communities that pivots around White and middle-class ideals about social class, family structure, employment, and kinds of engagement with schools; these ideals worked to maintain the status of White and middle-class families (Duhn, 2012b). On investigation, I found that this was in part due to long-term state induction training and professional development for teachers on the Ruby Payne (2005) framework, which taught that "poor children are generally deficient in the cognitive, linguistic, emotional, and spiritual resources needed to escape poverty" (Dudley-Marling, 2020, p. 55).

Ruby Payne's (2005) framework seeks to teach educators how poverty impacts their young students' learning, work habits, and decision-making through what she calls "hidden rules" of people in poverty. Payne teaches her readers how to use the knowledge of those rules to respond through support, instruction, discipline, and relationships.

It is a theory that imputes the problems in a "culture of poverty" to Blackness as well as to poverty itself. Following their ingrained deficit thinking, preservice teachers sometimes struggled with expanding FoK work beyond the thinnest approaches (Sherfinski et al., 2021). Some preservice teachers may not yet have the tools to engage with their students' cultural resources in teaching, learning, and assessment in meaningful ways that allow them to independently rupture authoritative discourses of the curriculum and improvise when they meet prescriptive curricula and tests (Bakhtin, 1981; Brown et al., 2021).

As a teacher educator, I used our study's findings about preservice teachers' experiences to locate new ways to help preservice teachers understand the importance of engaging students' and families' cultural resources in the classroom (Doucet & Tudge, 2007). I introduced the approach of engaging students' and families' FoK through literature and ongoing 1:1 and critical friends' conversations as well as by guiding preservice teachers to engage more with mentors, children, and families whenever possible. FoK portrayed through readings and other sources did not always match the ways in which students and families were discussed at school, such as in this example from a preservice teacher from the earlier days of the program:

> I kind of steered clear of [FoK] because there are so many kids at Chilton Elementary who, their family lives are just appalling. It's so sad, and they don't want to talk about it. So, I feel like I don't want to talk about it with them. But . . . I could ask them about their families or send things home; but my thought behind that was like, well, what if they don't want to talk about [their lives], and what if we don't get our things back?

These comments were not isolated. White and middle-class teachers and preservice teachers have said that low income and/or racial minority families do not care about education; that it is easier to keep families separate from school because families might "raise a fuss" if they strayed from the textbooks; and that poor kids simply can't afford to mess around with the "risk" of children engaging in hands-on projects when there are basic skills that they need to master. I also have heard that "inquiry is not necessary because poor kids already play too much at home."

Teachers enrich learning opportunities when they can draw on knowledge from ethnographic home visits (Karabon, 2017), and these visits enhance academic concept development as well (Barton & Tan, 2009). Creating spaces to work between schools, homes, and communities can be difficult because teachers must carve out these spaces within the standard curriculum (Sherfinski et al., 2016). Yet this could be an entry point for preservice teachers and teacher educators to find ways to penetrate these barriers through place-based education.

THE NARRATIVE PORTFOLIO AS A COUNTER-NARRATIVE TO FAILURE

The narrative portfolio became a tool to work toward a more democratic form of accountability in my teacher education program. In the narrative portfolio project, I used strategies to tacitly unravel the "fabric of habits" (Foucault, 2007) while (re)weaving place-based education with lenses on critical theories of the field. The narrative portfolio created opportunities for democratic dialogue because it was a shared space among preservice teachers, teacher educators, and mentor teachers.

The narrative portfolio, an in-depth form of local documentation, "spoke back" to standardized assessments by providing spaces for preservice teachers to demonstrate their knowledge of theory and practice as it was enacted in natural settings of school and community. The original format for our narrative portfolio was born out of a series of conversations among teacher educators in my college, who had, like myself, experienced e-portfolios while teaching in their doctoral institutions. From this sharing, Dr. Sharon Hayes and I created the unique form of our narrative portfolio at Mayville University to intentionally teach key theories in the field through inquiry-based action research and leadership projects. Through the narrative portfolio process, teacher educators supported preservice teachers to design instruction, practice teaching, document/reflect, and dialogue with others about their work. The narrative portfolio, rooted in ideas of place-based education, acknowledged the need for meaningful assessment and offered an alternative to overreliance on mainstream testing of teacher quality. Table 3.1 shows how democratic accountability elements were connected to the narrative portfolio.

Table 3.1. Democratic Accountability in the Narrative Portfolio

Element of Accountability	How the Narrative Portfolio Supports It
Emphasis on democratic discourse	The portfolio is coconstructed between the university and school with input from children and families through action research. Parts of the portfolio are assessed across six semesters and revised with feedback. At three points mentor teachers, university faculty, and peers review the portfolio. It includes a specific study of democratic education (i.e., Beane & Apple, 2008).
Builds on promising practices	The practices of place-based education and the portfolio derive from and are highly respected in teacher education.
Based on and fosters trust of the profession	The quality of the work is dependent on deliberative discussion and debates about practices that matter to all children and families. These are actively taught in teacher education. The place-based education and action research elements may improve conditions within local schools.
Includes active participation and joint decision-making among relevant local stakeholders	Input from mentor teachers, children, and families is important to both the construction and the assessment of the portfolio over time.
Builds capacity for internal accountability mechanisms that focus on intelligent professional responsibility	Creating the portfolios in a dialogue allows for building a community of practice into the profession that is critically reflective and professional.
Programs accountable for preparing teachers to enact deliberative and critical democratic education so students can engage in democratic deliberation	Place-based teacher education is rooted in studies of critical democratic education and some of the projects, such as lessons, inquiries, and action research, engage more deeply with projects that build opportunities to engage democratically.
Multiple complex local and external measures and accountability tools	The portfolio is used along with many additional tools to better understand preservice teachers' learning and growth. It provides a complex reading on how they are growing in their knowledge of teaching for equity, diversity, and social justice over time.

Source: Cochran-Smith et al. (2018).

Transforming an ePortfolio Into a Narrative Portfolio

ePortfolios use technology like a container to house multimedia artifacts such as audio, video, graphics, and texts. ePortfolios use hyperlinks to organize the materials and evidence connected to important outcomes in order to document preservice teachers' performance and showcase their work for potential employers (Thomas & Liu, 2012). Because ePortfolios are web-based, they lend themselves to collaborative reflection if educators choose to use them in that way (Liu, 2017).

I used a variation of ePortfolios called *narrative portfolios* as an entry point to change teacher education. Preservice teachers' ability to speak about their practice was developed through portfolio and other work over their three years in the professional program. Reflecting more democratic approaches to assessment in which multiple and complex local and external measures and accountability tools are used, the portfolio provided a multi-perspective account of each preservice teacher.

The narrative portfolio is situated in a strong framework of inquiry and created developmentally, with careful attention and support from multiple instructors. The narrative portfolio is a communication tool and space for documentation and both individual and collaborative critical reflection. I viewed the portfolio as key to developing preservice teachers' resistance to neoliberalism through the strategies of reflection, dialogism, I-You vs. I-It relationships, and diffraction.

Dual purpose. The portfolio was designed to respond to the neoliberal context as an ePortfolio while also providing a space for more democratic and humanizing learning as a narrative portfolio. We needed to design the portfolio this way in order for it to be accepted widely in the program. To help preservice teachers navigate the dual purpose, I taught preservice teachers how the portfolio promoted critical reflection and dialogue among different audiences at different times in the program. The narrative portfolio could function in different ways in response to various benchmarks, like admission to the teacher education program, critical reflection, gaining admission to the graduate sequence, deeper critical reflection, showing competency understanding, and using lenses. The portfolio was revised by the preservice teachers, if they desired, to showcase their work for employment.

The portfolios contained educational philosophy statements, narrative observations of their teaching from liaisons and teacher education coordinators, narrative feedback and letters of recommendation from mentor teachers and professors, and letters from parents and students. Transcripts, resumes, and Praxis and edTPA scores could be included as well. The narrative portfolio was a space to negotiate and navigate goals; however, this was not the main intention.

Narrative portfolio. The narrative portfolio was designed to outsmart the neoliberal accountability cluster by reclaiming democratic and humanizing aspects of teaching and teacher education. Fundamentally, the narrative portfolio was created to disrupt the notion of the objectification of data (Bradbury & Roberts-Holmes, 2018). In the narrative approach to assessment, there is still "data" around which meanings are made. The data was not numbers that narrow, however, but rather multivoiced narratives and layered perspectives on teachers and teaching that have expanded interpretations and understandings in order to support, as well as learn from, students.

In terms of assessing an activity, ends arise within an activity, not at the beginning of the activity (Kliebard, 1970). The most significant parts of an activity are those that we could not anticipate. Tyler's argument that ends must be predetermined before activity begins limits the possibilities of children's learning, and also of preservice teachers' learning. This is a point that the narrative portfolio captures in its attention to complex moments of shifting understandings.

Inquiry and Lenses

Place-based education offered an alternative to the narrow neoliberal focus by bridging local and global notions of education with focus on issues of equity, diversity, and social justice, pushing toward democratic notions of accountability through the Inquiry Strand. The Inquiry Strand was a series of weekly small group meetings in cohorts "looping" with the same instructor, when possible, over a 3-year period. I encouraged preservice teachers to reach inward to examine their own and their families' FoK. All of the preservice teachers were in somewhat different places regarding knowledge, experience, and openness. Most were very interested to learn about the theory and practice of teaching at deeper levels.

In teacher education, inquiry-focused communities of practice used eight lenses as entry points toward critically reflective practices and place-based concerns. The eight lenses include:

1. Funds of knowledge (FoK) (Moll et al., 2005)
2. Inclusive education (Sapon-Shevin, 2010)
3. Democratic education (Beane & Apple, 2008)
4. Erasing opportunity gaps (Gorski, 2018)
5. Culturally relevant, responsive, and sustaining teaching (Ladson-Billings, 2009; Paris & Alim, 2017)
6. Fixed and dynamic frames (Johnston, 2012)
7. Critical and family literacy (Vasquez, 2014)
8. Dialogic teaching (Reznitskaya, 2012)

This work revolved around recognizing, exploring, and addressing dilemmas of self, practice, and social responsibility. The preservice teachers went through a scaffolded series of experiences in which they read, discussed, and used the literature on the eight lenses. Lenses are simply ideas guiding an analysis of place. I shared the lenses with mentor teachers in the schools and some mentor teachers read full-length texts such as *Reaching and Teaching Students in Poverty* (Gorski, 2018). I explained the lenses in simpler terms and expanded the language of the original "10 Characteristics of the Novice Teacher" into a language more rooted in diversity and social justice as an entry point (Appendix B).

To begin to do place-based work, preservice teachers and their teacher educators use varied lenses when learning about the places in which they student teach.

Weaving Lenses and Strategies

Preservice teachers metaphorically "weave" lenses and the place-based strategies of sensing and resisting neoliberalism discussed in Chapter 2 to create pedagogy and curriculum. To examine the metaphor of weaving more carefully, imagine the actual material process of weaving a piece of fabric, traditionally created from threads spun from natural fibers, moving the weft in and out through the warp and back again using textured and colored yarns to create and strengthen the product. Metaphorical weaving does not involve material fibers, but it involves combining the critical and the pragmatic. The intended result of this weaving is that preservice teachers will not only sense but also address the challenges that neoliberal policies and practices present. A challenge to this kind of work is that practices are "by their very nature relativistic and ambiguous" (Lenz Taguchi as cited in Mueller & Whyte, 2020, p. 73). Some may not perceive deconstructive approaches in teaching and teacher education to be robust because they are not grounded in one particular theory and not the educational norm or "best practice."

Indeed, in the teacher education program, sometimes people saw elements of the curricula as separate from one another and were worried about this. The products seemed to be delivered for the goal of testing and accreditation requirements. However, people also recognized the layers of interpretation, power, and authority that needed to be navigated as part of the curriculum development process (Pinar, 2004). The weaving of strategies and lenses allows preservice teachers the opportunity to question curriculum, teachers' roles, and the meanings and purposes of schooling (Cochran-Smith & Lytle, 1999), as well to see how neoliberalism does and does not support FoK (Gonzalez et al., 2005). This weaving process is rooted in carefully listening to their students, communities, and places; understanding and responding to national and local standards and mandates; and inquiring about children's FoK so that preservice teachers can counter the deficit perspectives that occur often when class or race borders are crossed (Schultz et al., 2008). I encouraged preservice teachers to examine their own and their families' FoK. As a preservice teacher explained,

> Moll's [FoK] research was one of the first things that we discussed [in our teacher education program]. That was something that strongly impacted me because I was seeing a philosophy and a stance for the first time, which I wasn't exposed to [before the program]. After we would have conferences with [teacher educators] one-on-one, we had those at least twice a semester as we went on, my small group leader would email or talk to you in the meetings about helping you piece information together through different resources and text. So, [they] make you question the route you were taking if it was appropriate, if it wasn't appropriate. If it was really rooted in this stance. (Wren)

Observing and incorporating Funds of Knowledge is an important way to build trusting relationships between homes and schools, relationships that support creating place-based education in the teacher education program. FoK are dynamic and ever-changing cultural knowledge and practices; educators can gather them during visits with families in their homes and they can be used to create new knowledge in classrooms by informing curriculum and pedagogy (Gonzalez et al., 2005; Perry, 2021). "FoK" refers both to the actual "funds" or content that families and children draw on every day and to the FoK approach that is a teaching and research process. Specific FoK reflect the social, economic, and productive activities of local people (Moll et al., 2005).

Coursework

Some of the main assignments for the Narrative Portfolio Project in the Teacher Education Program are included in Table 3.2.

Admissions and Exit tickets, ongoing dialogue journals, and Teacher Researcher Notebooks (TRNs) supported preservice teachers' thinking related to readings, discussions, memories, and work in the communities and schools. They studied ethnographic research methods (Frank, 1999) as well as several approaches to Action Research including critical ethnography (Caro-Bruce et al., 2007; Phillips & Carr, 2014). In their final year of the program, they designed a full Action Research study, wrote a Research Brief, gained all necessary approvals, and crafted a Portrait of Becoming (Appendix C). The action research used in the program evolved from earlier action research shaped by the National Council for Accreditation of Teacher Education (NCATE)'s requirement that an assessment should show a substantive change in children's learning.

Action research became more open-ended in its scope and approach by engaging with deeper "how," "why" and "what" questions exploring context,

Table 3.2. Assignments and Uploads for the Narrative Portfolio

Semester of Professional Program	Name of Assignment/Course
Spring sophomore year (pre-admit)	Whose Knowledge Is of the Most Worth Interviews FoK Photojournal Sharing Teachers' Union Guest Lecture/Waiting for a Superman Critique Admissions Portfolio
1-Fall junior year Practicum 1	Admissions/Exit Tickets Teacher Researcher Notebook (TRN) Inquiry of Self Where I'm From Poetry Out of the Box Project
2-Spring junior year Practicum 2	Portfolio Vignette 1 Admissions/Exit Tickets TRN Inquiry of Student Virtual Backpack Project
3-Fall senior year Practicum 3	Portfolio Vignette 2 Admissions/Exit Tickets TRN Inquiry of Context Journey Box
4-Spring senior year Practicum 4	Portfolio Vignette 3 Admissions/Exit Tickets TRN Inquiry of Practice Family Outreach Project
5-Fall graduate year Full-time student teaching	Portrait of Becoming—Action Research Project (see Note) TRN
6-Spring graduate year Self-designed Contract Hours	Portfolio Vignette 4 TRN Shadow a Community Leader Project Distance and Online Learning Professional Development Project Antiracist Education Book Club Project Professional Development Plan Project

Note: Designates sample assignments included in Appendix C.
Source: Author

learning experiences and advocacy, instead of only pre- and post-academic intervention comparisons. For example, a preservice teacher, Maya, instead of requiring 4th-grade children to memorize the battles of the Civil War, as her mentor teacher typically required, started with the children's own conceptions of freedom:

- "Everyone has the right to choose against something and for something. You are not free if you're killed for something you believe." (4th grade student 1)
- "Freedom means friendships from different races, and happiness between contries (sic) and states." (4th grade student 2)

Maya then used the children's concepts of freedom as the skeleton from which they began to flesh out their historical and sociopolitical knowledge gained through studying their local contexts. The preservice teachers found that Civil War confederate General "Stonewall" Jackson was lionized in town squares when he actually fought on the side of slavery—some local families, community members, and festivals commemorated Jackson's prowess and thus his role in perpetuating White supremacy. Action research drew upon critical literature and theories of the field such as examining the social context of education as part of culturally relevant and sustaining place-based learning, instead of being located in only narrow cognitive psychology approaches, like time on task and other behaviorist interventions. In this way, action research represented a direct move toward more democratic thinking about accountability through complex assessment. My version of place-based education was designed to learn about the communities the preservice teachers student taught in. This work was done by intentionally scaffolding preservice teachers' development through carefully designed readings, activities, learning tasks, and dialogues over the 3 years of the professional program that were carried over into their school-based clinical experiences.

Longitudinal Narrative Vignettes

The narrative portfolio offered a space for preservice teachers to become stronger educators by individually and collectively reflecting on and reimagining place. The portfolio organized specific strategies and lenses for documenting work and crafting stories of practice (narrative vignettes). The vignettes were longitudinal in that they were created over time—the preservice teachers began crafting these during Year 1 of their program and continued creating new narratives and revising old ones in their portfolios.

Documentation. Documentation, which has been called "visible listening," (Rinaldi, 2001) helps children and their teachers to change their identities from products of test-driven schooling, passive recipients of knowledge, to joyful and thoughtful learners. Documentation is an invitation to reflect on values in dialogue with others, to co-construct knowledge, and to potentially change one's own views (Rinaldi, 2012). Teachers keep notes, make videos, take photographs, and retain copies of student work, in order to document the full educational process. It is, admittedly, a partial and subjective view of the learning of each child yet it is a fuller and deeper view than test results can offer. As Rinaldi (2001) says, "Observation, documentation, and interpretation are woven together in a spiral movement in which the parts cannot be separated" (p. 4). Documentation of place-based learning provides the "skeleton" of preservice teachers' narratives. Profoundly, the teacher learns to teach through observing, documenting and interpreting *with* the children and with colleagues (Rinaldi, 2012).

Documentation is a form of assessment that shows the limitations of testing because testing only shows knowledge of the test's content, but documentation offers evidence of children's educational work and developing understanding, which I believe represents true learning. Documentation supports democratic accountability because it creates an ethical and democratic community in which to inspire knowledge and communicate with the place. As Fyfe (2012) explained, documentation is not measurement. Measurement is an exact science: looking at a standardized notion of quality through a standardized unit. The traces of learning seen in documentation are not standardized units, but rather spaces that make reflection and interpretation possible. In other words, documentation fits with a formative rather than a summative or evaluative form of assessment.

Vignettes: the portfolio stories. The primary data source in the portfolio was 4–6 narrative vignettes of 5–12 pages each in which the preservice teachers reflected on their teaching practices through a framework of one or more theoretical lenses. Creating and revising the vignettes required preservice teachers to identify generative, learner-focused, appreciative, and/or disruptive moments from their classroom practices (Wetzel et al., 2017). The vignettes began with the children they worked with and their places. This reflected the understanding that teaching and learning most often should begin and end with the child, in relationship with the teacher (van Manen, 1991). Elements of the vignettes included:

- richly descriptive and well-documented praxis-oriented stories narrating and critiquing their practices, alone and with support
- input from their communities of practice, including critical reflection during video and artifact analysis
- multiple cycles of teacher educator, mentor, and peer feedback
- input from mentors and sometimes children and families about the vignettes.

Vignettes are written performances of practice that let preservice teachers weave discourses that are at least in some ways different from and even resistant to the "fabric" of neoliberal education. They are preservice teachers' multilayered and multimodal stories of their classroom and community practices with children, families, and communities, created in various small groups and classes, revised over time in response to dialogue and new learning, and posted in their portfolios so that they could be easily shared with multiple groups. The preservice teachers' vignettes wove discourses in constructive and co-constructive ways and emerged differently in different classrooms, connecting and weaving with each other across all of us in conversations.

The narrative approach supported preservice teachers in making connections to children's learning and in guiding their learning in "third spaces" (Quintero, 2020). Third spaces included home dialects of children's families and their FoK, as well as the children's lives and experiences (Bhaba, 2004). It was a relational approach that necessarily worked in complex communities of practice and responded to prescriptive, pressured contexts in the local public schools.

The preservice teachers' vignettes helped disrupt technocratic education in moments of classroom life because they were ways in which communities made sense of place while also making the place meaningful within their own cultural contexts (Bird, 2002; Mueller & Whyte, 2020). I hoped that their stories would help bear the load of places shaping humans and humans shaping places by allowing structured places to become habitable ones through multiple entry points that the preservice teachers noticed and/or created (de Certeau, 1984). For preservice teachers, this could be uncomfortable work, as I will discuss subsequently, but work that was essential for their learning and growth.

Mentorship and Collaborative Support

Mentors and teacher education colleagues learned about the narrative portfolio process through communications made in the PDS network. Teacher educators communicated with the Teacher Education Coordinators (TECs), who then shared information with the mentor teachers. Faculty clearly explained the lenses, and connected them to the 10 Characteristics of the Novice Teacher when possible (Appendix B). They offered training sessions for portfolio reviewers in the weeks before Portfolio Night, the concluding event for graduating students. Additional individual training and support were available on an as-needed basis.

Action Research as a Method

Preservice teachers' action research was a semester-long inquiry during student teaching, supported by mentor teachers, communities of practice, and critical friends, a highlight of the narrative portfolio. Action research can be defined as:

> A process of learning to think and act critically, recognize and negotiate political systems, and to focus passion on one's identity as a teacher. Such a process evolves out of a desire to become a caring, intelligent, transformative educator and includes honing the art and science of planning, assessment, and a critical reflective practice that includes the interrogation of one's own paradigm while in active exploration of ways of thinking and acting beyond those said boundaries. (Phillips & Carr, 2014, p. 272)

"Action research takes teachers and students beyond the experience and study of places to engage them in the political process that determines what these places are and what they will become" (Gruenewald, 2003a, p. 640). With roots in early childhood traditions such as the project approach (Helm & Katz, 2016), Reggio Emilia education (Rinaldi, 2012), and anti-bias education (Derman-Sparks et al., 2015), action research contributes important tools for studying and improving teacher practice at both the early childhood and elementary education levels. This is vital in order to push back against the decontextualized contexts of teaching and learning that have been so common in the early years (Hatch & Groenke, 2009) yet are so dangerous to the growth and development of all young learners, particularly children of color, and those in poverty (Sherfinski et al., 2016). I have found that action research teaches preservice teachers how to answer their own place-based questions.

Portfolio Work and Communities

Local working-class family members I was able to interview in a study of the community's early education beliefs and practices, and discussed previously in the literature (Sherfinski, 2017), believed that portfolio sharing helped them to understand the school context better and open up to relationships. For example, a parent interviewed for that study said, "You don't know what the [children] are actually doing on a daily basis until you see a video that shows it" (Jane). Jane said later in the interview that her son, Garrett, being a part of the narrative, and her son's uncle being a part of a family project highlighted in the video, reinforced the family's connection to being part of a learning community.

Preservice teachers in the present study engaged children and families like Jane's with their portfolio and action research work. For example, Heidi was a brilliant preservice teacher who did not pass the edTPA. She was inspired by the work of Barbara Broadhagen, a Wisconsin educator known for her democratic classroom practices (Beane & Apple, 2008). Heidi went on to become certified through another testing pathway available that year, and worked with a partner at her rural PDS on an action research project that used the SeeSaw app to create electronic portfolios for young children as a tool to bridge homes and schools. This work created a space for children as young as kindergarten age to document their best work. Teachers guided the children to lead their family–teacher conferences; they used the SeeSaw portfolio to support the conversations.

Heidi's action research report was included in her narrative portfolio where she presented a vignette that connected the project to the lens of democratic education (Beane & Apple, 2008). She used this as a basis for professional development in her PDS, and kindergarten teachers continued to use this model after Heidi graduated. Additionally, her multimedia narrative on using SeeSaw portfolios to promote democratic conferences with kindergarten children and their families became required reading in my online early childhood literacy course taken by practicing preschool teachers, and her idea rippled through early education centers in the state and region. In this way, I see the narrative portfolio as a tool for building capacity for internal accountability mechanisms focused on intelligent professional responses (Cochran-Smith et al., 2018).

Portfolio Night

Portfolio Night was a special annual event for graduating preservice teachers, with a massive potluck dinner and everyone wearing smart professional dress. In 2020 and 2021, Portfolio Night was virtual, due to COVID-19.

Each presentation group included four preservice teachers, one or two mentor teachers, and one or two university teacher educators. Portfolio Night was cherished by participants, according to feedback received over the 7 years: "I was able to listen to others who have been place-based, and how they look at it differently" (Joanna, Preservice Teacher). Teacher educators seemed to learn and grow from the sharing experience: "It's nice for [preservice teachers] to come in to the group and talk about their experience . . . I think every time I do it, I learn something new" (Janice, Teacher Educator).

A couple mentors I interviewed struggled to understand the role of the portfolio, especially at the beginning, when they were accustomed to the preservice teachers being evaluated on the 10 Characteristics of the Novice Teacher. However, all of the mentors noted that they became more comfortable with the narrative portfolio as they got more actively involved in the teacher education program in various ways, through mentoring, leading small groups, studying the lenses, and participating in the various portfolio reviews. In the next chapters, I show the effects of all of this hard work and support on the preservice teachers' place-based approaches.

QUESTIONS FOR REFLECTION AND DISCUSSION

Creating Your Place-Based Curriculum
- How might you go about weaving your own curriculum in your place?
- Who might be a part of weaving your curriculum?
- What support would you need in weaving your curriculum?

Goals of Place-Based Education
- What are your initial goals for your place-based work?
- How are these goals shared within your teacher education program or school?
- How are these goals shared within your local place?
- How might these goals be fluid and flexible?

Exploring Action Research
- How might action research promote your place-based teacher education goals?

Designing Narrative Portfolios
- How might narrative portfolios address your place-based teacher education assessment goals?
- How might you and your colleagues work together to create a structure to support preservice teachers' development through documenting, crafting, discussing and revising narratives? What would be your first step?

WHAT'S NEXT?

In this chapter, I discussed the context of my teacher education program, with its roots originally planted firmly in the Tyler rationale, which sets out specific objectives for learning in ways that may limit opportunities for developing place-based relationships. The narrative portfolio project created a "rupture" in the former more traditional and neoliberal approach to teacher education, providing a much needed space to (re)claim deep place-based inquiry in early childhood and elementary education. Next, in Chapter 4, we will take a look at how preservice teachers' actual place-based narrative portfolio work unfolded in our local communities.

CHAPTER 4

Resisting Neoliberalism Through Place-Based Narrative Portfolio Work

Twelve preservice teachers are highlighted in Chapters 4 and 5 of this book. Their names are Amy, Cora, Destiny, Frankie, Imogene, Joanna, Lexie, Maya, Millicent, Reece, Sophie and Wren (all pseudonyms). They were chosen for their interest in place-based education and their ability to illustrate how they navigated place in the Five-Year Teacher Education program using strategies of reflection, dialogism, I-You vs. I-It thinking, and diffraction (please refer to Table 2.1 for definitions of these terms).

The preservice teachers who used these four important strategies for disrupting neoliberalism in their work provide an important perspective because they engaged in place-based education across the years of the pandemic, in a combination of face-to-face, hybrid, and remote classroom settings.

In this chapter, I first discuss how preservice teachers were introduced to their professional development school (PDS) communities through a place-conscious process of "getting lost." Then I explain how learning to listen to their students' silences was also a necessary part of place-based education. To illustrate preservice teachers' place-based practices, I show four vignettes, which are stories of place-based classroom practices from preservice teachers. The vignettes show how preservice teachers used their creativity and strength to engage in place-based education by constructing understandings of place. In doing so, the preservice teachers pushed back against the neoliberal practices that they found to be barriers to teaching all children and to creating richer relationships with children and families. Specifically, the narrative portfolio provided a space to bring theory and practice together and intentionally create a community to engage with the neoliberal critique in complicated ways. Thus, the narrative portfolio and the inquiry that surrounded it opened up spaces for more democratic and relational educational possibilities that brought the crucial nature of education as a public good into preservice teachers' cognitive, social, and emotional "maps" and those of their students. The narrative portfolio and inquiry allowed the teacher education program, schools, and especially community members to begin to have more voice in the children's learning.

GETTING LOST IN PLACES

Intentionally, I guided preservice teachers to first "get lost" in their PDS communities as part of the inquiry project, in order to get out of their "bubble" to see their places with fresher eyes. The chapter "Getting Lost in Logan" by Power (2011) is about the "disembodied, dislocated" (p. 53) place-conscious work that becoming part of a PDS community entailed. By meeting a place in multiple "cultural contact zones" (p. 60)—by driving through the PDS community, by walking through it, or by hanging out within it—preservice teachers could learn more storylines about social and cultural identities that bring the natural and cultural elements of a place together. A cultural contact zone is a space where cultures meet and grapple with each other (Pratt, 1991), as I will describe in this chapter. These storylines simultaneously erased and honored places in complex ways. While Logan is a rural county in West Virginia, "Getting Lost in Logan" is actually set in a suburb of Brisbane, Australia, halfway around the globe from West Virginia.

"Getting Lost in Logan" served as a mentor text for weaving lenses and strategies together in preservice teachers' own narrative portfolio work in their communities of practice and had a powerful impact on many preservice teachers' thinking. Likewise, readers might find this diffractive process generative in relation to their own places, which would almost certainly be different from both Brisbane and West Virginia.

Driving

The preservice teachers did their clinical fieldwork in approximately 20 P–5 elementary schools located in a five-county PDS network. Preservice teachers drove more than an hour each way from campus to their school communities. It is a mountainous area with good freeways leading to miles of country roads snaking toward schools that are often larger and newer than one might expect due to the consolidation of one- and two-room rural schools over the past 3 decades. Each town has its own character—yet when preservice teachers drove through their communities they could not see those characters at first, noticing instead the samenesses; the gas station, the dollar store, the post office, the old homes in need of repair. Driving provided a broad overview, but without the next steps, it might be easy to slide into stereotyping their school communities.

Walking

In spending some time walking through their PDS communities, schools, and playgrounds during the first weeks of school, preservice teachers learned from speaking with children, families, and mentors that families lived in these communities for generations. They noticed that there were one or more children of color, including ELLs, most often from Mexico; their parents often worked in agricultural or service industries. Preservice teachers learned from the residents that the communities had been sundown towns, meaning that Blacks had to leave the vicinity before dark (Brown, 2020), and that their PDS schools, if they existed before the *Brown* decision of 1954, were formerly racially segregated schools (Stack, 2008). They also learned from their early discussions with mentors, principals, and community leaders that the overall poverty rate is very high; nearly all schools are Title I and serve all children free breakfast and lunch.

Teachers learned that local employment is in the service sector, coal mining, farming, lumbering, natural gas fracking, health care, and education, and many workers are unemployed seasonally or more permanently. They learned that most of the communities have no childcare centers, and kin care is prevalent. They also learned that the opioid crisis is very real and affects families, as do other health issues.

Preservice teachers learned by walking (and eating) their way through the communities that festivals are common in each county and bring reason for celebration with 4-H competitions, music, bake-offs, and craft sales. They learned that hunting, fishing, camping, 4-wheeling, and dirt bike riding were favorite activities among families. And they learned that church is important to most families, with Baptist, Pentecostal, Evangelical, and conservative Catholic denominations being popular along with mainline Protestantism.

Hanging Out

By "hanging out" in classrooms and communities over time, preservice teachers learned about their early childhood and elementary students' basic needs and mental health. They learned that special education services were strained as policies allowing certification via Praxis gutted college and university special education programs, causing less emphasis on solid practices such as co-teaching between special and general educators and more emphasis on self-contained special education services. They heard their mentor teachers say that behavioral issues children displayed were escalating more and more each year. They sometimes became frustrated when they learned that there was little direct interaction between teachers and families as policies have increasingly limited volunteering and home visits in some professional development schools (PDS).

By hanging out, they learned firsthand the realities of how elementary schools struggled with test scores and were forced to use narrow curriculum such as iReady and the *Journeys* basal reader series designed to promote extensive skills practice and instruction aligned to state assessments. By hanging out, they learned that political talk was no stranger to classrooms; even the youngest children brought knowledge of politics from home to school. They learned that many families and teachers were very conservative and supported Trump during the recent elections, but that there also was social, cultural, and linguistic diversity even within the most seemingly homogenous school.

By hanging out, preservice teachers often saw that childhoods in this context were shaped by how teachers created boundaries and borders that were based on children's race and class status through classroom discourses and practices. By hanging out, Joanna, a preservice teacher, and her critical friend heard through the grapevine of a hidden outdoor wildlife learning site that had been forgotten by her school. Making the outdoor learning site accessible for all people in the community became a project for these two preservice teachers. "Recognizing that places are what people make them—that people are place makers and that places are a primary artifact of human culture—suggests a more active role for schools in the study, care, and creation of places" (Gruenewald, 2003a, p. 627). "The extinction of experience" (Pyle, 2001) is a haunting phrase referring to the double jeopardy of humans' self-imposed isolation when people cut themselves off from rich pedagogical possibilities of contact with nature and are then less able to see natural and cultural diversity. Dominant storylines of place deny our connection to natural spaces like the community wildlife site, and mark sites for future economic exploitation (Gruenewald 2003b). Deconstructing dominant storylines is therefore part of resisting the colonizing tendencies of neoliberalism (Somerville, 2010).

Listening to Silences

Neoliberalism, White supremacy, and poverty affected the communities and classrooms in my study, as I discussed in Chapter 1 of this book. In my teacher education program, I addressed these problems by teaching the importance of a listening stance, which means that preservice teachers entered the classroom with questions as well as answers, and with an understanding of the potential limitations of their views (Cochran-Smith & Lytle, 1999). Explicitly teaching preservice teachers how to listen for those silences that arise when people don't expect to be listened to in empathy (Schultz et al., 2008) was part of the narrative portfolio project and inquiry work, crucial in neoliberal and high-stakes testing times. For example, they needed to learn how to listen for extractive settler colonial narratives, stories that serve to privilege the role of White supremacy by confirming "rights" to land and its products—such as coal and natural gas—for the highest benefit of a particular group, as this is a past that is not closed, but remains an active presence in the place (Nxumalo, 2015). Thus, driving, walking, and hanging out, all opportunities to listen and observe, were important activities for preservice teachers, with the understanding that there was always more to learn.

VIGNETTE 1. CRITICAL REFLECTION ON PLACE

Preservice teachers in my program were taught to explicitly use critical reflection on place to support their students' learning and to continually ask what is working in meeting their teaching and learning goals, for whom, and in what ways (Zeichner & Liston, 1996). In place-based education, this work has special significance when one considers what it might mean to, for example, practice education that sustains nature and diverse cultures in rural places where nearly everyone is White.

Amy's Work

A preservice teacher, Amy sought to deepen her practices in a rural classroom by using Rinaldi's (2012) pedagogy of listening, a promising practice inspired by the highly regarded Reggio Emilia early childhood schools. The pedagogy of listening practice promotes democratic discourse and making multiple voices visible by documenting and discussing them to create a space of connection between school and community (Ceppi & Zini, 1998). In Amy's work, the documentation and discussion of her students' individual and collaborative work promoted critical reflection (Krechevsky et al., 2013) and the generation of narratives (Sisk-Hilton & Meier, 2016) for reflection on action (Schon, 1983).

By working with preschool students to create photos, drawings, and videos of their place-based projects and then stepping back to interpret them together using evidence of learning and reflecting on the actions of her teaching, Amy set up a classroom in which teachers and children could move beyond worksheet-type activities that did not promote much thinking. In this context, the simple act of gaining new insights about how children learn in their places set up a doubled cycle of reflection (Liu, 2015) in which Amy first reflected on business as usual in the classroom and then worked to change those practices.

What is notable here is that Amy included her mentors in the reflective cycle by asking them to work together with her to change her practice to be more place-conscious (Gruenewald, 2003a), through creation of a project to research where the foods the children ate at school and home came from, and to help the kids understand why sustainable agriculture is important for local communities facing food access challenges. Her mentors were willing to bend the practices they were teaching Amy to include fresh thinking and collaboration. Amy read the place-based education and culturally responsive teaching scholarship and translated it for her mentors, who then were willing to trust their professional knowledge and act as "partners in crime" with Amy to engage place-based inquiry, making learning visible through documentation in this farming community during a global pandemic. The community of practice they were co-constructing was not top-down, but shared knowledge among preservice teacher, mentor, and paraprofessional, all of whom brought somewhat different knowledge and experience with place to the table.

Critical reflection during the pandemic. In Amy's classroom, place-based education was shaped by the conditions of the pandemic, in which field trips could not be conducted as usual. Instead, Amy and her mentors brought the field trip to the children (Figure 4.1).

Amy's action can be seen as similar to those suggested in the "Getting Lost in Logan" chapter that she studied in her community of practice. Amy

Figure 4.1. Amy's Documentation of her Teaching Practice

This week I wanted to move the majority of our farm unit to a virtual setting. I wanted to give the students a real-life experience of going to the farm, but due to COVID-19 restrictions, we could not take the students on a field trip. However, my paraprofessional lives on a farm and has farm animals, so my mentor, paraprofessional, and I went on a little excursion to film a video exploring Living Well Farm. While at Living Well Farm, we were able to film cows, horses, chickens, a tractor, a barn, and some hay bales. In this video we were able to show the students different aspects of their farm and even some of the products from animals, like eggs. After the video I recorded a short clip asking the students to create their own farms. They could tell us about their farm by using the microphone, they could draw a picture, use toys or figurines, take pictures, or however they may choose.

moved beyond disembodiment and dislocation by getting out into her PDS community in new ways that she might not have done pre-pandemic, to better understand community agriculture and her students' and colleagues' FoK. This required reconfiguring relations within the community of practice, as described below. This was challenging for Amy, who identified as White and suburban, and who felt a bit traumatized from a former classroom placement where the paraprofessional castigated her for being a "city girl" who "drove a certain kind of car" and "didn't know to put 2 bean seeds in the pot in case one refused to grow" (Amy). During her final student teaching experience, Amy said that although it was disorienting to have to adapt to new mentors, she had found a place in the community.

In her interview, Amy said that COVID-19 was an affordance in some respects because it set the stage for her to support her students' thinking through technological platforms that otherwise would have not been available in her rural school:

> It kind of worked better with COVID because they were doing half-virtual/half in-school. I could pull some of their online work and pictures that they had from home and share it in the class and have them talk about, "This is different from what I did" or "This is the same about what I did" and why it's different and why it's the same. It helped other students develop their thinking, but it really helps me when I could target the similarities between students or differences between students or if students didn't do anything at all because sometimes that was the case in virtual learning. It makes me realize, as a future educator, how important it is to keep up with each of my students and what they're understanding or what they're not understanding or what they're thinking versus maybe what they're keeping out because it's just not relatable to them, all the things they see in their home life. For documentation, I really wanted to understand my students better so I could better teach them, so I could better explore with them.

Amy included a sample of Greta's documentation of her home place (a farm) in her narrative vignette to use as evidence of how she used documentation to help understand Greta's Funds of Knowledge (FoK) from farm life (Figure 4.2).

As I discuss in Chapter 5, place-based work differs between rural, suburban, and urban settings. In that chapter I share additional examples of teachers' creativity during the pandemic in different places (for example, the local city harbor near the school, another place that resonated with their daily lives).

Figure 4.2. Greta's Documentation

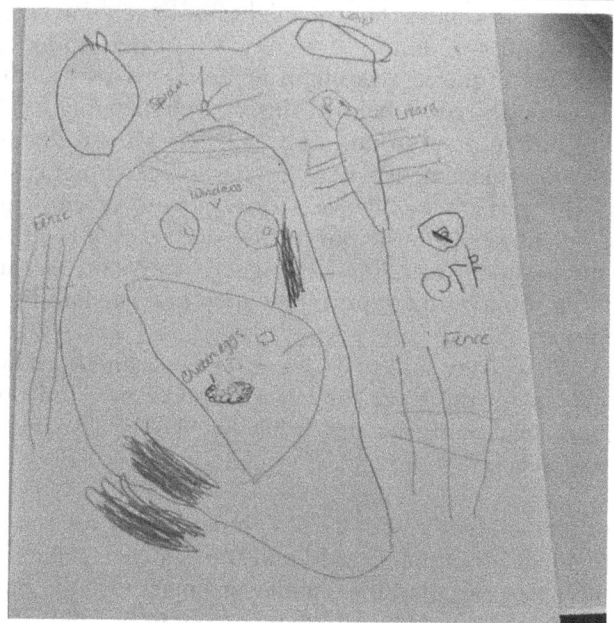

Greta drew a picture with a spider, lizard, fence, windows, and chicken eggs. Greta also shared a video of the goats and pigs that she has at her house. While at school Greta has told me, "The pigs and goats are stinky!" For Greta, her thinking was geared toward animals and how they were kept, which she has had experiences with at her home. (Amy)

Struggling with documentation. Amy studied her students' documentation of their learning, used it to understand her students' FoK, and centered it in classroom activities designed to promote dialogue among students, yet it was "a struggle":

> I looked at the stages of development and I know that [4-year-olds] think more about themselves, kind of egocentric. However, I think that sometimes it's the case of course, but not always. My kids had the ability to relate their lives to their learning and I think that was very powerful for them and I just wanted to give them the time to do the thinking and talk for themselves because I felt so often the time in preschool they're like, "If you can't cut this, we'll cut it for you. If you can't think about this, we'll just tell you."

Struggling with documentation for the purposes of critical reflection showed the ways in which Amy might change her teaching in order to promote better outcomes for her students' learning. This was a space to practice the joyful, democratic life so important for young children's learning. In this space, individuals might grow in a community, understand their own and others' FoK, and be accountable to each other and themselves.

Multiple viewpoints in teacher education. Documentation affords understanding multiple viewpoints in classrooms, as shown in this example from Amy's 2nd grade practicum placement. Students' Funds of Knowledge affect how they view topics within the classroom. The cultures of their homes and available resources have an effect on academic achievement. One day at school, Amy's mentor was discussing the seasons with the students. She asked the students if they knew what the four seasons were. The first boy raised his hand and said, "Deer season!" Amy's mentor said, "No, that is not a season." A second boy then raised his hand and said, "Oh! I know. Rabbit season." Once again, Amy's mentor said, "No, it doesn't revolve around hunting." However, these seasons were viewed through the two boys' perspectives. Even though they were not technically the right seasons, deer and rabbit season could have been connected to the season they were in, to support their FoK. As Amy watched, she realized that the boys were accurately reporting their own, locally-acquired understanding of seasons. Later, reflecting on the scene, she saw that it could be an opportunity to connect the two kinds of season: to say that "deer and rabbit' season was related to "fall season," and in so doing to tie the students' FoK to the vocabulary being taught in a respectful way. Based on her understanding of the opportunity gap lens that she learned about in her coursework (Gorski, 2018), Amy said that she set "high expectations . . . for the students who are in poverty; their places need to be in our curriculum and not so foreign to them." By critically reflecting and re-situating the relations between the children's FoK and the curriculum, Amy found ways to practice place-based education that prepared children to think and do creatively and in community.

VIGNETTE 2. DIALOGISM WITH PLACE IN MIND

Making change as an educator often requires more than *only* stepping back and recognizing the problem that exists and then acting upon that knowledge, as in critical reflection. One must also learn to listen to many voices that might become tools of disruption and make sense of them (Bakhtin, 1981). Preservice teachers may think and act dynamically in ways that are ultimately only fragmented and partial due to their experiences that have shaped their thinking about education (Brown, 2009b). For example, they might reflect and see the scripted curriculum as a tool of neoliberalism and transform it as much as possible in their lesson designs. In partially rupturing neoliberalism, they might inadvertently choose another authoritative discourse. They might choose to teach in a charter school because they believe that they might be free of traditional curriculum there, instead of choosing to teach in public schools in hopes of changing the traditional curriculum to support all students' learning (Brown et al., 2021). Thus, it is the role of the teacher education program to teach preservice teachers the facts about the social context of education so they can find a situation that allows them to practice according to their beliefs about education (Schultz et al., 2008).

Joanna's Work

Older teachers trained in West Virginia were not taught how to offer culturally sustaining opportunities to students, and mentoring programs staffed with these teachers have not kept pace with new ideas and challenges. Although there was support through communities of practice and critical friends in the teacher education program, preservice teachers often needed to rely strongly on themselves to make sense of their places because they did not always have mentors who were open to working in a community of practice. One such preservice teacher was Joanna, who struggled with mentoring relationships while at the same time studying the history, culture, geography, social aspects, and ecosystems of her school community.

In her role as a preservice teacher, Joanna continually navigated what was persuasive. In "walking" through the community's Facebook site, she learned that the local bank literally lost its iconic Victorian turret years ago. When the building, originally a theater, fell into disrepair during an economic recession, the community could not afford to restore and maintain the turret, and the town's leaders decided that it must be removed.

Joanna used dialogism—the process of listening to multiple voices and listening to what is most persuasive—to rupture the deficit discourses from her mentor teacher and broader society. These discourses said that everyone has equal access to a good life, but that those in poverty tended to make bad choices and thus deserved to suffer. According to Joanna, her mentor, who was a White and middle-class parent from the community, described the phenomenon he saw in both the classroom and the community: "We have the takers and the watchers and then we have the givers and the doers." The mentor's statement seemed related to White middle-class advantage-seeking discourses used by community educator parents (Brantlinger, 2003). Such community discourses may be situated within spatialized economic critique, which states that uneven development is a necessary condition for the acquisition of wealth and power. The spatialized economic equation posits that the production of wealth depends on extracting surplus labor and resources from one geographical region to benefit people in another (Gruenewald, 2003a).

It seems that her mentor teacher's statement might reflect a situation of social class reproduction in a place that has long benefitted some members of the community but is currently in a "bust" part of the economic cycle. The decision to weave students' lives into her practices was mediated by Joanna's use of strategies in this rural context oppressed also by standardization and testing. By driving, walking, hanging out, and listening in her classroom and community, Joanna heard voices that contributed to her discerning how she might rupture the binary that superficially positioned children and community members as "deficit" versus "deserving."

Role of teacher educators. Through continually meeting with and cultivating a mentoring relationship with her small group of teacher educators, Joanna, Amy, and the other preservice teachers learned that when they reflected on and redesigned their teaching, they were actually using strategies and lenses: "Sandra [my professor] said, 'That's a strategy, and that's a strategy, and that's a strategy.'" Sandra's voice as a teacher educator was a powerful influence on her students, helping them to think more broadly and holistically to decide for themselves how to navigate the many tools of teaching. It was one that they internalized and that helped them to negotiate their internally persuasive discourse and separate it from the authoritarian discourses they heard around themselves.

The power teacher educators have to "implant" voices is something I also cultivate in the preservice teachers who soon will be on their own. There is a danger, however, in that preservice teachers could interpret teacher educators' voices as authoritarian rather than educative. However, from the evidence in this vignette, it seems that preservice teachers in my program were using teacher educators' voices to help remind them of how they might think more carefully and critically about place. The teacher education program layered in many formal and informal assignments and experiences in which they learned to sort through their possibilities to act.

Rupturing place binaries. As Joanna learned through her place-based readings, the creation of maps helps navigate wanderings and wonderings of place (Power, 2011). Joanna described a map-making task she designed for her class, and specifically her work with a kindergarten boy. From "walking" through student data at school, she learned that his test scores indicated that what he knew academically resembled someone who would be entering first grade; his scores were by far the highest of any child in the class. From hanging out with him, she saw that he struggled more than any other child with creating his heart map, designed to show what he loved about his place (Figure 4.3).

> When asked, "Is there anything else you have in your heart that you would like to draw?" my Kindergartner's response was, "Can I see what they drew in the book again?" I believe he was trying to show me the "right" answer. The next steps for him would be asking him to think critically and share his thoughts after his response to the question, "How do you know?"

Figure 4.3. Heart Map

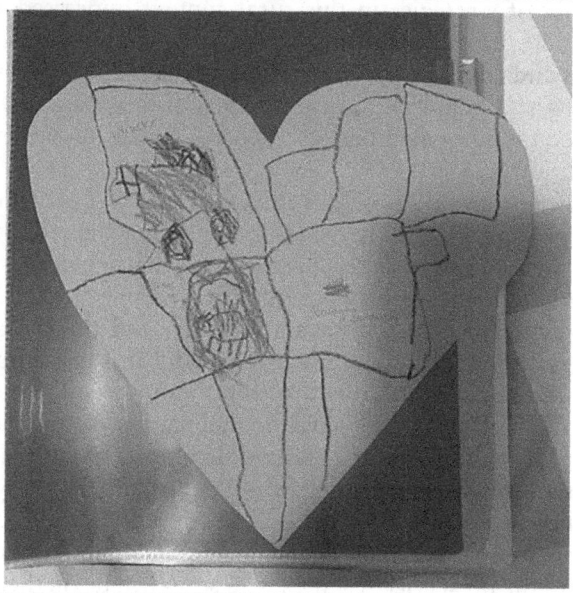

Joanna's reflection showed that, aware of the importance of holistic teaching in the early years, she decided she would teach this kindergartner to think about his own internally persuasive answer, about what he knew to be true, and to provide evidence about how he knew that, by drawing on her seminar reading about hearing silences in the classroom (Schultz, 2010). Joanna detected that he was trying to show the "right" answer—possibly a form of silencing what he knew and loved, perhaps as a form of power or protection; sometimes children wish to protect their academic identity and not expose aspects of culture or place they believe may disagree with being school-smart.

In place-based pedagogy, listening for silence addresses children's rights to silence without rendering them invisible (Schultz, 2010). Joanna learned to trust her kindergartner to think deeply and carefully and to begin to weave his own stories of self, of knowing and claiming what he loved. Like Joanna, he was learning to weave together discourses as he co-constructed understandings of his place.

People learn through their interactions with the people around them, in the places they inhabit, and preservice teachers' questions could be important to helping children make sense in ways that were good for them (Schultz et al., 2008). In her high poverty community, Joanna acted on what was internally persuasive, using inquiry to rupture her mentor's binary of "takers and watchers vs. givers and doers." This is necessary work for place-based education, in which children come to learn to love the earth and then, perhaps, to save it (Sobel, 2013), and in which there may be a need to contribute to understandings of social class, and to protect and preserve one's home life in a school setting that may feel threatening (Schultz, 2010).

As a teacher educator, I took the opportunity to share (with permission) Joanna's work with her kindergartner, and the work of Amy who sought to expand on students' local meanings of seasonality. I presented the work of Joanna and Amy to first-year preservice teachers in my Differentiated Instruction course. I was able to use Joanna's and Amy's work to provoke new preservice teachers to consider how they might resist neoliberalism. I share a page from my own reflective teaching journal, considering how this sharing unfolded:

> Since the first-year preservice teachers in my Differentiated Instruction course were just starting the program and many were not from rural areas, I wanted to expose them to some local texts on rural FoK. I asked them to analyze Amy's deer hunting "season" story and Joanna's heart map story for:
>
> *The presence of FoK—how family and community practices mattered in the stories
>
> *How the lowest level of Bloom's taxonomy, "remembering," was taken up in the stories
>
> *How class, race, gender, and perceived academic ability contributed to the stories
>
> *How FoK might inform how we differentiate the content of lessons
>
> *How testing and children's perceived abilities might be affected by rural norms, and by poverty
>
> I wanted to help transform the first-year preservice teachers' thinking through the ways they thought about and interacted with students in their initial practicum and designed, taught, and reflected on their differentiated lesson plans for my class.
>
> I assigned Amy's and Joanna's stories to small groups. It was very interesting how when I asked a representative to explain the story to the half of the class that did not read and discuss it, the students omitted details about the children's class, race, gender, and perceived academic ability. They also left out details about the context of testing for gifted education in Joanna's heart map story, even though these details were essential for reading it from a critical perspective. They also

omitted how the goal of teaching was remembering (the lowest level of Bloom's taxonomy). When analyzing Amy's deer hunting "seasons" story, the preservice teachers emphasized the importance of elevating "good" cultural knowledge (like hunting) before pivoting to teach their students the "school way" we view seasons. There was no debate that hunting and farming would not be good knowledge for school children (their FoK was not under debate; the question was whether to let it go or use this as a teachable moment). The preservice teachers also stated how important it was to model open-ended questions for Joanna's kindergartner who was advanced academically but very narrow in his perceptions. They believed that he had not been exposed to critical thinking much and had been rewarded for being "right" throughout his life.

I was glad about these interpretations since the preservice teachers themselves often have a hard time seeing beyond correct answers. Yet I wondered why the preservice teachers ignored race, class, gender, perceived academic ability, testing context, and services such as gifted education, since these have been points of discussion thus far in our class this semester and previous classes also continually examined these topics.

I noticed the preservice teachers' reluctance about discussing important elements of their students' identities, and decided that they needed to think about identity from a postmodern perspective. The postmodern perspective draws on poststructuralist concepts and combines them with other theories, including theories that move beyond a global north view, to create a challenge to normative understandings of gender, sexuality, race, ethnicity, and more. The postmodern perspective is needed to question normative understandings because humans "interact in a range of discourse communities, each of which creates a politics of truth and determines what can be said and done by different subjects in that community" (Blaise & Ryan, 2020, p. 82). That being said, even in the most technocratic, prescriptive, and standardized contexts of schools, "because power circulates in relation to knowledge there are also spaces within the discourse of schooling where children and parents and teachers may be able to exercise more agency and power than policies" (Blaise & Ryan, 2020, p. 82). Why, I asked myself, were "my" preservice teachers not speaking about these crucial issues when asked to engage in analysis? What did I need to do differently as a teacher educator? Engaging in this reflection provoked by preservice teachers allowed me to shift my own thinking and eventually come back to antiracist teaching, which I discuss in the next chapter.

In sum, dialogism was an important strategy for preservice educators to negotiate multiple meanings related to place, and to listen to silence in the classroom. Dialogism provided the preservice teachers a way to discern discourses that may promote alienation, versus caring relationship formation, as I discuss next.

VIGNETTE 3. TRANSFORMING I-IT TO I-YOU

The COVID-19 pandemic created a unique hybrid educational context between home and school, in which preservice teachers used their internally persuasive discourses to identify the places in which they might cultivate I-You relationships with families and children. I highlight below two interesting situations for relationship-building that emerged during the pandemic—shifts in technologies and outdoor learning. With support from their teacher educators, preservice teachers used their creativity and strength to define new contact zones for getting to know families and children, and then transformed barriers between home and school so they might see assets rather than deficiencies, and coconstructed emerging relationships that might have more sustained possibilities for curriculum and teaching. This work drew upon and expanded the intergenerational relationships that were often a part of local experience, a key component of critical place-based education (Gruenewald, 2003b). It was a way to push back on neoliberal silencing of families' agency in education.

Millicent's Work

In her very traditional student teaching placement, Millicent committed to calling every parent twice per week for the duration of her student teaching semester to inquire about how they were using the school-prescribed materials and to ask, not only if families were following a prescribed teaching format required by her school and mentor, but how they were using the materials provided in ways that reflected their unique family practices. She used this opportunity as an entry point into progressively deeper conversations. In her action research paper, Millicent reflected:

> I asked if the families have come up with any strategies by themselves at home that they have found beneficial with their child. I had all my students' families answer this week, except for one student. I was able to have conversations with all my focus students' families, and I was thrilled with everything their families shared with me. Families of my focus students told me these things below:
>
> *Mom #1:* We haven't really been using the flashcards that y'all sent home but . . . we've been using the letter tests that you send home to review the letters she doesn't know. She is really starting to get better with remote learning and stays focused longer so it's been a lot smoother process.

> *Mom #2:* I use his letter tests with him and point to random letters for him to identify. If he does not know the letter, we sound it out together. I go over the flashcards with him, but I go from Z to A instead of A to Z, so he is not just singing the ABCs and reciting the letters.
> *Grandma:* I play an alphabet song on YouTube for my grandson while we go over the flashcards so he can sing along.

What I found very interesting after analyzing these conversations is just how different of a take these families had on the same materials provided. These families used both the flashcards and the letter tests we send home very differently with their child, which shows that there is not just one way in which something can be useful and helpful to a learner. . . . Families are coming up with these amazing strategies that are enhancing their child's learning of their letters, and they are doing it in the midst of one of the most crazy and stressful times any of us have ever seen.

Using "old-fashioned" technologies in new ways. I was Millicent's small group leader for action research. Throughout our conversations during her student teaching semester, Millicent's "eyes were opened" (her words). She found, as she read in the literature on home–school relationships we were reading (Lawrence-Lightfoot, 2003; Whyte & Karabon, 2016), that families were more relatable than she imagined at first. She was moving from more of an "I-It" relation of difference between teacher and families, to an "I-You" feeling of mutual respect and understanding by disrupting assumptions of families based on stereotypes related to class and to living in rural spaces in Appalachia.

> Shockingly, all my families were so easy to get in contact with. It was crazy. I have families with parents who were divorced, for instance it was only Mom doing the communicating but she was a night nurse, she worked at night. So, it was hard to communicate with her but she would always call back because we would leave messages. We formed a different way of communicating with her, not doing it every week, but she would let us know. So we just communicated together to figure out something that worked.

In some ways, Millicent's work is far removed from place-based education in that there is little described here for families and children that is experiential or multidisciplinary. Yet Millicent addressed the historical disconnect that positions most Appalachian families as "deficit" and moved beyond the banking conception of education when she valued families' ideas (Freire, 1970). Millicent said, "We're always taught to create a classroom community." Reflecting on the project of doing so provoked her to start asking, "How can we take this a step further? We're talking to our families a lot. They're a huge part of this pandemic remote learning. How can we create a community among them? Could it be sustainable? Is it effective? Does it do anything?"

Millicent was beginning to see the classroom as a created space and seemed to be starting to see that her classroom community might be influenced not only by her choices, but also by who the students were, and what they had learned from their homes and communities, rather than only by what they had learned at school. Millicent created a community newsletter in which she regularly sent home strategies that families had come up with for improvising the teachers' activities from the prescribed curriculum. This was a practical way to share ideas among families and transform the power dynamic so that families' voices were heard. Her concerns for "effectiveness" and "doing" showed that she held on to traces of her understanding that relationships were for the goal of producing learning outputs ("involvement"), while also seeing her students and their families as assets rather than deficits within the learning community. This was a collaborative effort that seems to show that families, even in traditional and conservative communities, were supportive of some of the preservice teachers' more progressive and place-based ideas.

Cora's Work

A new kind of cycle affected teaching and learning for the preservice teachers when the world seemed to shut down due to the COVID-19 pandemic in March of 2020. They needed to shift the place of schooling and revisit their home places. For Cora and nearly all of the preservice teachers, their PDSs closed their doors and preservice teachers' family homes became their new classrooms. Because multigenerational families are common in West Virginia, and became more so during the pandemic, some of the preservice teachers homeschooled their younger siblings, nieces, nephews, cousins, and others during the initial stages of the pandemic; Cora did so with her little niece.

Cora's niece deeply missed her preschool teacher and friends, especially since the transition to home was so abrupt. Cora's work was emotional and relational as well as academic—to help her niece remember her preschool relationships while connecting her with place-based learning in the present circumstances, "mindful of our messy togetherness and beginning to understand . . . our inescapable struggles and interdependent existences" (Yazbeck & Danis, 2015, p. 29).

Learning with multiple generations at home. Prescriptive pedagogies and materials were brushed aside as preservice teachers like Cora came together with family members to represent the world in ways that pleased them. This was not a romantic task. Home places were devastated by income loss, death, and illness. Multiple generations of family members lived together out of need. This shed a new light on FoK as some preservice teachers had opportunities to learn about the assets of their own extended families that they may not have considered previously, even things as simple as being outdoors together, walking in the woods, and collecting firewood.

Preservice teachers needed to (re)learn to belong, participate, and relate (Duhn, 2012a) in ways that were experiential, multidimensional, and intergenerational (Gruenewald, 2003b). In many cases, preservice teachers needed to become their own teachers with less direct and formal support from mentor teachers and teacher educators than they would have otherwise experienced. Cora explained in her portfolio what she learned when she was forced to move back home and educate her 4-year-old niece, while maintaining her own university teacher preparation:

> We live in Southern West Virginia so many of the things that we saw in The Gruffalo [Donaldson, 2006] story (mushrooms, mice, foxes, owls, snakes) could also be found right in our backyard. We went on quite a few nature walks to search for things in nature that we saw in our story. . . . As we walked, my niece was so excited searching for animals and plants that we found in our story. "There's a mushroom," exclaimed my little niece as we walked. We also found different insects, birds, trees, dogs, salamanders, tadpoles, a cat and even a mouse. After our walk, we discussed the similarities and the differences in the animals, insects, and plants that we found on our walk compared to what we found in our story. I asked my niece to create the characters out of playdoh. As she worked, she described the different colors she would need for each one. . . . We had to improvise with some of the colors because we didn't have brown or purple to use for the Gruffalo. I decided to allow her to use playdoh rather than draw the characters like I had originally planned because she loves playdoh. It is such a special treat for her to get to use it.
>
> Engaging this style of teaching using my niece's interests and Funds of Knowledge was very different for me. . . . While teaching at my PDS, I was so used to using material that was already provided. . . . To see how interested my niece was compared to the traditional ways that I had used before . . . proved that taking the extra time to plan was worthwhile.

Cora and her niece were open to exploring their place with fresh eyes, as if it might end at any moment. Indeed, the young girl helped her aunt Cora see things differently—at age four, she was physically closer to the ground and spied what Cora "never would have thought" to enrich her teaching; in this way, Cora's niece helped cultivate an "I-You" relationship, too.

Cora recognized that all people, including White, low-income Appalachian families, have knowledge that can be used in teaching (also

Perry, 2021). This is the mechanism of a fundamental shift in power from "I-It" to "I-You" that can be used in non-rural contexts too. For example, suburban and urban schools and communities in many places of the United States and other countries have gardens that are used for learning purposes, such as the suburban elementary school in Wisconsin that has been the subject of my research, and with whom I have shared ideas back and forth about place-based possibilities across contexts.

The edTPA asks preservice teachers to select students with particular performance levels and needs to highlight in the exam, and Cora was "programmed" to think about children that way through her preparation. As Hicks (2002) writes, "Children and teachers together can contest and transform the relations that position children as 'failures' because they voice and enact working-class identities and values, or Black identities and values" (p. 21). This alternative opportunity to experience engaging with FoK helped Cora to see another way to think about children, space, time, materials, and her own role as an educator, a view that she can transfer to public school teaching in creative ways in the future. It is a way to break from the doubled deficit disorder experienced by young children bottled up in neoliberal schooling—not only culture deficit disorder but nature deficit disorder as well.

Cora and her niece documented the journey together and co-constructed the narrative vignette that Cora included in her narrative portfolio, deepening the intergenerational I-You relations that often begin to crack in a neoliberal culture of schooling that esteems only individuals fit for lives aligned with the culture of success (Sherfinski et al., 2016). This example shows the power in getting preservice teachers out into their places *with* students, to experience them, and to imagine the "I-You" potential for curriculum, teaching, and learning.

Diffraction, the next strategy presented, was used when reflecting, discerning, and cultivating relationships did not emerge as strategies, or when preservice teachers were not allowed to take strong enough action toward transformation. Sometimes preservice teachers needed to go around the barrier that was stifling opportunities to teach.

VIGNETTE 4. DIFFRACTION: BENDING AROUND BARRIERS

The preservice teachers had to figure out how to bend around obstacles: voices of authority, constraining policies, limits in time and space. Many things stood in the way of creating place-based education, but Amy and other preservice teachers engaged diffraction with the support of teacher educators to bend around those barriers. I discuss three common barriers in this section.

Barrier to Place-Based Education #1: Community Members' Wrong Perceptions of Young Children's Capabilities

Amy taught in a rural farming community. She faced challenges doing place-based education with young children during the pandemic. Her original plan was to Zoom with experts from the College of Agriculture to build on children's knowledge of farming practices. Unfortunately, the scientists there said, "We don't have time for the attention span of preschoolers," and "You need to talk to them like they're babies." The scientists would not allow the preschoolers to visit the farm because "they were nervous about the animals getting sick" (Amy).

How Amy used diffraction as one tool to bend around the barrier. Amy decided to persist in figuring out how to do place-based education during the pandemic. She explained how she decided on building a cow simulator (Figure 4.4) in her classroom:

> Any time we talked about farms, the children only wanted to talk about cows and they wanted to "moo" and they wanted to talk about where milk came from. . . . "If I can't get them to a farm to milk a real-life cow, if I can't get real cows to come in, how can I make this possible for them?" I was actually brainstorming with my mentor and aide and we were like, "We could probably make an udder out of a glove or something, we could poke holes through the bottom and just have them pull and it'll squirt out like how you would milk a real cow."

Challenges and limitations. Although Amy's work was creative and it did support children's thinking, a milk simulator might be supplemented with rural children's FoK to co-construct richer knowledge about milking. Amy assumed that children, even those who live on farms, cannot help with farm animals at home and that school rather than their home place was where the children would learn to milk their family's animals. She said, "I think that them getting to see this is what they can see in their community outside of school, they can go home and some of them actually have farm animals and now they can be like, 'Well, I can milk the cow because I learned how to do it in school.' So it's relevant for them." In fact, I found that in my work with school communities, many rural students as young as pre-kindergarten already had direct experience helping their parents milk cows, and those children's FoK might be leveraged in the classroom to deepen understandings of this relevant task. Further, children in suburban and urban areas often have interests in farms as well, as they are connected to their own contexts of food accessibility. Nevertheless, Amy's persistence in creating a teaching experience is admirable. It may not always be easy to engage with

Figure 4.4. The "Milker"

hands-on explorations of students' local issues, but there are often ways that teachers can bend around the barriers of access to resources, even during a pandemic.

Barrier to Place-Based Education #2: Learning Formats Were Not Motivating

Joanna's mentor teachers relied on paper and pencil tasks in the classroom. These unmotivating learning formats increased in quantity during the pandemic because mentor teachers found them easier to manage, particularly when children's movement around the classroom was restricted. As a way to stimulate her students, Joanna decided that the children needed place-based literacy work that they could figure out on their own at home through hybrid instruction during the pandemic.

How Joanna used diffraction as a tool to bend around the barrier. Joanna demonstrated how ordinary objects can resemble letters, or be placed to form them. Then she asked each child to be a "letter hunter" at home, to find C or E or L in household objects or in printed material and when out in the world with their families. They copied these letters into a notebook or photographed them and sent them to Joanna via their portfolio app.

> But I noticed, overwhelmingly, I was very surprised when I came back to school and all students had participated and all were eager to share their documentation. My students were very excited that they found

Figure 4.5. "L"-"C"-"E": Letters at Home and in the Community

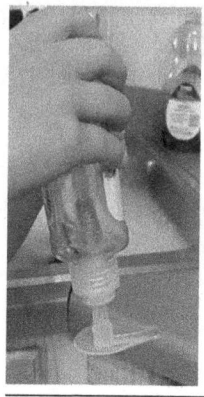
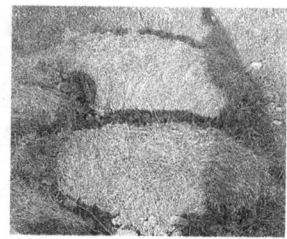
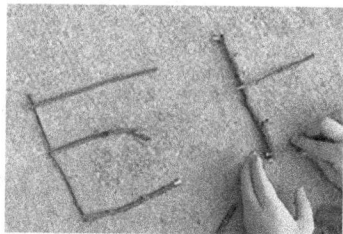

the "E" all the way at their Nana's house. They couldn't believe that the letter "E" was beyond our four walls of our classroom and that it could be somewhere else that they knew.... Place was what brought the class together.

Figure 4.5 shows the letters created by three different children—one child found that his family's kitchen hand soap dispenser turned upside down makes an "L," a second child saw that the hay bales sitting in his family's yard made a "C," and a third child created her own letter "E's" out of sticks that she found outside.

Challenges and limitations. Joanna's mentor liked the project she invented but was not committed to place-based education as classroom philosophy. "I felt like I had made some really good strides and I was seeing such great results in the homework that I was assigning, as opposed to what she was assigning" (Joanna). Joanna noticed that her mentor cared, but didn't want to change her curriculum:

> My mentor made the comment to the students: "Oh my goodness, maybe Ms. Joanna needs to make the materials for the remainder of the year and I can use them next year." Which was very kind, but also kind of defeated the purpose because I was trying to use images relevant to those specific students. So, next year she would need to make the images relevant to those students again.

Barrier to Place-Based Education #3: Prescribed Time for Learning Did Not Allow for Conceptual Understandings to Develop

Wren was required to teach a scripted phonics program that timed flash card work down to the minute. Her mentor rebuked her when she stopped to discuss any aspect of the work in more depth with the children. Limits to time were the obstacle Wren had to work around.

How Wren used diffraction as a tool to bend around barriers. Wren worked with her teacher educator, Sandra. They probed and pushed each other's thinking to reconceptualize time in order to combat the scripted curriculum and critically analyze the nature of assessment to design a performance task that honored children's starting points. Wren explained: "I told Sandra, 'My mentor teacher really wants this [scripted phonics curriculum] done every day.' And Sandra said, 'Try to get it done in 25, 30 minutes. And then you have the extra 20 minutes to make it what you want it to be.'" Wren then used her extra time for her portfolio research project:

> I wanted to try and have the students recognize their sight words in song lyrics. I asked [my early childhood professor] if she could help me because I had all these different ideas that I wanted to try. We worked through two components of the sight words and the music and tried to combine them and make tasks that were engaging and emphasized either one or the other. She was so helpful with it because I felt like maybe this was just a crazy idea that I've wrapped up in my head and it's not really attainable in a classroom setting. And she was like, "Oh, this is such a great idea."

Wren's responsive curriculum design supported her students' FoK between home and school:

> Kenny would watch an Ozzy Osbourne show with his dad. After we completed our sight word search in song lyrics, he came into school and was so excited. He just couldn't believe that he heard his sight words while he was riding in the car with his dad. They were listening to their favorite song, and so he was singing the lyrics to "Crazy Train", emphasizing our Dolch sight words when he sang, "I'm **going off the** rails **on a** crazy train . . ." So even in just the short little part of the chorus, he was able to recognize multiple sight words. I just thought it was awesome because, "Wow, he's using this."

As a teacher educator, I took the opportunity to share (with permission) Wren's diffractive resistance to the scripted curriculum in her rural school with the 1st-year preservice teachers in my Differentiated Instruction class. I present a page from my reflective teaching journal below, to show readers how I perceived my students' response to Wren's work:

> A preservice teacher raised her hand in my Differentiated Instruction class and said, "How are we supposed to differentiate scripted

instruction when we are mandated to follow the program *with fidelity* and teach every kid exactly the same way?"

This was a powerful moment for me because I was able to share Wren's story with the class. I called Wren one of my "sheroes" because she was so committed to supporting her students' FoK in a rural school that she compartmentalized the prescribed program, turning it into a "check off" task. Once she quickly checked off the neoliberal requirement, she had time left to engage with her students around their home knowledge including the exciting connections to "Crazy Train." Preservice teachers who were also experiencing scripted curriculum were excited because they had not yet figured this out. Wren's story was becoming institutionalized as a diffractive strategy for resisting neoliberalism.

Challenges and limitations. Wren explained that she "really was pushing hard to have FoK and place-based education seen in the classroom. And I think the mentor teachers were more reserved about it." She said that she wanted to model for veteran teachers that place-based education was different than their scripted curriculum, but still possible to accomplish. Wren explained that action research being required for the portfolio assessment opened the door to her being able to engage place-based education in elementary school, and it opened the door for me to share this with beginning preservice teachers as well.

Depending on the context, diffraction may include working with various subgroups within their community of practice more flexibly, and listening to support children, families, and communities more democratically.

CONCLUSION

In my teacher education program, documentation of preservice teachers' thinking served as an accountability tool to help them navigate the neoliberal education context. It prepared them to see why, where, when, and how to intervene, and when it was better to "bend around" barriers with their practices rather than to work face-front within the system or simply wait for the right moment in time to intervene, in ways that were place-based rather than prescribed by authoritative discourses. Preservice teachers, as shown in the vignette examples in this chapter, navigated place in a way that helped everyone get out of their "bubbles" while recognizing and respecting local communities and one another. It demonstrated the shared vision preservice teachers constructed individually and collaboratively, and revealed examples of how teacher educators assessed learning and promoted accountability for humanizing places and relationships.

QUESTIONS FOR REFLECTION AND DISCUSSION

Walking, Driving, and Hanging Out
- Try looking at your own teaching context in a new way—explore the spaces unfolding in your place by walking, driving, and hanging out. What do you notice that you have not recognized before? How does what you notice matter for the ways in which you practice as an educator?

Using Critically Reflective Teaching Strategies
- How might stepping back to reflect on your actions as an educator influence what you know and can do?

Using Dialogism as a Teaching Strategy
- How might analyzing the voices of power and authority that influence your teaching shape what you know and can do?

Using Relational Teaching Strategies
- How might actively seeking to relate with all people (including young children) and nature more equitably influence how you teach, and how you might know?

Using Diffractive Teaching Strategies
- What political and pedagogical challenges seem too difficult to address in conventional ways? How might diffraction help you to "think and act outside the box" as a professional educator working to address equitable education for young children, families, and communities?

A Ripple Effect?
- How might creating more socially just learning spaces "ripple" to new learning contexts? Why is this so important when considering the role of place-based education?

WHAT'S NEXT?

In this chapter, I introduced my readers to the actual inquiry-based action research work that the preservice teachers studying in my teacher education program did to resist neoliberalism in early childhood and elementary contexts. In the next chapter, I show how by (re)engaging with an antiracist approach in the narrative portfolio project, preservice teachers and teacher educators were able to construct and co-construct social justice teaching to both challenge White supremacy and support the learning of children in poverty.

CHAPTER 5

Pairing Our Place-Based Approach With Racial Justice

In this study, preservice teachers developed place-based strategies of resistance to the neoliberal culture of education. They used critical reflection, dialogism, diffraction, and "I-You" vs. "I-It" thinking to resist and transform their places. In the previous chapter, I showed how preservice teachers used these strategies to understand and transform some of the challenges facing children, their families, and local communities. In evaluating the program and engaging in deeper reflection, I found that it is also crucial to engage in place-based education because White teachers in the United States are inadequately prepared to address racial dynamics within their classrooms (Doucet & Adair, 2013) and place-based education can fulfill this need because it can support culturally sustaining education. White teachers need to learn to work through their "issues, questions, and hang-ups" related to race dynamics (Doucet & Adair, 2013, p. 94) to support all children's learning; we recognize that White teachers are capable of doing this work (Ladson-Billings, 2009).

The history of testing and standards is one of exclusion and ranking, revealing its function to legitimize racism (Ladson-Billings, 2003). That is perhaps part of why Critical Race Theory (CRT) is under fire of late, because it has the power to help reveal the inequitable context of testing and standardized education that privileges White and middle-class individuals (Luna, 2016). In this study, the neoliberal context revealed White teachers' need for support around race, in part because when the program's time and money were siphoned into privatized, standardized assessment streams like Praxis and edTPA, it was harder for preservice teachers and teacher educators to create space to engage in critical work together.

The problems the program has suffered in adequately supporting all preservice teachers in critically navigating a complicated multicultural society are not the fault of neoliberalism on its own, however. In recent years, I have come to realize that the eight lenses (FoK, Culturally Relevant and Sustaining Teaching, Inclusive Education, Democratic Education, Dialogic Teaching, Critical and Family Literacy, Reaching and Teaching Children in Poverty, and Fixed and Dynamic Frames) are powerful but not enough to support preservice teachers into the future. I realized that a specific focus on antiracist education was missing from the narrative portfolio lenses and overall approach to place-based education.

In this chapter, I discuss how I intentionally taught for racial justice and how racial justice began to affect preservice teachers' conceptions of place-based education. These efforts toward racial justice work challenged the neoliberal accountability cluster at multiple levels. Toward the end of the chapter, I turn my analytic lens to preservice teachers of color, considering how they were served by the place-based teacher education program.

ANTIRACIST EDUCATION

There are two different directions that college and university programs have taken toward globalization in the midst of increasing standardization and testing pressures. One is to conform to the demands of accreditation schemes, which may nominally address diversity (Ladson-Billings, 2003). Ladson-Billings poses the question of whether teacher education programs will produce a "palatable fusion" of multicultural education that is Whitewashed and lacking in substance, or whether the future work will be deep and self-sacrificial, generative with many opportunities to think critically and deeply, and to learn. Standards-based reform has been extraordinarily successful at pushing out opportunities for educators to respond to children's and their families' FoK, such that antiracist and other critical pedagogies are needed (Brown & Barry, 2020). I learned how important it is to weave antiracist pedagogy into the place-based framework.

Antiracism work is teaching and activism that actively confronts racism in society and peoples' daily lives (Kendi, 2019). Antiracism work has a history in the education of young learners (Doucet & Adair, 2013); it has not only been reserved for those children and youth who are in the upper elementary and secondary years. But changing one's attitudes and beliefs about the existence of racial inequalities is difficult for preservice teachers working at any level. Preservice teachers may have an "out of sight, out of mind" approach to engaging in racial justice work, akin to colorblindness (Karabon & Johnson, 2020). Antiracist education is a promising practice by which people can see color and engage in racial justice work instead of turning away. It involves identifying and opposing racism among individuals and in institutions and social structures and challenging all types of policies, beliefs, and behaviors that perpetuate racist ideas (Kendi, 2019). The Black Lives Matters (BLM) movement has been powerful in drawing attention to the importance of antiracist work.

It has been useful to consider why I have not included antiracist education as one of the lenses used in the teacher education program. In many ways, it is due to my colorblindness and anxieties as a White teacher educator. I used the first edition of the book *What If All the Kids Are White?* by Derman-Sparks and Ramsey (2011) my first year teaching in the program (2011–2012) because I thought it would be very appropriate for this place given the racial demographics. It is an antiracist early childhood textbook that provides a solid and compelling argument for why antiracist education is crucial in every place, including rural and Appalachian early childhood education. But the response I received challenged me as an educator.

Preservice teachers pushed back against that text in my Teacher Leadership class because many of them saw "reverse racism" as a serious issue affecting their families and themselves. To challenge their beliefs that reverse racism exists and is a threat to their well-being, I believed that the preservice teachers needed to see demographic data showing how racial demographics are shifting, and the ways in which communities with large proportions of children of color are affected. The first edition of *Reaching and Teaching Students in Poverty* (Gorski, 2013) answered that need. It was palatable to the students because it used supporting children in poverty as its focus, and it satisfied a spectrum of preservice teachers in the program because it focused on concrete practices that they could do in the classroom to boost their students' achievement. It also embraced other lenses like culturally relevant and responsive teaching and specifically challenged the "culture of poverty" (Payne, 2005) framework taught by the state at that time, but it did not take an explicitly antiracist position; and perhaps that was another reason my students preferred it to Derman-Sparks and Ramsey's book. I began threading Gorski's book throughout multiple courses beginning in 2013 and shared it with mentor teachers as one of the lenses for the narrative portfolio.

Strangely, I later buried that memory of doing explicitly antiracist teaching my first year. It was only through looking back at the "archive" of my teaching journals and, oddly, receiving the following letter as I was writing this chapter, that I began to see more clearly how social justice teaching might loop back and support individuals' abilities to think critically.

A "line of flight" (Deleuze & Guattari, 1988) is a moment when something new happens that is unplanned, unpredicted, and results in the production of new knowledge and meanings—it is a kind of rupture, but rupture for the general purpose of understanding and knowledge production. This letter (abridged version below) arrived in December of 2021, as I was working on this chapter of the book. It served as a "line of flight" for me. The letter was from a mentor teacher who had been a preservice teacher in my class a decade prior, during my first year of teaching at Mayville University, when I taught antiracist education. It said:

> Dr. Sherfinski,
> I want to take a moment to tell you thank you. I'm certain you don't remember me, but I have very fond memories of you and what you

taught me. What I learned in your course at Mayville University echoes through the work that I do today. . . .

I remember one time, you had assigned us a reading about legos, resource allocation, social justice ["Why We Banned Legos," Pelojoaquin and Pelo (2006/2007)] . . . I don't remember all of the details, but we had an interaction that I think about frequently. For some reason I was in a bad mood. I have no idea why, but I was salty to say the least. The article asked us to question how we provide equity in the classroom. I wrote some self-righteous, entitled, ridiculous answer and was ready to argue. (Keep in mind that social justice, equity, and culturally relevant education was and still is the most important part of why and how I teach . . . so who knows what my issue was that day . . .) Anyway, the way you responded to me was gentle, kind, understanding, but monumental. When I look back on my career, I attribute, my dedication to equity, to you meeting me where I was, but holding me accountable and reminding me that knowledge is not a limited or non-renewable resource. All students can learn and grow. I don't know that I can put into words all of my gratitude for that moment.

Fast forward 10ish years, after teaching in the Southern and Western parts of the US, I have found myself back in West Virginia teaching and working with preservice teachers.

I know you are in the middle of grading right now, so I hope this helps you remember how "worth it" what you do is!

May Jones
West Virginia PDS Mentor Teacher

This letter represented a line of flight for me because I learned that May, a graduate from 10 years ago, was currently a mentor teacher for some of our preservice teachers, and was committed to social justice. A follow-up phone call confirmed that she was deeply engaged in antiracist education. I received May's letter at a time when I wondered if we would ever be able to build triad relationships that centered social justice or antiracist education. I found from our conversation that May was willing and able to work together to begin to create more three-way spaces among preservice teachers, mentors, and teacher educators, to support our growth as antiracist educators.

Strengthening Antiracist Education

In 2018, three things happened that shifted the ways in which I began to see the strengths and weaknesses of the narrative portfolio.

First, an evaluation of preservice teachers' learning through the narrative portfolio brought up deeper questions about approaches to place-based education. At that time, I was oblivious to the fact that there was not a lens specifically focused on antiracist education. Ironically, the omission of antiracist education occurred while I was advocating for social justice and reconceptualizing the ways in which I taught and assessed preservice teachers in my program.

Second, I applied for and received a post-tenure sabbatical to study early childhood education in the state of Wisconsin. I did this in part because I felt that in West Virginia I was becoming increasingly out of touch with urban and semi-urban educational contexts. I had networks that allowed access to these contexts in Wisconsin, and spent 4 months working with a racially, linguistically, and economically diverse suburban elementary school there (Sherfinski, 2022). In returning to Wisconsin, I noticed increased racial diversity in suburban and rural schools from the previous decade, and greater neoliberal intensification and privatization. I recognized that in only a heartbeat in time, West Virginia would experience more intense place-based challenges related to racial diversity. I renewed my thinking that antiracist teaching was imperative, in order to support White preservice teachers' development, and to enhance P–12 education as well.

Third, dynamic new faculty members were beginning to revitalize the teaching in courses like Social Studies and Diversity, from an antiracist and Black feminist perspective. These three things encouraged me to intensify my work for social justice through action research, inquiry, and the narrative portfolio assessment system.

Policymakers' Reinforcements

I have no illusions that doing antiracist education in West Virginia or anywhere else for that matter is easy, in part because I recognize that place-based histories influence how individuals recognize or deny their cultures—an issue that is worsening due to recently passed and impending legislation. At the time of this writing, Kamala Harris is the first woman of color to be a United States Vice President. She represents a shift in identities, politics, and policy orientations from her predecessor, Mike Pence. While momentous, this changeover in the White House seemed to increase policymakers' attention on controlling how sex and race are (or are not) discussed in public school classrooms. At this time, intensified legislation that seeks to control public school teaching by erasing mention of the systemic and historical nature of racism and banning any teaching that makes students "feel bad" about their race and/or sex has either been passed or is currently pending in state legislatures across the United States. Between January 2021 and January 2022, 39 states had introduced 156 of these bills, 12 had become law in 10 states, and 88 were currently live and specifically affecting K–12 schools (84 bills) or higher education (38 bills), with mandatory punishment for those found to violate them (48 bills) (Sachs, 2022).

It is also important to consider how sexuality, gender, language, (dis)ability, and other issues relate to race issues in that they are also highly politicized and used by some policymakers to create laws that further marginalize groups and individuals. These issues can be opposed in the same way as race issues, through legislation that seeks to ban opportunities to critically discuss marginalized identities in public school classrooms, and that can act in ways that strengthen discourses of oppression. Recent efforts by policymakers to censor LGBTQ+ identities expanded along with policymakers' efforts to constrain critical discussions of race (Sachs & Friedman, 2022). For example, Florida's "Don't Say Gay" bill prohibits teachers from discussing gender identity and sexual orientation in the primary grades, and places on teachers the constraint to make judgments of "developmental appropriateness" of such discussions for any grade beyond primary education (Florida HB 1557, 2022).

In higher education, new laws that undermine free inquiry, expression, and critical thinking are beginning to have deleterious effects on college classrooms (Young & Friedman, 2022). These policies may press faculty to consider the language they use to label programs and events, and to not assign texts or include course sections dedicated to critical race theory (Young & Friedman, 2022). We must confront these pressures in teacher education because we have preservice teachers who come to the program wanting to become social justice educators and expecting to engage with the tools that they need in order to do so (Hawkman, 2017).

In my state of West Virginia, SB 498, called the "Creating Anti-racism Act of 2022 Bill," is pending a crossover vote as I finish this book. SB 498 reinterprets the regular meaning of antiracism, which is a way to address racism as a structural phenomenon rooted in White supremacy. Instead, SB 498 states that public K–12 and university educators teaching that "academic achievement, meritocracy, or traits such as hard work ethic are racist or sexist or were created by members of a particular race, ethnic group, or biological sex to oppress members of another race, ethnic group, or biological sex" or making "an individual feel discomfort, guilt, anguish, or any other form of psychological distress because of the individual's race, ethnicity, or biological sex" (West Virginia SB 498, 2022) are in violation of the law.

Given these developments, a flourishing future for all of us necessitates becoming more conscious and creative about educational possibilities. This is at a time when teachers' professionalism is threatened by policymakers and still challenged by the ongoing effects of a global pandemic.

COVID-19 AND ANTIRACIST TEACHING

COVID-19 smashed our worlds in the spring of 2020. As it did elsewhere, it flattened 5-Year teacher education program spaces to the lifeline of the

Zoom portal and the individual worlds we each inhabited. Responding to local districtwide leadership's decisions, early childhood and elementary preservice teachers in our program experienced different contexts in each of the five counties in which their professional development schools were located.

In the fall of 2020, the preservice teachers were in class face-to-face with their students anywhere from one to four days per week. One preservice teacher did her student teaching completely online as her classroom was the designated "virtual" classroom at her grade level. Other schools provided paper packets and/or online instruction, using platforms such as Schoology, SeeSaw, and Google Classroom when the children were not present in the classroom. Schools took varied approaches in their attention to social distancing and sanitizing protocols within their classrooms. All of these differences took place in local schools and created spaces for discussing place-based education. Furthermore, the edTPA was cancelled for the program that year, creating breathing room for preservice teachers to have one less responsibility cutting into their time in the classroom, and allowing instead space for exploring new ideas like antiracist education.

During the 2020–2021 school year, the preservice teachers had the challenge of doing full-scale action research projects while student teaching during the pandemic. This was part of the required course sequence.

Besides COVID-19, increasing racial violence in the United States and the growth of the Black Lives Matter (BLM) movement were important influences driving changes in my program. Surprising to me as a teacher educator were the ways in which the challenges of COVID-19 and the work of BLM created spaces for some of the White preservice teachers to begin to practice more socially just and antiracist forms of teaching young children. I first want to highlight the case of Sophie, who created her action research study and portfolio approach on the subject of supporting kindergartners' learning of difficult knowledge surrounding the pandemic. Exploring the theme of "dark" and difficult knowledge in kindergarten became an entry point to her antiracist unit during the spring 2021 semester. In the following sections I discuss challenges preservice teachers faced in the PDS network, how I approached teaching for antiracist education, and the outcomes I saw for the preservice teachers.

Dark Funds of Knowledge

Children's lived realities are never fully bubble-wrapped. Dark Funds are the knowledge and epistemologies that do not match with middle-class curriculum standards for success in schooling, but that reflect the realities of local children, families, and communities (Zipin, 2009). Dark Funds of Knowledge include knowledge about bullying, mental health, opioid use, alcoholism, discrimination, and other challenging issues. These difficult topics that have long been Whitewashed from classroom discourse can be important learning aspects because they reflect lived realities of children and families (Grant & Sleeter, 2012) and have affected the lives of some preservice teachers as well.

In Appalachia, Dark Funds of Knowledge are often related to the extractive economy (Sherfinski et al., 2022). Neoliberalism promotes negative consequences both for the environment and for environmental participation, but this is not only a rural problem. Many teachers, unfortunately, do not want to engage the environmental and human problems that are relevant to their students' lives (Ladson-Billings & Dixson, 2021). For example, Black students in urban schools might be set up to "save" the rainforest rather than test the toxic levels of lead and other chemicals in the water that they and their families drink. This form of masking children's and families' lived realities through curriculum and teaching is in part achieved through not engaging or mis-engaging opportunities for understanding children's and families' worlds. "Not tapping children's Dark Funds of Knowledge is a subtle act of not honoring all students' cultural resources that contributes to the act of othering and perpetuating cultural superiority" (Karabon, 2021, p. 4).

In West Virginian communities, culturally responsive place-based teaching is often a pressing need because it is difficult to understand one's own culture as well as other people's when culture is silenced and also commodified (Derman-Sparks & Ramsey, 2011; Sherfinski & Slocum, 2018). This phenomenon is pervasive for White preservice teachers generally (Sleeter, 2017) and for those White preservice teachers enrolled in rural teacher preparation programs (Karabon & Johnson, 2020; Sherfinski, Jalalifard, et al., 2019). A main reason that White preservice teachers feel they cannot engage with conversations about race is that they never learned about race and racism in school, at home, and in the community; families and teachers don't often talk about race when they do not have any direct relationships with people of color (Derman-Sparks & Ramsey, 2011). Understanding the linkages and power relations that connect communities that perceive one another as fundamentally different is vital (Vascellaro, 2011).

Difficult Knowledge and the Pandemic

Understanding children's lived experiences, rather than separating them from their Dark Funds of Knowledge, is a humanizing act that some preservice teachers supported through place-based education developed with the aid of the narrative portfolio approach. The pandemic brought the issue of mask-wearing and individual rights versus public safety front and center in schools and local communities. The narrative portfolio became a tool for preservice teachers and their classrooms to confront this issue, as in Sophie's case of using diffraction to address the politics of wearing masks in schools during COVID-19.

In the rural community that Sophie taught in, wearing masks was viewed as an invasion of privacy and freedom. Thus, teaching the facts about the pandemic risked families' pushback against the activities. Yet Sophie was committed to teaching children the truth about the disease and its effects:

> I strongly believe that what students are learning in the classroom needs to be relevant to their lives outside of the classroom. . . . I felt like we were doing an injustice to the students if we tried to teach them the same way as every other year because this year is nothing like every other year. By incorporating COVID-19 into the curriculum I also realized that I needed to discuss difficult topics with students such as sickness, loneliness, and death. I wanted to give the students an opportunity to talk about how hard it is to live through the pandemic and realize that they are not alone and that there are things we can do to protect ourselves and others from this terrible virus.

Sophie's action research project was creating COVID-19 alphabet books, with each page of the book corresponding to a letter and aspect of the pandemic beginning with that letter (Figure 5.1). Sophie and the kindergartners discussed vocabulary, for example what a "zoonotic" disease means (spread to humans from a wild animal). They also discussed challenges of Dark Funds of Knowledge related to the pandemic as it was affecting their class directly, such as parents' unemployment (disproportionately in the service industries), being unable to see loved ones, more family moving into the same residence, and the death of a live-in relative.

In this very traditional classroom, Sophie introduced discussions of public health that taught the children a specific vocabulary of facts. She encouraged the children to discuss how wearing a mask affects the health of others positively:

> *Child 1:* I wear a mask to protect my teacher!
> *Child 2:* I wear a mask to protect other people like MiMi, Grandpa, Mommy, Bubby.
> *Child 3:* To protect my family and friends.
> *Child 4:* You have to have a mask to help everybody and Ms. Sophie and to help PaPa not get sick.

Sophie also used traditional approaches to quizzing the children on letters, sounds, and vocabulary, lessons typical in this kind of classroom, as vehicles for teaching facts about public health. This was a trade-off between novel content and the traditional learning style she made to be able to engage with the difficult neoliberal context in which she was situated. Sophie taught the children to notice and talk about the multiplicity of identities people hold within local places as they relate to more global contexts (Massey, 1991). In

Figure 5.1. COVID-19 Learning in Kindergarten

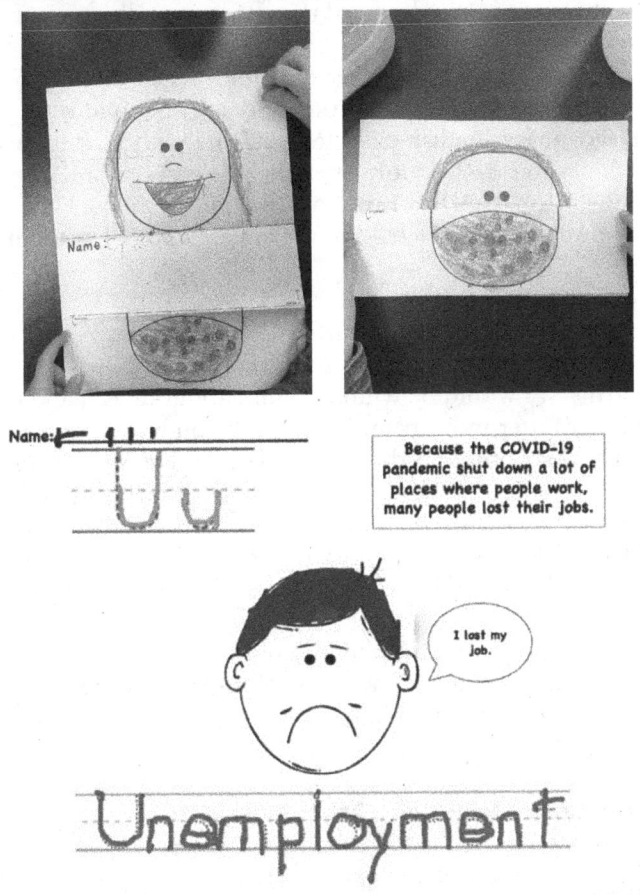

order to do so she had to create a kind of rupture in the classroom. Sophie addressed difficult knowledge directly in the classroom through teaching facts about COVID-19. Yet she did not shake up everything. She recognized the significant forces of neoliberal testing culture in her school and chose to address public health as her social justice challenge, for now. Through her work with the narrative portfolio, Sophie's views on children's subjectivities as knowers and doers in relationship with caring teachers were reinforced:

> Through my research I have learned that "protecting" the student from hard things is unnecessary and even potentially harmful. Like adults, young students experience extreme emotions in response to difficult things that happen to them. I knew that living through a

worldwide pandemic was not easy for me, and it wasn't easy for my students either, and they deserved the chance to talk about that.

Because Sophie earned a teaching certification in special education as well as elementary, she was required to student teach a second semester, which she did in a secondary English class for students with learning disabilities. Coming off her successful action research in kindergarten, she created a portfolio vignette on a Black Lives Matter poetry unit. This experience folded into how Sophie reflected on the importance of teaching difficult knowledge:

> You can incorporate anything with the younger ones . . . we talked about xenophobia [letter "X" in the alphabet book] with my kindergartners. I would be willing to talk about racism and even the Black Lives Matter movement. I just think you have to put it in their terms. But a lot of times, I think when you do the work to put things in terms for younger students, it can be super powerful because you have to simplify it down to what it really means. And some of the things that students will say about it are super powerful too, because it's simplistic, but it's also, sometimes it's just very insightful.

Although not all preservice teachers had the kinds of realizations that Sophie did, her example shows the kinds of understanding and action that are certainly possible for White and rural Appalachian preservice teachers to achieve.

Teaching for Antiracist Education: Two Lessons

The description below is a composite of my reflections on doing antiracist education in my classes and preservice teachers' reflections on what they learned during the program as they created and discussed their narrative portfolio projects.

Lesson #1: Social context and identity work. There were three ways I foregrounded identity work in my courses. The first was to create identity-focused activities and share them in order to build community, the second was to discuss news events that related to teaching work, and the third was to bring in guest speakers to share about the possibilities of racial justice affinity in the rural and Appalachian community.

First, I used a resilience-focused curriculum called *Onward* (Aguilar, 2018) centered on helping teachers understand themselves and their students and families, care for themselves and their students, and avoid burnout. This was important because classes were online and each preservice teacher was student teaching in varied places using different instructional formats, which increased the preservice teachers' feelings of isolation and fragmentation during the pandemic. The political context was important as well. Some White preservice teachers said they thought about their social identities in a previous social studies class, and were now past thinking about them. Some White students said they felt stressed when social identities came up because, since the 2020 U.S. presidential election, they now were "minorities" and feeling "beat up" in their classes and everyday lives.

Second, we studied the news events that took primacy during the pandemic, like the U.S. Capitol insurrection of January 6, 2021, when five people died as an angry mob stormed the U.S. Capitol claiming that the presidential election results were rigged in favor of the Democrats. In my Teacher as Leader class, I introduced a brief article from *The Conversation* (Schonfeld et al., 2021) that presented classroom responses to the insurrection from several educational perspectives. The article suggested addressing the topic, spending ample time using it as a learning opportunity, focusing on White supremacy, helping children deal with the violence they witnessed on television, connecting to the past and future, and learning what "dissent" means. The preservice teachers generally embraced this format of discussion because they felt they were educated about several possibilities and invited to discuss them. End-of-semester feedback was along the lines of, "Listening to our opinions and thoughts on a matter made it much easier to talk in the class." This is the same orientation I provide to preservice teachers through the eight lenses used with the narrative portfolio.

The preservice teachers reported that their mentor teachers were not addressing the insurrection, in part due to the narrowed curriculum forced into early childhood and elementary school by neoliberalism: "My mentor teacher can't even teach any social studies or science, they are not going to take time out to teach about the insurrection." Even though their mentor teachers were under extreme pressures and constraints during the pandemic, teacher education was a space to discuss and imagine place-based approaches. Participants tended to think that the global happens only in other places (Duhn, 2012b), a notion that required additional resources to disrupt. That led to the third activity. I worked with a racial justice affinity activist, who was also the mother of a preschool child and a kindergartner, to promote professional development in developmentally appropriate ways honoring FoK, and then to continue ongoing work in this area through organizations such as the National Association for the Education of Young Children (NAEYC) and the National Council for Teachers of English (NCTE), which has resources for elementary educators as well as secondary teachers.

Teachers for racial justice ally with Black children and families in the local schools and classrooms. For example, a local mother/activist shared insights from her own young biracial children's racial identity development to help illustrate for the preservice teachers possibilities for supporting the development of young learners in classrooms. The speaker explained opportunities for organizing racial justice affinity groups among teachers and families that might look at demographic data on suspension rates and grade retention. The preservice teachers spoke highly of this presentation, and some of the ideas rippled into their antiracist book club projects done later in the course.

Although some preservice teachers mentioned personal discomfort around revisiting their social identities, I found it important for preservice teachers to carefully consider demographic data and examine how their students' and families' lives were affected by their social identities. Unfortunately, this work is difficult because the state's local test reporting is less commonly found disaggregated by race/ethnicity and free and reduced lunch now than it was during the No Child Left Behind era. I have now found alternative ways to approximate this data to see how children of color and low-income children are affected by structural issues in schools and society. For example, adverse childhood experiences (ACEs), if ignored, can have lifelong effects on children. While ACEs occur across all racial and ethnic groups, children of color and those who live in poverty are more likely to experience ACEs, and disproportionate racial and ethnic representation is seen in areas with predominantly White populations, such as rural and Appalachian settings (Iruka et al., 2020). A preservice teacher, Maya, explained how demographic information about the changing racial context of rural and Appalachian communities helped her but would also affect the teachers she worked with to begin to understand antiracist education:

> With the teachers that do not see the students, who do not see the diverse population . . . why are they going to think that they need to be an antiracist? There is just no proof in front of them that that is a necessary change yet. . . . Projections of what our public-school demographics are going to be like, I think that that would be the game changer. . . .
>
> If we cannot elicit the internally persuasive voice, we may end up with a reaction.

Lesson #1 challenged the neoliberalism of both our teacher education program and the local schools because in framing the lesson, teacher educators and preservice teachers recognized two aspects of antiracist work. The first was to use demographic data and the second was to listen more carefully. Both Dark and positive FoK were useful in supporting relational place-based approaches to teaching (Poole & Huang, 2018). Lesson #1 further challenged neoliberalism by giving preservice teachers concrete tools to see, hear, and transform issues of racial injustice that infect educational institutions and communities. These tools gave preservice teachers multiple entry points to "struggle for their souls" (Ball, 2003) within the neoliberal accountability cluster. The tools were available for preservice teachers to use to address the challenges at hand, and thus efficient and effective pathways to creating change.

Lesson #2: Antiracist book club discussions. I structured small-group book clubs on antiracist education in the Teacher as Leader course; groups of four to six participants planned and led their own meetings. I offered a selection of relevant titles and each group chose one to read and discuss. This course was designed around Darling-Hammond et al.'s (1995) four faces of teacher leadership in PDSs; one of these was the use of curriculum development as a teacher leadership task, which inspired the book club format as a dialogic curricular structure. The first book club selected *How to Be an Antiracist* (Kendi, 2019). The second book club selected *Stamped: Remix* (Reynolds & Kendi, 2020). The third and fourth book clubs selected an antibias early childhood book called *Don't Look Away* (Iruka et al., 2020)

For teachers, antiracism work involves taking risks, because there will be criticisms. However, to not do the work in anticipation of criticism is paralyzing. Yet doing antiracism work can bring positive emotions such as hope and inspiration as one works to heal the wounds of alienation and dehumanization that racism creates (Derman-Sparks & Ramsey, 2011). A crucial aspect of supporting preservice teachers' learning in this form of place-based education was understanding preservice teachers' vulnerability, for example, recognizing the risks they took in talking with young children about race and racism (Vascellaro, 2011). After engaging in studies of antiracist education through reading and discussing *How to Be an Antiracist* (Kendi, 2019), Wren was more accustomed to listening and intervening in racial discourses. In a first-grade classroom that semester, Wren was confronted with the opportunity to be antiracist:

> One little girl who is mixed race, it came up that she has a crush on one of the boys in the class who was White. So when we were going in for recess, I heard one of the boys in our class say, "Oh, well, you can't like him because you're supposed to be with a Black boy. You're supposed to like him." And she was like, "No, I don't. I'm not Black. I'm both."

Wren explained in her interview that she commonly heard microaggressions in her classroom, but they went unaddressed by her mentor teacher. But that day, armed with more knowledge and understanding from studying antiracist education, Wren stepped in:

> I took the time to say, "It doesn't matter the color of their skin. It doesn't matter if they're a boy or a girl. It doesn't matter if they have

blue eyes, brown eyes, green eyes, anything. We can like who we like, and we should be accepting of all of our friends in our class."

Although she saw her work as "just a small little aspect," Wren still felt that, "given the research we've done with the readings and the books and the different articles, it really needs to be addressed more, especially in these rural areas, because her family and her siblings are probably one of two families in the school that have this diverse view and ethnic makeup." When confronted with racism at her PDS, Wren listened for what was internally persuasive, bent around the commonplace colorblindness of her school community, and addressed racist thinking. Wren's work was humanizing because it helped her 1st-grade students shift their "I-It" thinking about relationships to "I-You" thinking. She wove the strategies of reflection, dialogism, diffraction, and relationships together with an antiracist lens.

A second insight that the antiracist book club work brought forth was an opportunity to talk very specifically about the challenges of children of color in the PDS schools. Maya saw the need for antiracist thinking in her PDS because her mentor teacher bullied children of color:

> I had a mentor teacher that would talk, would gossip about her students, one of them. "The girl has problems! The girl needs certain services, her family is not stable, she does not have a positive role model at home."

In her interview, Maya revealed that her White mentor teacher seemed to use Maya, a preservice teacher of color, to confirm her deficit beliefs about students and families. In her case, "those who endure the violences of settler colonialism also sometimes bear the burden of resolving it for those who most profited from it" (Ashton, 2015, p. 83).

Maya was treated as a temporary guest in the mentor teacher's classroom, welcomed on the condition of Whiteness: that Maya should agree with the mentor's deficit position of a child and their family based on race, a form of "conditional hospitality" (Derrida as cited in Ahmed, 2012, p. 42). Instead of humanizing discussion about race in the classroom, her mentor positioned Maya in an I-It relation by using her knowledge not for caring for students but in twisting Maya's "racial authority" as a POC to confirm the mentor's White supremacist thinking. The mentor's process seemed to secure her ownership of the classroom by attempting to get those who the dominant group may see as less than human to deny their agency (Wynter as cited in Adair & Colegrove, 2021).

Instead of falling into this game, Maya refracted an I-You relation with the child and served as a reflective and antiracist role model for her mentor. For Maya, *Don't Look Away* (Iruka et al., 2020) was a powerful text because it helped her to find new ways to turn the conversation back to the context and needs of the child:

> Why are we talking about her like she is your friend that betrayed you? She is a child. Instead of talking about her and acting like we are sick of her, let's talk about how we can help her!

Specifically, Maya saw that the *Don't Look Away* book showed the importance of understanding the role of race, as well as intersectionality related to aspects such as geography, in placing children in challenging positions of trauma and difficulty beyond their control. Instead of looking to blame children, Maya learned and shared strategies to understand where children are coming from, so that their Dark Funds of Knowledge become part of the conversation as well as working toward awareness of the positive FoK each child possesses (Poole & Huang, 2018).

Maya continually used her knowledge of racial justice and the local political context to design sensitive curriculum projects for her students. In the first example, I elaborate on Maya's 4th-grade Civil War project first discussed in Chapter 3 of this book. In her interview, Maya detailed the political and pedagogical implications of her work:

> In these tumultuous political times, especially positioned as the teacher with my own views and biases, knowing that the kids are following in the footsteps of their families in whatever ways they are, we can not necessarily change the racism off the bat, but we can plant seeds. When I asked those students, "What does freedom mean to you?" and they were positioning that definition in the midst of Civil War content, their definitions were even transcending into today's world. If they were adults making political decisions that actually were reflective of those definitions that they made for themselves, I think we would have a really great place. But it takes that inquiry into our history, and our inquiry into all learning experiences for the students to come out with positive meaning that we can only hope that they are going to carry with them.

In the second example, this one from 1st grade, I discuss Maya's postmodern literacy project based on the children's book *Black and White* (MacCauley, 1990). Maya created a reader's "mystery" theater to support the children's grappling with uncertainty, at a developmentally appropriate level, as she explained:

> *Black and White* is a mystery. It is four stories, and as you flip the pages, each story has its own life, but there are connections that are

subtle. The kids would think, "These two definitely connect, but I don't know about these two." It was really, really, really fun. I taught multiple perspectives and critical literacy in a child-friendly way. I think that critical learners need topics that maybe aren't always as heavy as the Civil War, but that are just as valid because they use the same skillset of deconstructing meanings.

Maya carefully navigated her neoliberal context, selecting the antibias lessons that she believed would be most appropriate and successful at the moment.

For all of the preservice teachers, the final project in our Teacher as Leader class at the university was to create family-, school-, and/or community-based antiracist book clubs that could be done during their first year of teaching. This assignment was very challenging for preservice teachers because now they needed to consider the specific relational aspects of engaging antiracist education as a form of teacher leadership and racial justice affinity. Destiny provided a good example of how she would work with a group of rural teachers to explore historical facts about the construction of racism through the book *Stamped: Remix* by Reynolds and Kendi (2020) (Appendix D). Each book club group collaboratively produced a plan specific for the book they read and the communities they worked in. Destiny's plan included ground rules for the group, meetings with discussion and hands-on activities, and ways in which to connect the knowledge the community groups co-constructed through their meetings back into the classrooms.

Not all preservice teachers believed that the place-based projects would work well in practice, but even those who were uncertain understood the key considerations and resources for effectively planning and doing such a project. They also learned important lessons about co-researching and planning in a team of colleagues interested in racial justice affinity. To illustrate what they learned, I showed a quote from Wren, whose book club read *How to Be an Antiracist* (Kendi, 2019). She explained that doing such a book club would be difficult in a rural and Appalachian community because she saw the attitudes and values of teachers on the whole as mixed:

> I think certain teachers would be open to it, but I also think the culture as a whole thing might not be as willing to or be accepting of some of the ideas that were presented. Because I know that some views [of other preservice teachers] were challenged in How to Be an Antiracist. . . . So I think it would be something that certain teachers would engage in, but I don't think it would be a schoolwide accepted type of situation book club.

A second illustrative quote is from Frankie, who had just received her first teaching position at the time of her interview. Her prospective school had relatively more racial diversity than most other counties in West Virginia, and certainly more diversity than the county she traveled to for high school. She used her different frames of experience as a way to sort through the possibilities of whether a community racial justice book club using *Don't Look Away* (Iruka et al., 2020) would be effective or not:

> I hate to say this, but the residents of the county where I went to high school are not very open to change, which kind of sucks. So, getting them involved, I think, would be a lot harder. But, I definitely think . . . where it's more racially diverse, the *Don't Look Away* book club would be something that I could definitely do. It would be beneficial, and it would be easy to get teachers and even community members involved.

Lesson #2 challenged neoliberalism by providing accountability and a supportive community to discuss the challenges and affordances of doing antiracist work. It spoke back to the neoliberalism of this place because preservice teachers addressed "the bubble" through designing place-based antiracist book clubs that many hoped to use when they were teachers.

At the same time that they made plans to roll out their book clubs, the preservice teachers felt fearful and uncertain when contemplating the possibilities of carrying this work out, even though they believed it was the most humane way to teach. Comber (2016) suggests that in culturally diverse and high poverty communities, place-based curriculum improves learning based on several factors, including whether children connect to the curriculum ("recognition"), whether the children use the curriculum ("take-up"), and whether the children use the curriculum in novel settings and instances ("translation"). Recognition, take-up, and translation were pertinent areas of learning for preservice teachers, too. My assessment in this study, however, showed that while many preservice teachers were learning to recognize and take up antiracist and place-based education at the end of the study, in 2021, translating their learning to new settings after graduation from college became a challenge, particularly for our White program graduates. It was becoming clear to me that one important aspect of place-based education was missing.

PLACE-BASED EDUCATION POST-GRADUATION

Huerta and Brittain (2010) understand *teacher political clarity and humanizing practice* to describe the call not to undermine the humanity of students of color or to take them for granted, whether they be preservice teachers or children, because we all deserve to be viewed as fully human. In considering teacher political clarity and humanizing practice in this chapter, I sought specifically to center the experiences of preservice teachers of color and preservice teachers who, after graduation, moved on to teach in schools educating children of color.

At the time of this writing, it was too soon to see the effects of place-based, antiracist, and antibias education on the preservice teachers as they graduated and went off to teach in the same or new places. The narrative portfolio project offered a structure that seemed particularly powerful in helping preservice teachers see individuals and culture in ways that were developmentally appropriate. Moreover, critical friends' relationships in the program emphasized developing preservice teachers' critical capacities to act as intellectuals in schools to make change, for example, through curriculum reform. "Place roots individuals in the social and cultural soils from which they have sprung together, holding them there in the grip of a shared identity, a localized version of selfhood . . . [s]elfhood and placehood are completely intertwined" (Basso, 1996, p. 146). People carry their roots from one place to another (Quintero, 2020), and inquiry and the narrative portfolio can be a place to mediate an integrated approach to doing so. For example, Tammy and I shifted geographies but have carried our roots. Purcell-Gates (1997) in her classic text on the Appalachian diaspora illustrated that shift among children and families as well.

Preservice teachers, likewise, shift to new places and spaces and take their roots from their communities, families, and other important relationships. For critical friends Reece, Imogene, and Lexie, the narrative portfolio was a way through which their trust developed; it has continued to grow throughout their first years of teaching in places geographically removed from West Virginia. These preservice teachers had struggled with the challenges of taking the required battery of teacher tests, as mentioned in Chapter 3, yet they succeeded in creating collaborative spaces to share their emerging teacher knowledge (Recchia & McDevitt, 2018). They used their different FoK as Reece is a person of color and Imogene and Lexie are White, to create understandings of how best to support their students. Reece, a West Virginian woman of color, embraced her new role as a 1st-grade teacher in an urban setting, creating a home visiting program to work with families. For Reece, place-based education was deeply influenced by culturally responsive teaching; she saw the two approaches blurring and blending in her everyday practices:

> I think that just being able to understand the inner workings of a child, just really getting that pedagogy and understanding this is who this child is and why, and then connecting it back to their family, their community in general allows me to be like, "Okay I need to bring this into the classroom." Really, just being culturally responsive, this is who they are and this is what I need to bring in. When we learn stuff, what goes at the end of a sentence, we say, "A period, sis." I know all the Tik Tok dances because they all know all the Tik Tok dances, that's just who I have to be in order to keep them focused.

Reece spoke of her students as powerful knowers of their social context. She believed that this was partially because of their identities as well as the teaching she was doing as part of their place-based inquiry. As in this case, when the least advantaged groups, such as Reece and her students, become the possessors of knowledge and have control over the curriculum and assessment in place-based pedagogies, fairness emerges as the new script (Connell, 1995). Desire and humor are also important parts of supporting students in using their cultural talents and skills while also learning the knowledge of the culture of power, needed especially in high poverty places (Brown, 2021; Comber, 2016).

Reece, like Sophie, who designed the COVID alphabet book lesson, also understood that learning might not always be joyful given the realities of her students' lives and their histories. She was adamant about creating place-based opportunities *through* connecting her urban students with local geography:

> The city has a huge inner harbor. . . . we're trying to teach the children about the city because they just think [of their neighborhood] and I'm like, "You guys can literally look out the classroom window and see the harbor." And so many of them haven't even been there.

The harbor, as Reece described it, was a daily reminder of her students' marginality (hooks, 2009). Across the modern-day harbor was the aquarium, the convention center, clean streets, and an absence of glass shattering, tires screeching, and children not making it to the hospital on time. In an all-Black school, in a former slave state, it is possible that some of the children's ancestors were once bought and sold as slaves at the harbor, and that the products of their labor were traded on the docks of the harbor that now hosts touristy businesses and attractions.

Lines are often drawn to segment and section spaces like classrooms and communities, even to create boundaries, barriers, and territories that segregate and colonize these classrooms and communities, walling off children's and teachers' opportunities to learn together in ways that are democratic and humanizing (Heimer & Ramminger, 2020). Because the official purpose of education is formally reduced in high poverty places to preparing workers for the global neoliberal economy, it is crucial that teachers, children, and communities develop an analysis of how the economy functions through space, geography, and social institutions (Soja, 1989). Places are socially constructed, and can be made differently based on the interests of different people (Comber, 2016). Reece started to do such critical place-based work by listening carefully for how extractive settler colonial narratives of the past are not closed, but remain an active presence in this place (Nxumalo, 2015).

Reece worked hard to use her own rooted understanding, her identity, to build on her students' understandings in her new place. She organized home visits to learn more about families' FoK and used this information to design project-based curriculum; she and the students took walking field trips and did nature studies. She took advantage of the technologies that corporate sponsors provided to support her young students' inquiries. Reece had ideas of how her students might engage with what is interesting to them, like the patch of ground on which cicadas called in the summer and left their shed exoskeletons, seeing their school greenspace as more than the space they walked by on the way into the school (Nxumalo, 2019).

Reece's project required a spatial and historical analysis of the global neoliberal context that the strategies and lenses we taught did not provide. However, Reece built on her FoK and that of her students, drew on her roots from her life including the weaving she learned in her teacher education program, expanded her reading and thinking, and connected it with what she learned from her students and their families on a daily basis. As a beginning teacher, she organically created place-based education that was decolonizing (Adair & Colegrove, 2021).

Imogene and Lexie were White women from rural areas and critical friends with Reece in the teacher education program. They continued their relationship as critical friends when they graduated and moved to their first teaching jobs, all in urban or suburban schools in different states. Imogene and Lexie mentioned in their interviews that they were "proud of" and "inspired by" their former classmate, Reece, and the work that she was doing at an all-Black urban school. Imogene and Lexie looked to Reece for ideas about supporting racially and culturally diverse students, and modeled themselves as much as they could on her concrete examples of culturally responsive approaches to supporting students of color. Reece spoke to this role positioning in her interview:

> I have a unique role as a Black woman in West Virginia where there are really so few Black people. I feel like it's kind of hard, but you need to just have to let people know you care. You know, I know that people sometimes look at me a certain way. They sometimes think that I'm like an exception or not like other people, and that's just simply not the case. Exposing people to a race and just being responsive is something I was passionate about and still am passionate about.

Reece went on to say that even though, in a way, she was seen as someone who doesn't quite belong in West Virginia because she is Black and the vast majority of the population is White, she wants to become a teacher educator, and sharing her knowledge about race and culturally responsive teaching with her peers will benefit children and families in places beyond her own classroom, and it is practice for eventually working "at a higher level" with many preservice teachers, a predominantly (but not exclusively) White group

(Sleeter, 2017). However, Reece did acknowledge that being a role model and consultant for her White colleagues could be "hard." In addition to this work, during my last communication with Reece as this book was going to press, she had been given three significant leadership positions at her elementary school—family liaison, Title I coordinator, and faculty committee chair—in addition to her role of teaching 31 children. Reece was positioned as the "go-to" leader of the school because she was seen as the one who possessed the knowledge and skills to support Black children and families in her place. Imogene and Lexie experienced complex challenges, theirs related to their identities as they moved from rural to urban and suburban places to teach. "Assumptions about particular people feeling a sense of belonging in specific places are often unfounded" (Comber, 2016, p. 37). This complexity is underscored in the literature on rural and White communities. Although preservice teachers from rural communities may be encouraged by their families to stay local, *urbanormativity* draws rural youth, and particularly those with some marginalized identity, away from their rural spaces (Terman, 2020).

Some of the graduates who grew up in rural areas believe that their White and rural communities lack structures to support social and economic opportunities for them. One theory explaining why rural graduates might leave their White and rural communities is urbanormativity. *Urbanormativity* is the view that the urban is normal and the rural is deviant, reflecting the "material and symbolic hegemony of urbanization and globalization" (Terman, 2020, p. 22) in relation to rural people and places. Imogene and Lexie, as they described in their data excerpts below, desired better comfort levels with students who were different from them in terms of race and language, which they believed they needed to do to belong in their diverse schools. Imogene stated:

> I learned very quickly to be able to understand someone who uses African American Vernacular English, that was something that I was not used to, coming [to a city school district], because you don't really hear that much [in my rural PDS]. So coming here, it wasn't a bad thing, it was just like, whoa. I need to step back and listen a little more closely. So, that was something I had to get used to.

Imogene showed that she was not only thinking of her own comfort level; she also understood that educational spaces need to be negotiated for children to learn (Somerville, 2011). Lexie added:

> I have a girl who literally came out from Ecuador at the beginning of the year, and she does not speak any English. . . . It's nice to see how willing other students are to help those kids. In [my rural PDS], I feel like you're on your own [if you are not a native English speaker].

Lexie showed in this quote that she was not only thinking of her own ease either. She recognized that children need to feel that they belong in educational spaces (Somerville, 2011).

For both Imogene and Lexie, negotiating between one's comfort level and one's students' needs for belonging in the classroom was an important part of the new teacher's role. Meritocracy, the pervasive societal discourse that claims that individuals who gain rewards earn them through their hard work instead of their race and class privilege, is reinforced when structural inequities inherent within the assessment "cluster," such as fixing teacher training, recruitment, and retention incentives to create and keep teachers who are "highly qualified," continue to be promoted after preservice teachers graduate—an efficient but also valid means of controlling the quality of the teacher education workforce and who might teach children in local communities (see Patel, 2015).

Yet, for White graduates specifically, critical friends support and the accountability theoretically guaranteed by their many credentials were not enough support in navigating urban and suburban places. Many well-prepared graduates did struggle at times, particularly when their teaching community did not share the same community characteristics (i.e., urban, suburban or rural) with their student teaching one (Sherfinski, Jalalifard, et al., 2019; Sherfinski et al., 2021).

Imogene came to her interview with blue hair. She revealed to me a ramp (local West Virginia onion) she recently had tattooed on her shoulder. With these gestures, she seemed to mark herself in ways that seemed incongruous with the culture of her current suburban school in a distant state. In her new place, feeling more comfortable as an "outsider" was a large part of how she wanted to view herself as an educator:

> I'm not the only outsider. Lots of kids are coming in from all over the place. I mean, I've got parents who can't speak English. They're clearly not from here. But there's almost a better understanding among all of us, because we're all like, this is a new situation that we're all in. For people that are outsiders, it's like a double new situation that we're all in, and we're just working through it together. And it's made some good relationships from it.

Place, culture, and identity were important aspects shaping how graduates engaged with place in their new settings. There is evidence in the above data excerpts of Imogene and Lexie searching for their own belonging in their new places, and wanting to understand people they viewed as different from themselves, a form of I-You thinking: as Imogene said, "A double new situation we are all in." Both Imogene and Lexie explained in their interviews that they looked to master the curriculum given to them by their school districts and to begin to feel more comfortable in their schools, to feel more at home in their new places. This is consistent with other published analyses of graduates' experiences whence working in teaching placements (Sherfinski, Jalalifard, et al., 2019; Sherfinski et al., 2021). Shortly after I interviewed Imogene for this research, she moved back to West Virginia.

CONCLUSION

Critical friends and teacher educators' support helped many preservice teachers develop nature sustaining and culturally sustaining parts of their practice, as shown in this book. Putting this work into practice after graduation was a difficult task, however, based on this data and that published in other studies (Sherfinski, Jalalifard, et al., 2019; Sherfinski et al., 2021). Reece, meanwhile, as a critical friend of color, unfortunately had a special burden and responsibility of doing the labor to support her White peers from the program after graduation as well as extra responsibilities at school.

edTPA and Praxis exams were positioned in the program as a kind of "ticket out" of the rural place for preservice teachers drawn by urbanormativity (Terman, 2020). But settler colonialism may hurt preservice teachers' ability to teach in new places because of the ways in which they "carry their roots." The literature on Critical Whiteness in rural and Appalachian communities is instructive on the processes that may affect White preservice teachers. Appalachian Whiteness is a "marked Whiteness . . . both stigmatized and idealized" (Scott, 2009, p. 805). Appalachian Whiteness serves a function of perpetuating racism within communities because it carries the notion of class victimization of White and working-class communities that has a homogenizing effect on those communities; furthermore, it reinforces the false narrative of meritocracy and Manifest Destiny that is taken to mean that these communities inherently deserve their claims to land (Scott, 2009). This situation may be worsened by anti-CRT laws that deny the complexity of White Appalachian students' and all students' intersectional identities (Powell, 2022). This situation ultimately hurts new teachers who do not have support to help them grapple with Whiteness, and were unprepared before completing their teacher education program to do so. Although not the focus of this study, I wonder about the effects of these processes on teacher retention, a challenge affecting education across the United States (Simon & Johnson, 2015).

"The taken-for-granted nature of place largely persists in educational theory and practice, yet 'place' holds the potential to expand and challenge understandings of how the self relates to the world" (Duhn, 2012a, p. 99). Children need to feel their teachers care about them as whole people (I-You) and less about everything else; this helps them to care about school (Valenzuela, 1999). Children also need teachers who can navigate the neoliberal and structural aspects of schooling that marginalize students in poverty and students of color. This is difficult for new teachers in the global neoliberal era. New teachers of color are particularly at risk of spending more of their time supporting colleagues in this context. That is why place-based teacher education needs to go beyond nature sustaining and culturally sustaining pedagogies to include critical place inquiry.

QUESTIONS FOR REFLECTION AND DISCUSSION

Planning for Antiracist and/or Antibias Education
- What challenges have you experienced in doing antiracist and/or antibias education in your personal practice? In your teacher education practice? In your community?
- How do preservice teachers' and/or teacher educators' ideas and examples presented in this chapter/book encourage you to think differently about how you might do antiracist and/or antibias education in your place? What is the next step that you would like to try?
- What international, national, state, and local organizations (in addition to NAEYC and NCTE mentioned in the chapter) are you aware of and/or can you find through your internet research and/or professional circles, that might support teacher educators and preservice teachers interested in investing in antiracist and/or antibias teaching?

WHAT'S NEXT?

Antiracist and antibias work is crucial, as I showed in this chapter, for constructing and co-constructing early childhood and elementary education rooted in belonging for all children and families, in multiple places and spaces. The next chapter introduces specific practice and policy implications of expanding critical place-based education that resists the status quo of settler colonial relations, seeking transformative spaces that support antiracism and address poverty through humanizing and democratic processes.

CHAPTER 6

Practice and Policy Implications

Shifting practices to take critical place inquiry seriously (Tuck & McKenzie, 2015) is crucial in teacher education. Race, space, and settler colonialism have affected opportunities to assess the learning of preservice teachers relative to the communities they student teach in, and have compromised accountability structures in ways that are not democratic and humanizing. In this final chapter, I articulate a shared vision for place-based education and assessment. I discuss how we might assess learning and hold one another accountable to support a place-based vision for teacher education programs, teacher educators, and preservice teachers considering new ways of weaving place-based education and assessment.

Curriculum and teaching should be about relationships, about becoming—what should matter is how education relates to human life (Stremmel et al., 2020) and how places matter (Gruenewald, 2003a). Policymakers' discourse, conversely, often centers on human capital approaches that discount the place of education as connected to and a part of (but not all of) children's and teachers' well-being and agency; these approaches claim a context of "freedoms" while they focus on marketization and performance in narrow and prescriptive ways (Ball, 2003). Popping these harmful neoliberal "bubbles" requires an expansion of teacher educators' and preservice teachers' approach to place-based education, one that recognizes the power of critical place inquiry (Tuck & McKenzie, 2015) to understand more fully the dynamics of place, space, racialization, and settler colonialism as they affect communities.

Kinloch (2018) has posed three questions that inform my understanding of what is required for teacher education to be properly accountable. Her three questions point readers to what educators should not miss in thinking about what is most important in teacher education assessment and accountability, and sum up much of what I learned and experienced in teaching inquiry through the narrative portfolio project that provoked more critical and antiracist approaches to teaching.

First, Kinloch argues that teacher educators cannot begin to understand how to engage with more responsible approaches to assessment in teacher education without understanding how place and space are dynamic and moving, shifting, and changing in their material structure and the meanings people associate with them, and how place impacts the lives, cultures, and identities of people in multiple, intersecting ways.

Second, she states that teacher educators cannot begin to address assessment in teacher education without recognizing the race-based opportunity gaps affecting students of color.

Third, she suggests that teacher educators cannot begin to understand how to approach accountability in teacher education more democratically without understanding the roles of culturally sustaining and revitalizing education in varied cultural, economic, and educational contexts.

In the next section, I explore how what I learned about assessment and accountability through the place-based narrative portfolio project might add to this conversation.

TEACHER EDUCATION PROGRAM ASSESSMENT IN THE "CLUSTER"

Assessment of teacher educators focuses on how well they develop their plans for the education of the preservice teachers who are their students. In turn it must also assess how well the educators teach those students to plan the education of their P–12 students (Sherfinski, Jalalifard, et al., 2019). Assessment should consider how the individual performs *and* how they view themselves as a learner or teacher whose practices are situated within a particular community (Brown, 2021). There should be a social and relational model of democratic learning that recognizes and supports the capabilities of all learners and their relationships with others (Adair & Colegrove, 2021). This democratic and humanizing assessment model should push back against the self-interested individualism seen in neoliberal assessment schemes that promote testing, standards, and accountability (Clark & Richards, 2017). Instead, assessment should be revised so that individuals are positioned as knowers who see themselves as active learners and members of learning communities (Adair & Colegrove, 2021). Place-based education offers many tools to support, document, and expand democratic and humanizing assessment practices in local communities, as discussed earlier in this book.

Accountability

Neoliberal teacher education judges quality and effectiveness with standards-based assessments like the edTPA. Results on these standardized assessments then determine in part both accreditation of schools and licensure of new teachers, and are assumed to provide *accountability*, meaning a mechanism for the state to hold programs and the people who work in them responsible for the academic output of the children in P–12 public schools (Darling-Hammond, 2020). Paired with incentives to recruit and retain teachers in high needs areas, accountability positions preservice teachers as human capital in an "input-output" model such that they might inject knowledge to classrooms in order to promote learning and remediate perceived "achievement gaps" (Olssen & Peters, 2005). The data-driven system includes a whole nexus of practices and logics that shape how the teaching profession is viewed by society and the ways in which educators, whether teacher educators, mentors, or preservice teachers, can be validated by data and responsive to data in the workplace (Lewis & Holloway, 2019).

Ultimately, accountability models may negatively affect the agency—or ability to act upon one's world individually and collectively—of teacher educators, preservice teachers, mentors, and P–12 students (Holland et al., 1998). Accountability models often limit the "choices and voices" (Brown & Mowry, 2015, p. 55) of all of these groups by stealing time and space away from engagement with more democratic and humanizing projects (Sherfinski, 2020, 2021; Sherfinski, Hayes, et al., 2019; Sherfinski et al., 2022).

Granted, all of these layers of baggage can make it very difficult for teacher educators and their preservice teachers to engage in disruptive practices. For individuals who have been socialized in neoliberal assessment and accountability systems, taking responsibility to "pop" the bubble might feel like trying to tread water for a very long time in a very deep pool. Yet, this disruptive work is important because telling new kinds of stories forms ripples that can disrupt deficit ones. Think of it this way: What if teacher educators and preservice teachers closest to this work took the time they needed to co-construct their assessment practices to create a system that works well for everyone? (Clark & Richards, 2017). What new stories might be told?

Status Quo Teacher Education Assessment

There are two status quo approaches to teacher education program assessment, both of which may serve to strengthen and reproduce the neoliberal system, with all of its flaws (Cochran-Smith & Reagan, 2021). The epistemological bases of these approaches are post-positivist and pragmatic. Those who use a *post-positivist* evaluation approach aim to study a program objectively, in a systematic and valid way. Those who use a *pragmatic* approach focus on how programs might use their evaluations when making program decisions.

In my 6 years of experience as an NCATE/CAEP accreditation SPA leader at Mayville University, the teacher education accreditation system used both post-positivist and pragmatic approaches. These frameworks, unfortunately, have done little to advance equity, social justice, and inclusion in teaching and teacher education (Young & Diem, 2014). They narrow expectations and set bars for the purposes of creating "quality" teachers who are capable of transmitting knowledge to children—a limited aim. More disturbing, post-positivist and pragmatic approaches to teacher education do not see preservice teachers, their teacher educators, and the children and families that they work with as fully human. That is in part because neoliberal policy discourses are often colorblind in their approaches to assessment, when in fact racial formations, and specifically anti-Blackness and settler colonialism, are intrinsic to how neoliberal education works (Tuck & Gorlewski, 2016).

By using post-positivist and pragmatic frameworks that mask the role of race, anti-Blackness, and settler colonialism in neoliberal education policy, teacher educators have not pushed back against policies that are colorblind and do not recognize the intersectional identities of children, families, communities, and geographies. In post-positivist and pragmatic paradigms, it becomes very difficult for teacher educators and their preservice teachers to address the political nature of teaching (Lipman, 2013). Thus, as a teacher educator, I needed to listen more carefully to the dissonance I sensed when doing place-based education from nature sustaining and culturally sustaining approaches, because I was partially entrenched in post-positivist and pragmatic aspects of teacher education and Whiteness. It took time before I heard a call to address the effects of settler colonialism on the teacher education program. Maya, one of our preservice teachers of color, said it well when she described the challenges of listening across differences when settler colonialism is thick and racial justice is at stake:

> There is a big world that [preservice teachers] are going to be a part of, and when they are blindsided, or threatened by the existence of other cultures that they don't know about . . . I think about dogs that bark at another dog they don't know. They are just so afraid, it's the fear that turns into aggression because there is the fear of unknown, and the fear of, "Is this going to hurt me? This is different from me." We have so much of that, racially, that still exists. We just need to socialize. We need to get everybody comfortable with the existence of others, it is all awareness.

As Maya stated, education is crucial to "humanize the educational process . . . to work toward breaking away from their unspoken antagonism and negative beliefs about each other and get on with the business of sharing and creating knowledge" (Bartolome, 1994, p. 176). This process is a form of inquiry as stance (Cochran-Smith & Lytle, 2009) that moves beyond "damage control" in teaching and teacher education (Tuck, 2009) because it is a constructionist rather than reactionary stance.

Teacher educators and preservice teachers can build better models that center children and their teachers in communities of practice that are more deeply connected to their places, so that the communities can work to recognize and confront the effects of race, space, and settler colonialism in those places. Humanizing in settler colonial contexts involves understanding and addressing racist ordering, the constant attempt to align the world within a hierarchy with Whites on the top and Blacks on the bottom, and how it is embedded and embodied in early childhood and elementary school classrooms (Tuck & Gorlewski, 2016).

Disrupting Settler Colonial Spaces

There is a contradictory positioning of subjugated Indigenous knowledge within the academy: It is valorized by critical scholars and defamed by those scholars who insist on Western conceptions of knowledge as valid indicators of quality and achievement (Semali & Kincheloe, 1999). In this dominant view, White and middle-class individuals are positioned both above and separate from the natural world and it is this separation and superiority that rhetorically justifies their assumed rights to extraction of the environment in the service of racial capitalism (Nxumalo, 2020; see also Sherfinski et al., 2022). White people often claim Indigenous knowledge and/or a position of cultural "deprivation" in which they speak about themselves as missing out on the economic status and security they worked hard for to distance themselves from complicity in settler colonialism and White supremacy (Pearson, 2013). It is a way of making sense of their racial privilege and class positions. Local knowledge is connected to global knowledge, yet at the same time it is "transcontextual" knowledge because it is borrowed, interpreted, and reinterpreted in other local contexts (Cochran-Smith & Lytle, 2009). Therefore, it is important when analyzing local knowledge to consider what is localizing and what is globalizing, and how and why those processes occur.

To resist racist ordering as it is used in teacher education assessment, teacher educators need critical analyses of the spaces in which preservice teachers must perform, supported by constructivist and constructionist epistemologies. Settler colonialism—in addition to extractions of labor and resources that silence the working class and people of color—is about settlement of land, it is about place and spatial violence. It required the destruction of Indigenous communities of color so that a path was cleared for settlement, and through mechanisms of assimilation, appropriation, genocide, and state violence, Indigenous presence is erased, such that Indigenous life, along with Black life, is dispossessed, and immigrant communities are exploited as well (Kashyap, 2020).

It is the experience of dispossession, and not proletarianization, which has shaped the historical relationships between Indigenous peoples and the settler colonial nation state (Tuck & Gorlewski, 2016). There are variations on this theme based on the place. For example, the volatility of boom/bust cycles is a strong force in West Virginia, with its numerous White and working-class identities related to its labor history (O'Leary, 2018).

Therefore, it is important that neoliberal policy analyses and critiques—and the assessment, evaluation, and curriculum work that influence and are influenced by these policies—recognize that critiques of neoliberalism should be expanded beyond place-based approaches that are naturally and culturally sustaining, to also address critical place inquiries that see the material effects of settler colonialism (Tuck & McKenzie, 2015).

Critical pedagogies of place help us move beyond critiques of neoliberalism that ignore the effects of race; that is because critical pedagogies of place connect to relationships between people and places, and to histories of places and how the nation-state, and the past and present people inhabiting these places, came to be (Gruenewald, 2003b). In West Virginia and other places our graduates teach, critical pedagogies of place are needed to reveal how different bodies are racialized in different ways, and how people who are "othered" in race-based hierarchies might relate to each other (Tuck & Gorlewski, 2016). These relationships are important for the ways in which we as educators might view place-based education and assessment that are attentive to neoliberal effects on local ecologies.

TRANSFORMING TEACHER EDUCATION ASSESSMENT

Transforming educational assessment will help ensure the democratic rights of all children and their teachers to experience dialogue, well-being, and equity without exclusion from the community because their cultural and linguistic talents and skills, or neuro- or physical presence, do not match the White and English-speaking norms of U.S. society (Brown, 2021). It is a humanizing process.

Transforming assessment in teacher education should help strengthen preservice teachers' democratic and humanizing educational approaches. These approaches both inform and are shaped by their capabilities to transform education with their young students, both when they are preservice teachers, and after they graduate from their teacher education programs. In my view, transforming teacher education assessment requires creating assessment structures that support preservice teachers to connect inquiry as stance to a critical and questioning edge (Cochran-Smith & Lytle, 2009). This aims for creating a profound shift to enhance learning, deepen relationships, and improve life chances. This work requires daily decisions to generate social change (praxis) (Freire, 1970). *Praxis*, according to Freire, is "reflection and action upon the world in order to transform it" (p. 36).

Transforming place-based education through an inquiry stance means that "practice encompasses students' learning as well as students', teachers', and leaders' ongoing investigations into the social, cultural, intellectual, relational, and political aspects of knowledge construction. This includes questions about what counts as learning, what learning counts, and to whom" (Cochran-Smith & Lytle, 2009, p. 133).

Because places face profound effects of race, space, and settler colonialism, praxis must deal with neoliberalism. Thus, transforming assessment in place-based teacher education requires practicing and analyzing practice through a process of weaving both strategies and lenses. In the context of place, it is assessment that captures and requires honest analysis of the "interplay of teaching and learning, the synergies of learning and leading, the synthesis of theorizing and acting, and the continuous reinvention of ways of connecting to and allying with colleagues, parents, and communities" (Cochran-Smith & Lytle, 2009, p. 132).

Transforming place-based education from a systems perspective might mean using tools like the narrative portfolio to create a more democratic space and structure for documenting, developing, revising, and sharing narratives individually and with communities over a dedicated time span. The relational structures embedded within the narrative portfolio (Douglass, 2017) that are continually evolving support more democratic approaches to assessment and accountability (Cochran-Smith et al., 2018).

Place-Based Teacher Education Assessment Is Equity- and Social Justice-Oriented

Teacher educators using transformative frameworks have a commitment to equity and social justice. Since at least the reauthorization of the Higher Education Act's (HEA's) Title II provisions in 1998, teacher education programs have taken a harder look at the field's own history of White supremacy (Cochran-Smith et al., 2018). Scholars have diligently revealed race, culture, and language inequalities that exist. Documenting how teachers and teacher educators take the next step to provide responsive, deeply contextual, equitable learning opportunities for children is, unfortunately, seldom seen as the goal of evaluation in teacher education (Cochran-Smith et al., 2018). Transformative frameworks require a fundamental change in the core of how we approach education because they address equity through a process of democratic engagement. Transformative evaluation is a constructivist process. Evaluators make judgments based on valuing goals that serve the public interest, in ways that center justice and equity for children, families, and communities.

Place-Based Teacher Education Assessment Is Place-Conscious

Place-consciousness complicates post-positivist and pragmatic conceptions of accountability, equity, and achievement by emphasizing the connections between education and places and re-constituting the status quo: "Any place-conscious challenge to the educational status quo . . . must redefine accountability as a way that takes local culture and local environment as seriously as test scores in reading and mathematics" (Gruenewald, 2005, p. 268). Place-consciousness recognizes that creating more democracy means more than only closing the achievement gap in school classrooms. Instead, it requires sustained, conscious engagement with places, with educators intentionally shaping communities that can cultivate democratic responsibility for their futures by "extending our notions of pedagogy and accountability outward toward places" (Gruenewald, 2003a, p. 620). Taking a constructivist and constructionist approach to place-based assessment and accountability can be challenging because the discourse of school reform lacks a vocabulary of place, which needs to be articulated to emphasize the significance of local spaces. The lack of development of place-conscious education is due, in part, to post-positivist conceptions of institutional accountability.

THE CHANGE PROCESS

Even though current trends of accountability and collaboration may limit place-based education, place-based education potentially offers a powerful entry point through which to initiate transformative change (Gruenewald, 2005). This vision moves away from the post-positivist and pragmatic ones. Instead of aligning place-based education with neoliberal orientations, I have suggested in this book that preservice teachers should become more dynamic in considering their meanings and goals of assessment and accountability in order to transform their places. For their students and themselves, preservice teachers and their teacher educators should live their work as fully human inquirers, for "knowledge emerges only through invention and reinvention, through the restless, impatient, continuing, hopeful inquiry human beings pursue in the world, with the world, and with each other" (Freire, 1970, p. 72). This involves a recognition that active citizens are curious, and enjoy doubt, and that the point of learning is not to find efficient answers, but to listen and actively inquire to both prepare for and then actually do critical and democratic work. All educators are at different places and engaged in the work of identity construction or "becoming"—this work takes place both alone and together (Wetzel et al., 2017).

Engaging in change requires that teacher educators as well as preservice teachers resist "mastery" models of teacher training designed to efficiently and effectively train "quality" teachers and "ready" children. This essentially replicates the banking model of education that Freire (1970) and countless others have railed against—the idea that teachers must deposit knowledge into children's heads in order to pull it out later when it counts on tests. Instead, we should think about any system as engaged in the work of supporting preservice teachers to become the teachers they want to be, through a process of thinking through and "trying on" strategies and lenses in a process of learning through practice (Grossman, 2011). This work requires that education itself is viewed as a process of "problem posing" instead of "problem solving" (Freire, 1970). That means that change itself is a messy process and none of us will ever fully "arrive" at a perfect end.

Making change through teaching and teacher education involves engaging a critical, inquiry-based stance in order to disrupt the status quo. Kinloch (2018) introduced four components, with "we" meaning teachers—(1) how we teach, (2) what we teach, (3) why we teach, and (4) who we teach—that I find very useful in thinking about change in teacher education. The four components engage place, space, and relationships in the process of change. How we teach, what we teach, why we teach, and who we teach justify work within and across schools, communities, families, and online spaces, reciprocal engagement in learning, the broader socio-political-familial-community contexts of learning networks that allow teachers and teacher educators to "explain, model, demonstrate, listen, observe, think about, question, do, and remake learning" (Kinloch, 2018, p. 5).

How We Teach

Specific to the practice of teaching and teacher education, and the role of assessment in teacher education, I learned through my study that inquiry as stance and place-consciousness, supported by the narrative portfolio tool, were robust pedagogical approaches for teacher educators. Understanding the roles of culturally sustaining and revitalizing education in varied cultural, economic, and educational contexts helped preservice teachers and me to begin to work toward more democratic and humanizing practices even as we went through societal challenges such as the COVID-19 pandemic, the U.S. Capitol insurrection, increasing privatization, and an accelerating standards-based reform context in teacher education.

What We Teach

Content knowledge expertise teaching and evaluative assessment was abundant under the Tyler rationale. Even teacher education programs that use action research and portfolios may have a lot of emphasis on content knowledge expertise and on evaluative assessment. Integrating knowledge of place-based approaches, strategies, and lenses gave preservice teachers and teacher educators the raw materials to weave their own knowledge and build understandings. I learned an understanding of how place and space are dynamic and moving, shifting, and changing in their material structure and the meanings associated with them. I also learned how place impacts in multiple, intersecting ways the lives, cultures, and identities of people. Teacher educators' knowledge and understanding should extend to expanding place-based approaches to include critical place inquiry given the shifting and complicated demands of race, space, and settler colonialism affecting preservice teachers' practices in their chosen places after graduation.

Why We Teach

Concerning the practice of teaching and teacher education and the task of assessment, I learned through this study that to create more democratic and humanizing spaces, place-based education should adopt a decolonizing approach. It should center on supporting communities that seek culturally sustaining and revitalizing practices, sustaining nature, and understanding critical issues of race, space, and land rights.

Who We Teach

Regarding the practice of teaching and teacher education and the role that assessment plays, teachers have the power and potential to make positive change, which requires recognizing children's personal, sociocultural, linguistic, and developmental capabilities and the race-based opportunity gaps affecting students of color. The preservice teachers in the study were mostly White women, and they trained in professional development schools with very high White and low-income populations. Yet the children and communities that the preservice teachers go on to teach in will vary. Understanding and doing place-conscious education, critical place inquiry, and antiracist education are crucial even when places are White. A place-conscious approach can address both local and global concerns.

Especially after the January 6, 2021, insurrection, it became clear that democracy is not a self-sustaining and solid system, nor is it guaranteed that its lessons will automatically be absorbed by preservice teachers, communities, and schools—they must be supported, assessed, and nurtured over time. Although shifts in society that are located in time and that will affect space are unfolding, still for now (2022) it is important to analyze place-based education as a process of expanding learning about "what structures are coming together" and "how coloniality will shapeshift into different forms to attend to those forms" (Patel, 2016, p. 125). Teacher educators and preservice teachers should be "co-constructors of improvements" (Sommer, 2021). Teacher educators and preservice teachers can take the lead in this endeavor by weaving place-based education that is more democratic and humanizing.

Avoiding Dis-Placement in Place-Based Education

My place-based narrative portfolio work is about living with contradictions because it argues that educators should position themselves alongside their preservice teachers as researchers of their own context, seeing children as capable and full of abundant potential (e.g., Dudley-Marling, 2020). Teacher educators should situate assessment practices by "affirming the prerogatives of professional judgment to critique and reject those policies and practices that are not in the best interests of students' growth and learning, while at the same time choosing to work within the system when policies and practices do serve students well" (Cochran-Smith & Lytle, 2009, p. 156). Formative assessment should also include "proximal" forms in which preservice teachers and their young students, and preservice teachers and their teacher educators, engage reciprocally in assessing one another to open up possibilities for diverse perspectives (Erickson, 2007).

Transforming requires peeling back layers of the stories of places, working in unfolding, ever more "contested grounds"—that is, "figurative spaces where diverging, contending views of what does and should count as core values, knowledge, policies, and actions open up possibilities for change in thinking and practice" (Derman-Sparks et al., 2015, p. 19). Stories can generate new stories about place and locate invisible or forgotten ones. Changing our relationship to places means changing the stories we tell about places as a part of the sociopolitical work that educators do. "Part of this process of research is developing a language and (inter)disciplinary practice that makes this conversation possible" (Somerville, 2010, p. 335). In this work, the ultimate border is the border between knowledge and power (Gonzalez et al., 2005). When time and space are continually shifting in ways responsive to global neoliberalism, it can be difficult for any educator to center their practice on relationality. How might we work together when stances do not align well?

Positive Deviance

"Positive deviance" is the idea that we need to build on the capabilities that people already have in their possession rather than tell them they need to change (Gawande, 2007, in Cochran-Smith & Lytle, 2009). The goal is to recognize that local people are capable of making change. A decolonizing framework recognizes the complexity within local contexts—that places are both local and global; they are impacted by issues of race, space, and settler colonialism whether they are diverse or White. Addressing the local and recognizing local people's agency does not conflict with the dynamic nature of places and need for democratizing and humanizing practices in those contexts.

Preservice teachers can engage in positive deviance. They are capable and thoughtful weavers of their own unique classroom practices who know that matters of curriculum should come from the varied sociocultural, linguistic and developmental capabilities of young children as individuals (Brown, 2009c). Preservice teachers' voices and choices might diverge from the voices and choices of their teacher educators and mentors; there are multiple democratic and humanizing ways to engage place-based education.

Engaging in culturally sustaining practices requires sustained support of teachers, through networks, professional development, and (ideally) administrative support, in communities that help teachers navigate the challenges of doing progressive educational work (Brown & Weber, 2016). An affordance of these networks is that teachers can work across geographic contact zones to share place-based inspiration, collaboration, and support (Land et al., 2019) and navigate between the urgency for transformative change and the reality that change does not happen quickly or easily in most cases (Derman-Sparks et al., 2015). When groups are working in challenging contexts with much contested ground, the change is rooted in everyday work in classrooms and communities, and many hours of individual and group analysis within communities of practice.

Looking to the future, I imagine teacher educators and preservice teachers in what are currently White spaces learning and using decolonizing place-based education approaches that seek to benefit from the expertise of people of color and working-class people to "disrupt" power and knowledge hierarchies and to work toward a more racially and economically integrated society. The decolonizing approach involves inviting the knowledge of local families and communities into the teacher education setting and placing stronger emphasis on that knowledge in the teacher education process (Dominguez, 2017; Sherfinski et al., 2021). Thus, it supports preservice teachers to begin to see their work as educators as part of a larger project of racial and economic justice (Anyon, 2014).

Figure 6.1 shows how I conceptualize transforming place-based assessment in teacher education. My model starts with teacher educators and preservice teachers engaging the how, what, who, and why of teaching with democratic, place-conscious, humanizing, and inquiry-based approaches. I created a semi-permeable (dotted) border between teacher educators and preservice teachers and the children, families, communities, and mentor teachers they work with to show the fluidity of movement as projects are created and enacted with support of the narrative portfolio tool. In this model, nature sustaining, culturally sustaining, and critical place inquiry are all important approaches to place-based education. All of these are woven together by the people, and the work is complicated, uneven, and nonlinear, unfolding as places and spaces shift over time.

SUGGESTIONS FOR PRACTICE

In the final section of this book, I suggest guiding principles for teacher education programs, teacher educators, and preservice teachers interested in place-based education and assessment. These suggestions, based on my experience, are possibilities that I hope may inspire future practice.

Practice and Policy Implications

Figure 6.1. Transforming Place-Based Teacher Education Assessment

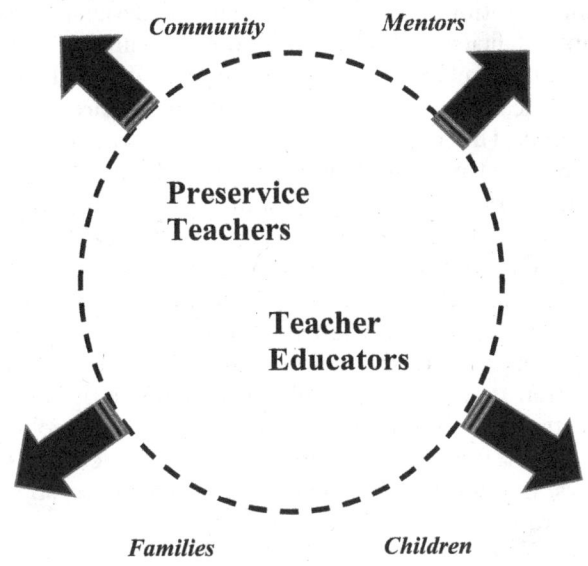

Teacher Education Programs

Teacher education programs should be held accountable to transformative approaches to teacher education assessment if they are serious about making a difference for children and families. It is important to recognize that even in challenging political and geographic contexts, there are ways to engage in place-based approaches. The work may be fluid and partial in my case, but it makes a difference for preservice teachers, their students, and their communities. Even when teacher education programs are required to submit data for post-positivist and pragmatic-oriented accountability programs, teacher education can formalize their commitments to transformation through the place-based education and assessment in which they engage. For teacher education programs, this means cultivating humanizing and democratizing spaces within the teacher education program's policies and assessment structures that intentionally craft spaces for transformative assessment, such as narrative portfolios and other place-based designs.

We have to look at how teacher education programs view learners. All learners are complex beings with social, emotional, cognitive, physical, and linguistic talents and skills. Educators of young learners have long acknowledged the holistic nature of children's development and the necessity of engaging a holistic view to promote rigorous, developmentally appropriate, inclusive, and equitable learning for all children (Brown et al., 2018).

However, in the neoliberal context, K–12 teacher educators in schools of education become positioned as "cognitive experts" designated to address perceived cognitive deficits in children and youth; faculty who prepare school counselors become experts in addressing emotional deficits in children and youth; and physical education teacher educators address the physical aspects of the child. This type of "expert" model partitions the whole child into discrete pieces. Unfortunately, in this paradigm, the social domain of learning and learners is erased from view and the importance of families and places is narrowed. Thus, democratic education has a diminished meaning.

The situation becomes even more complicated and confusing for preservice teachers in early childhood and elementary education when expert-oriented partitioning is actually labeled "humanizing," as sometimes is the case. When preservice teachers and their teacher educators are told to engage in education that addresses children's cognitive deficits to satisfy the teacher education accountability "cluster" and P–12 neoliberal goals, it can be difficult to remember the cultural and linguistic talents and skills of young learners. Given these challenges, here are my suggestions for teacher education programs:

- Part of transforming is having spaces for people to imagine better states of things. Teacher educators' programs might design relational structures like communities of practice and critical friends groups to support preservice teachers in place-based inquiry work, both during their program and as they transition to new settings after graduation.
- Lenses (critical theories of teaching and teacher education) and strategies (ways to push back against neoliberalism) are both crucial for teacher education programs to teach to preservice teachers as pedagogical tools to support their inquiry.
- Teacher education programs should be responsive to all of their preservice teachers. By this I mean that it can be deflating for preservice teachers who wish to prepare for their life's work as serious educators who will make a difference in their places to find that their teacher educators do not address important issues influencing their abilities to teach in local places, such as the effects of race, space, and settler colonialism.
- A simple narrative portfolio tool can facilitate important reflection and democratic conversations about teacher practice, as Cochran-Smith et al. (2018) suggest. The important thing is to have a place for preservice teachers to collect, reflect, revise, refine, and share their work with many people over time.
- Placements matter—opportunities for practicum and student teaching placements with mentors who want to grow in their understandings of place-based education are important. Ensuring

that all preservice teachers have opportunities to work in culturally diverse placements can support preservice teachers' growth, with strong scaffolding.
- Mentoring sessions for mentor teachers, adjunct professors, GTAs, and teacher educators new to critical theories of teacher education—and specifically ideas of place and race, space, and settler colonialism—help everyone learn together. These individuals might also co-teach courses and sit in on communities of practice for additional learning opportunities.
- Shared assessment projects and special events—for example, video clubs and research celebrations—built into teacher education program structures help forge relationships among teacher educators, preservice teachers, mentors, families, and community members.
- Institutions should recognize that instituting a new policy to pay preservice teachers' standardized testing fees may be helpful to recruit individual preservice teachers, but does not result in second-order, transformative change (Cuban, 1990) such as shifting toward place-based education.

Teacher Educators

- How teacher educators pose the problems of the field affects the ways in which preservice teachers see their work as teachers. A transformational approach that facilitates reflection and action, as well as other strategies, in support of preservice teachers' development, has the best chance of deeply and holistically affecting education.
- How teacher educators see preservice teachers, the children they teach and their families, and the communities they teach in, goes a long way to support transformative change.
- White teacher educators should question the ways in which Whiteness influences their life, knowledge, and approach to teaching place-based education, and use these understandings to re-envision how they do teacher education. Working with or starting racial justice affinity groups if they do not currently exist, perhaps in collaboration with other organizations, is an important part of place-based education.
- Teacher educators should seek to understand the issues at stake related to accreditation, teaching, learning, and assessment. That way, teacher educators might both advocate for and create transformative approaches to assessment in their places.
- An affordance of place-based education is the co-construction of new ideas and theories by teacher educators and others. Teacher educators must find new ways to use and share these in practice.

Preservice Teachers

- Preservice teachers are always becoming in the sense that they are always learning, but they should believe in themselves and feel confident that they have arrived as thoughtful, active decision-makers.
- Preservice teachers should use lenses and strategies to weave practices in their places. Creating new knowledge is a great affordance of place-based education. As they develop new theories alone and with others, preservice teachers should use and share these ideas.
- For preservice teachers, it can feel intimidating to question the standards and testing regime because it has been so ingrained in schooling. Talking with understanding teacher educators and critical friends about their feelings could help—they have been or are currently in the same boat.
- Preservice teachers should not be afraid to get to know children and their families at more than a cognitive, surface level. After all, educators are tasked with building communities of learners, and it is difficult to build a supportive, authentic and trusting community when the educator does not know who children and their families are.
- Understanding children's and families' Dark Funds of Knowledge (Zipin, 2009) is a way to honor all children's cultural resources, and preservice teachers are capable of this level of sensitivity.
- White preservice teachers might feel mixed emotions when examining the ways in which Whiteness influences their life, knowledge, and approach to teaching place-based education. Belonging to a racial justice affinity group is a proactive way for preservice teachers to contribute to humanizing changes in local communities.
- Because communication among teachers is so key for developing place-based pedagogy (Comber, 2016; as shown in this book), preservice teachers should work with peers and teacher educators in critical friends and communities of practice, or similar groups of place-based inquiry collaborators. They might continue these groups after graduation to support one another's growth and thinking as they expand and deepen their use of lenses and strategies, and engage in place-based action research.
- Preservice teachers should ask questions about assessments that affect them. Teaching and learning should be transformative for preservice teachers and for the children, families, and communities they work with. If assessments are not transformative, preservice teachers should use their voices to ask why.

- Preservice teachers should seek employment in public school contexts where they can use their knowledge and skills of weaving lenses and strategies to make democratizing and humanizing changes for children, their families, and communities.

CONCLUSION

It would be naïve to think that place-based education would be immediately welcome in every setting. However, if one can show that a rich, interdisciplinary, place-based education program not only cultivates reflective and responsible practitioners, but engages young students and benefits the community in democratizing and humanizing ways, one can better argue for transforming assessment in teacher education. The narrative portfolio and associated place-based inquiry and action research study was a welcome space for creating relationships and thinking and acting more critically in local places. The examples in this book, taken from varied communities, show that there is promise in early childhood and elementary education for place-based teacher education as transformational for high poverty and culturally diverse communities, and for preservice teachers and teacher educators. There are multiple entry points for beginning to make this change.

QUESTIONS FOR REFLECTION AND DISCUSSION

- How do you/your teacher education program address the How/What/Why/Who of transformative assessment? How might you share those ideas with others in our field?
- Figure 6.1 shows one way to think about transforming teacher education assessment. Try drawing your own conceptual diagram of transforming teacher education assessment in your place. How might it help lead to a vision for change?

WHAT'S NEXT?

The final chapter of *Rooted in Belonging* discussed the need for transforming teacher education assessment to address the challenges of race, space, and settler colonialism. As readers consider their own approaches to transforming teacher education assessment, Appendices B, C, and D present tools we have used in our teacher education program that readers may wish to consider as they imagine how they might redesign assessment.

APPENDIX A

Methodology
Capturing Meanings of Place-Based Education and Assessment

BACKGROUND FOR THE STUDY

The case study involved examining the experiences of preservice teachers (cohorts graduating 2015–2021), faculty, and mentors (n=32) with the narrative portfolio process in the 5-Year Elementary Teacher Education Program at Mayville University (a pseudonym), located in a rural and Appalachian setting. To accomplish this required the preservice teachers (n=24) and me to reflect on the multilayered contents of the portfolios and the inquiry processes related to the portfolios, which were created by preservice teachers with children, families, and mentors in and out of school classrooms, primarily through action research (Phillips & Carr, 2014).

Preservice Teachers' Action Research Protocols

In the teacher education program I studied, preservice teachers secured permissions for documentation work as required by the schools and program. For this study, the preservice teachers documented only the work of students whose parents or guardians gave permission; the children's identities were obscured. Preservice teachers got permission from the families and gave permission themselves for the artifacts used to help narrate their stories shared in this book.

METHOD

The case study (Yin, 2009) was initiated with approval from the Institutional Review Board (IRB) and relevant administrators in 2017, and a second phase was added with IRB approval and administrative acknowledgment in 2021, which added an examination of the experiences of preservice teachers during the pandemic. Pseudonyms were used for people and place names. I used subtle masking techniques for job titles, roles, some locations, and occasionally the genders of participants when I felt it was necessary to maintain confidentiality, which is particularly important in rural spaces where everyone seems to know everyone. I also aggregated the graduation years of the preservice teachers to maintain confidentiality. Photographs and assignments do not include identifiable data.

Study Phase 1: Narrative Portfolio Work Pre-Pandemic

Evaluating the narrative portfolio project. In Phase 1, I studied the narrative portfolio qualitatively in order to evaluate its educational effectiveness in supporting participants graduating in the years 2015–2018 (four cohorts). Phase 1 was foundational for this book because it provided a systematic look at how the narrative portfolio was functioning as a tool relative to other forms of assessment in the program, as discussed in Chapter 3. There were two main components to Phase 1. The first part was an analysis of the preservice teachers' portfolios (n = 138) over time, comparing cohort to cohort in order to look for changes over time. The second part was semi-structured interviews with program graduates (n = 12) and teacher education faculty and mentors (n = 8). All of these participants were White and female, with the exception of two teacher education faculty/mentors, who were White males. I was careful to wait to invite preservice teacher interview participants until they were graduated from the program so that there was not a power relationship related to grading attached to the research. The semi-structured interviews, about 45 minutes average in length, were audio recorded and professionally transcribed verbatim.

Analysis of Phase 1 data. To prepare the data, university students not connected with the teacher education program downloaded portfolios and de-identified them before returning them to the researcher. This provided anonymous artifacts for analysis. The primary Phase 1 data were analyzed and triangulated with the support of two doctoral students. I looked at what lenses the preservice teachers used, and how they used the lenses, by engaging in multiple rounds of coding and memoing (Saldana, 2015). Peer reviews of the data were done with several colleagues (Merriam & Tisdell, 2015). The de-identified portfolio materials provided a developmental storyline of practice that the interviews helped me interpret further in order to see changes in the preservice teachers' thinking and teaching over time (Clandinin & Connelly, 2004). Phase 1 findings spurred me to work harder to address the deficit perspective of children and families that the preservice teachers often expressed.

Study Phase 2: Narrative Portfolio Work During the Pandemic

Phase 2 participant selection. Phase 2 built on Phase 1 by narrowing the focus of the narrative portfolio and Inquiry work to study place-based education as it was done in my program for the most recent three years (2019–2021). I purposively selected the teachers highlighted in Phase 2, a total of 12 individuals who recently graduated from the teacher education program. I taught all but one of these women as preservice teachers at one point or another, and supervised half of them in Action Research and Teacher Leadership courses for the final year of their program. Six of the participants worked with Dr. Sharon Hayes in Inquiry for all 3 years of the course sequence.

The sampling for Phase 2 included individuals who used a place-based education framework in their inquiry projects, and exhibited some interest and dedication to this approach. I did not choose the best nor the worst preservice teachers by grade point average, test scores, or reputation to participate in the research. I wanted some racial and cultural diversity in the sample.

Two of the 12 participants in Phase 2 were unable to do interviews, but all of them were generous in sharing artifacts of their Inquiry work (Table A.1). Study involvement included an interview and sharing their portfolio teaching artifacts that reflected place-based education and their journeys of becoming a teacher. Each participant shared a substantial amount of material; portfolio artifacts included things like their full digital action research reports (50–100 pages with embedded links to lesson plans, photos, videos, etc.), research presentation PowerPoints (20–30 slides), community service learning project designs, and background work that supported the development of their thinking.

The semi-structured interviews (n = 10) lasted about one hour each, were done over Zoom due to the pandemic, and took place after graduation. The interview questions were mostly the same as the Phase 1 preservice teacher portion, with more emphasis spent on the context of the pandemic and BLM in Phase 2. The interviews were professionally transcribed verbatim. The two women who did not provide formal interviews were able to speak with me informally about the artifacts they shared.

On reflection, Phase 2 was an improvement over Phase 1 because, although I did not have a comprehensive set of anonymous portfolios in Phase 2 as I did in Phase 1, I had the ability to connect the interview to the participants' artifacts, which made for richer conversations (Brinkmann & Kvale, 2014). I co-constructed meanings to a greater degree through the mediation of the artifacts.

Data analysis for Phase 2. The Phase 2 data contributed to understanding a "reclaimed" form of accountability in which preservice teachers pushed back against neoliberal education in the context of a global pandemic instead of "saving" rural and Appalachian communities, the main theme of the Phase 1 data. I believe that the shift I found across the two study phases was in part because of the emphasis on place-based

Table A.1. Pandemic Preservice Teacher Participants (Phase 2)

Pseudonym	Race	Gender	Number of Interviews	Number of Artifacts	Types of Artifacts
Participant pseudonym (n = 12)					
Maya	POC	Female	1	4	Narrative Vignettes, Portrait of Becoming, Shadow a Leader PPT, Individual Action Plan
Cora	White	Female	0	2	Narrative Vignettes, Portrait of Becoming
Imogene	White	Female	1	5	Narrative Vignettes, Portrait of Becoming, Where I'm From Poem, Inquiry of Context PPT, Scrapbook
Destiny	White	Female	0	6	Narrative Vignettes, Portrait of Becoming, Antiracist Book Club Project, Individual Action Plan, Shadow a Leader PPT, Admissions Portfolio
Reece	POC	Female	1	2	Narrative Vignettes, Admissions Portfolio
Amy	White	Female	1	7	Narrative Vignettes, Portrait of Becoming, Inquiry Celebration PPT, Inquiry of Student PPT, Inquiry of Context PPT, Family Newsletters, Family Surveys
Joanna	White	Female	1	4	Narrative Vignettes, Portrait of Becoming, Inquiry Celebration PPT, Inquiry of Context PPT

Methodology

Pseudonym	Race	Gender	Number of Interviews	Number of Artifacts	Types of Artifacts
Participant pseudonym (n = 12)					
Sophie	White	Female	1	5	Narrative Vignettes, Portrait of Becoming, Individual Action Plan, Shadow a Leader PPT Inquiry Celebration PPT
Frankie	White	Female	1	7	Narrative Vignettes, Portrait of Becoming, Individual Action Plan, Shadow a Leader PPT Inquiry of Context PPT Inquiry of Student PPT, Inquiry Celebration PPT
Wren	White	Female	1	3	Narrative Vignettes, Portrait of Becoming, Inquiry Celebration PPT
Lexie	White	Female	1	2	Narrative Vignettes, Place-based Science Project
Millicent	White	Female	1	4	Narrative Vignettes, Portrait of Becoming, Individual Action Plan, Shadow a Leader PPT
Total			10	51	

education in the program in recent years, in response to the challenges seen in the Phase 1 data.

Phase 2 drew on narrative analysis approaches because I saw the data as preservice teachers' stories (Riessman, 2007). To analyze the 12 individuals' stories I placed each one's data together—their interview (if available) and artifacts. While the interviews and portfolio narratives relied mainly on the voices of preservice teachers, preservice teachers' narratives also draw on the refracted voices (Lawrence-Lightfoot & Davis, 1997) of policies, curriculum, administrators, educators, parents, and children present in the research. These voices mostly emerged through the preservice teachers' utterances (spoken and written) and gave important information about interrelationships existing in communities relative to place (Clandinin & Connelly, 2004). I relistened to the interview tapes in their entirety to check the professionally transcribed transcripts for errors. Then I read and reread each interview transcript and the related artifacts at least two times, taking notes on the emerging themes specific to what the neoliberal teaching context was like and how the subject used place-based education to push back against it in creative ways. I used a deductive coding framework based on the literature, defining processes that inhibit or support more complex and democratic engagement, such as tectonic instrumentalism, contact zones, reflection, dialogism, relationships, and diffraction (Saldana, 2015). I then used narrative analysis methods (Riessman, 2007) within each of those identified processes to analyze how the preservice teacher described the engagement and how she used it in her teaching (if she did). I noted the context, the personal meaning-making she communicated related to the process, and the pedagogical moves made in that context. Two main themes of place-based practices emerged and I wrote extensive analytic memos on each one, incorporating my notes and evidence from interview texts as well as work samples (Saldana, 2015). These themes fell into "homes and schools" and "creating an antiracist place." The two memos became Chapter 4 and Chapter 5 of this book, respectively.

Self-Study of My Teaching Practices

> Memory is not just the recall of past events and experiences in an unproblematic and untainted way. It is rather a process of remembering: the calling up of images, stories, experiences and emotions from past life, ordering them, placing them within a narrative or story and then telling them in a way that is shaped at least in part by the social and cultural context.... Memory (and remembering)... is not an abstract concept but a practical and active process of reconstruction whereby traces of the past are placed in conjunction with one another to tell a story. Memory is not just about the individual; it is also about the community, the collective, and the nation. (Abrams, 2010, pp. 78–79)

Memory is a central concept to studies of place. For example, in his classic study, *The Poetics of Space*, Bachelard (1964) asks his readers to remember a house they lived in previously—its particularities and what lives were lived there; this is a case of how memory, place, experience, and identities are woven together over time. People live their lives in places, and our relationship to them alters who we are (Gruenewald, 2003a). However, the erasure of memories is an issue that place-based researchers push against. That is because the settler colonial states in which researchers may live may be notorious for their White privileged class's desire to erase the history of their colonization of others in which stolen people perform labor on settlers' stolen land; they wish to make it seem as if by destiny they always deserved to be here, inhabiting this place (Veracini, 2011). The erasure of memory also carries over to the classroom, where individual accountability for learning, individual test taking, and opportunities to climb in the meritocracy are assumed, no matter who one might be. If one does not succeed, it is a matter of laziness and/or a bad home life—not structural barriers that may hurt one's opportunities. When community members have very few opportunities to experience the struggles of people of color and/or working-class people, and have perhaps worked within the system successfully themselves, they understand fairness to be when the same system that benefitted them is reproduced for everyone, including their own children. This is how Whitewashing and other forms of memory laws work; they require memory work on the part of educators to resist and speak back to them.

When I moved to West Virginia in 2011, I started to informally journal about my practice as a teacher educator in my new setting (Frank, 1999). My approach, for which I gained required approval, was a variation on memory work (Bobick, 2018; Haug, 2000) that included collecting my individual experiences based on my everyday life as an early childhood and elementary educator and accreditation SPA leader. In memory work, the individual's experiences "contain deposits of what has been left behind . . . elements, both of awakening and resistance" (Haug, 2000, p. 174). Memory work validates individual understanding as a foundation of data as narratives are composed of lived experiences that hold potential for rethinking interactions (Ellis, 1998). The self-reflective research was done, in part, related to my teaching in the Teacher as Leader course sequence in which I modeled being a reflective practitioner by studying my teaching and making educational decisions based on ongoing data analysis (Cochran-Smith & Lytle, 2009). I collected one or two "notebooks" (thick files) from each of eight academic years. The multiple voices found in my journal and ongoing dialogues with colleagues, students, and mentors helped make both authoritarian and transgressive voices audible to me so that I could reflect on my understanding of the context and implications of audit systems in teacher education as they influence my students and myself (Bakhtin, 1981). When I look back at how I thought, wrote, and spoke even several years ago, I notice that I did not always position other people as equal partners in building knowledge. My memories exist in the social milieu, not only in social constructions inside my head, exemplifying the "living" nature of discourse, the heteroglossia I have used to make my own research and writing decisions, which continue to change. Memory work has aided triangulation and crystallization, and it helped me reflect on how my identity and biases influence how I interpret the world, thus contributing to the validity of the research (Merriam & Tisdell, 2015). The portion of self-study from the spring of 2021, especially, helped inform my analysis of data for the antiracist teaching parts of Chapter 5 through triangulation with the interviews and artifacts from the graduated preservice teachers.

Relationships and Trustworthiness

I wish that I could say that this whole project was participatory action research in which everyone from community members to kids and families, teachers, administrators, preservice teachers, and teacher educators all worked together to create a critical pedagogy of place that made deep changes in the communities to address issues of neoliberal audit culture and White supremacy. Like most efforts, this work was fragmented and partial in both its implementation and its outcomes. To promote trustworthiness, I did member checks with several participants (Merriam & Tisdell, 2015). In Phase 2, I sent each of the 12 participants a brief synopsis of what I planned to share in the book and they had a chance to respond. Three colleagues did peer reviews of my interpretations that added to the analysis, and a respected local teacher and mentor did peer reviews of this entire book manuscript as well.

APPENDIX B

Lenses of Teacher Education and Revised "10 Characteristics of the Novice Teacher" for PDS Mentors and Faculty Professional Development

(This is an abbreviated version of the handout we used. In the original version, each lens is well defined, with examples and references.)

Teacher education aspires to cultivate spaces for prospective and practicing educators to collaboratively engage in learning and to develop innovations that influence education across the nation and world. These communities of learners, which include educators situated in diverse contexts and in various places in their careers, study the complexities of teaching and learning, including the intellectual, creative, affective, ethical, historical, cultural, social, and political aspects of these endeavors. Our shared goals include cultivating deeper and broader stances through problematizing the status quo, developing theory/practice connections, and exploring content and pedagogy through multiple lenses and perspectives. In partnership, we engage in advocacy and action that address the inequities and disparities faced by students, families, and communities in diverse contexts.

In order to work toward these goals, prospective teachers use a number of lenses and characteristics to connect what they have done and are doing in their classrooms to purposes of education and to teaching and learning that are fair, professional, and address the learning needs of all students. Some of the lenses are organizational and represent institutional arrangements and systems of beliefs and practices. The lenses include democratic education (Beane & Apple, 2008), culturally relevant and sustaining pedagogy (Ladson-Billings, 2009; Paris & Alim, 2017), erasing opportunity gaps (Gorski, 2018), critical and family literacy (Vasquez, 2014), Family Funds of Knowledge (Moll et al., 2005), inclusive education (Sapon-Shevin, 2010), fixed and dynamic frames (Johnston, 2012), and dialogic teaching (Reznitskaya, 2012).

Other lenses our prospective teachers use to understand and inform their teaching are more specifically focused on content and pedagogy. These lenses include strategies for erasing the opportunity gaps for students in poverty, fixed and dynamic frames, dialogic teaching and learning, family funds of knowledge, and culturally responsive pedagogy.

All of these lenses inform, and are embedded within, the revised Characteristics of the Novice Teacher (Hayes, 2015).

> **Characteristic 1: We believe that learning to teach is a lifelong endeavor and a teacher should have a commitment to and skills for lifelong learning.** As our communities, world, and profession continue to evolve, we must be committed to extending, elaborating, and transforming our own knowledge and understandings, independently and in collaboration with others.
>
> **Characteristic 2: We believe that a teacher should be an effective communicator,** someone who can express and receive ideas, messages, or information through appropriate spoken, written, and nonverbal forms to and from a variety of audiences, which include students, families, colleagues, the community, and the profession.
>
> **Characteristic 3: We believe that a teacher should recognize that teaching is a professional, moral, and ethical enterprise, should understand moral issues and ethical practices in educational environments, and should have developed ethical frameworks that facilitate effective teaching.** Teaching is an inherently moral and ethical enterprise, and teachers' perspectives, attitudes, assumptions, and actions affect the interests and welfare of others. Teachers face uncertain and value-laden contexts in which choices must be made among competing values and ends. Therefore, teachers must understand moral and ethical issues and the way they use power, as well as how their assumptions, perceptions, and biases influence what happens in classrooms and schools.
>
> **Characteristic 4: We believe a teacher should be a facilitator of learning for all students.** Every student is entitled to an equitable education that provides them with opportunities to achieve to their fullest potential and accomplish their dreams. Teachers must come to know their students as people with lives in and outside of the classroom, in order to provide them with the experiences and resources necessary to learn what they need and want to know.
>
> **Characteristic 5: We believe a teacher should have an in-depth knowledge of pedagogy,** which includes: (a) an understanding of human development, learning theories, and their application; (b) a repertoire of knowledge and skills that ensure the teacher is able to create a learning environment and classroom culture that supports the learning of all students; (c) a knowledge of instructional models and strategies; and (d) a knowledge of the various philosophical stances that inform our understandings of teaching, learning, and the purposes of school.

Characteristic 6: We believe that a teacher should have an in-depth knowledge of content, which includes the range of existing information in a discipline, as well as the structure of knowledge within the discipline, and the processes used to construct knowledge in the discipline. A teacher uses this knowledge of content to select and organize what will be taught, to interpret new knowledge in the discipline, and to decide what additional content knowledge they should acquire.

Characteristic 7: We believe that a teacher should effectively integrate content and pedagogy. A teacher must understand the dynamic relationship(s) between content and pedagogy in order to create the best opportunities for student learning.

Characteristic 8: We believe that a novice teacher should be a reflective practitioner, one who attempts to make sense of the complexity of teaching and learning both independently and in collaboration with others. Engaging in reflection empowers teachers to engage in professional development that improves their subsequent practice and the quality of learning for their students. Engaging in reflection on practice can become an opportunity to develop *inquiry as stance*, which is the idea that educational practice is not simply instrumental in the sense of figuring out how to get things done, but also, and more importantly, it is social and political in the sense of deliberating about what to get done, why to get it done, who decides, and whose interests are served. Thus, working for and with an inquiry stance involves a continual process of making current arrangements problematic; questioning the ways knowledge and practice are constructed, evaluated and used; and assuming that part of the work of practitioners individually and collectively is to participate in educational and social change.

Characteristic 9: We believe that the novice teacher should be aware of and have respect for human diversity. A teacher must not only develop a deep knowledge of cultures and diversity, but must also consider how to integrate this information into all subjects and skills routinely taught in school. A teacher must work to create and sustain a bias-free and equitable learning environment.

Characteristic 10: We believe that the novice teacher should be liberally educated. Such an education prepares a teacher to:
  (a) integrate knowledge from a wide variety of fields, cultures, and perspectives into the curriculum,
  (b) value an ongoing search for knowledge that provides opportunities for deconstructing and reconstructing their understandings,
  (c) embrace multiple perspectives and new ideas, and
  (d) take action to promote social justice in a world characterized by technological, cultural, and societal diversity and change.

APPENDIX C

A Portrait of Becoming

(Assignment designed by Sharon Hayes)

This semester we would like you to create a narrative portrait that documents your journey of becoming a teacher. For prospective teachers, creating/constructing narratives of their experiences provide a way of being and becoming a professional. Teachers think in terms of stories of their practice, and they use these stories to understand and question their lives with students in classrooms in order to make sense of what did take place and to explore the possibilities for what might or should be. These stories can be used to provoke dialogue with listeners who can engage with the storyteller in critical reflection and can learn with and from each other as they interpret, deconstruct, and reconstruct lived experiences. Narratives can also do political work and encourage social action; in fact, particular narratives may embolden us to interrogate the status quo and advocate for transformation. Ultimately, narratives "help guide action and are a socioculturally shared resource that gives substance, artfulness, and texture to people's lives. They form the warp and weft of who we are and what we might or might not do" (Sparkes & Smith, 2008, pp. 295–296). Thus, prospective teachers may better understand the influence of their stances/beliefs/practices and the teacher identities they are constructing as they capture their experiences in narratives and then interpret and reflect on the stories they tell both independently and in the company of others. This semester, you will write up your Inquiry as a portrait of the journey you and your students took as you learned with and from each other. We encourage you to use a variety of artifacts and/or media to bring your narrative to life for the reader.

> *Title:* A Portrait of Becoming: The Stories of a Teacher and Their Learners [Or you may create your title, which might reflect the nature of your experiences with your students this semester.]
> *Teacher:* Your name
> *Learners:* (names of your students, if you choose focus students, or if you make use of all your students in your portrait, you might say "Class of 23 third-graders")

This portrait of teaching and learning describes ... (finish this sentence stem in a sentence or two that summarizes what the reader will discover as they read your portrait).

OUR PLACES

In qualitative inquiry, context is critical to understanding our experiences in particular spaces/places. To begin, you'll write a paragraph detailing what you'll describe, document, and discuss in this section, which includes three subsections. Thus, you might provide a rationale for how your understanding of the places where you teach, learn, and live is important for your study. You might share with the reader that you will describe and illustrate the larger community in which your school is situated, your school, and your classroom.

Our Community

You'll want to provide a rich, thick description of the community in which your school is situated, focusing on the strengths/assets, resources, and traditions of the community. Think in terms of "Getting Lost in Logan" (Power, 2011) and how you've learned about your community from various perspectives/vantage points. One possibility is taking us on a tour of the community, inserting visuals that illustrate the geography and culture, the beauty of this place. While you may include some demographics when it makes sense to do so ... keep in mind that you are telling the stories of this place, paying particular attention to human and nonhuman aspects/features of the community that influence what happens in your classroom.

Our School

Similarly, you'll provide a rich, thick description of your school ... the physical context, as well as the human, nonhuman, and affective components of the culture that has been created and the vision that has been established for teaching and learning in this space/place. This may include demographic data, the school's mission, vision, traditions ... but keep in mind that you are telling a story, rather than simply reporting statistics. Again, you want to be sure you include those aspects of your school that might support or constrain your teaching practice, the study you design.

Our Classroom

Once again, you want to provide a thick, rich description of your classroom ... think in terms of the Inquiry of Context and consider the following aspects as they might influence your study: space/places, object, time periods, events, acts/activities, actors, interactions, goals, and feelings. In particular, you'll want to zoom in on those aspects of your context that will be influenced and/or changed during your study to illustrate what is happening now, as you'll be illustrating/discussing the consequences of those changes from week to week as you implement your study. You will want to describe/discuss the physical learning environment, the curriculum, as well as the culture/feelings of the place ... what kinds of identities/worlds are possible for the learners (which include teachers) who live and interact in this space?

LEARNERS AND TEACHERS

In this section, you will tell stories about yourself, about your students, and about other teachers/adults in the room if you wish. When you describe yourself, you'll want to discuss your passion for teaching ... the beliefs/stances you hold dear and how you expect to live them in your practice this semester and beyond. You'll also want to provide some insight into "where you're from" ... who you are outside of the classroom and how those aspects of self influence your learning environment, curriculum development, teaching, and interactions with students.

You will also want to tell stories about your students that are created from multiple sources of data you have collected, including kid-watching. Begin by looking for the patterns, as well as the contradictions/paradoxes you discover as you analyze the data you collect about your students. While you might provide some demographic data, you want to focus on what you are learning about your students' personal, cultural and community assets ... describe/illustrate their everyday experiences, cultural and language backgrounds (funds of knowledge) and practices, and interests. While you want to talk about students' similarities, you can also focus on particular students as "cases" of the unique strengths, talents, characteristics of the students in your classroom. Be sure that your portraits of your students are multifaceted and complex ... illustrating the assets/resources they bring, which can be used to support their learning this year.

BEGINNING THE YEAR: LOOKING AND SEEING AS AN ETHNOGRAPHER

In this section you will introduce the reader to your project. Instead of merely stating your purpose, you will describe/discuss some of the experiences/dilemmas you've encountered that led to the purpose of your study. In other words, you'll share the stories that led you to determine changes you wish to make related to the learning environment, curriculum and/or instruction ...

that contributed to the design of your study. You will look and see as an ethnographer and use multiple data sources (observation, participation, interviews/conversations, artifacts) to tell the story of how you uncovered the struggles of your students that needed to be addressed and that informed your activism and advocacy.

Because teacher research is inherently personal, the emotional stake/passion you have in your study is an important part of the story you need to tell as you share your research journey. You want to describe/illustrate for your readers how you uncovered/discovered your dilemma, how this discovery helped you to question your own beliefs and assumptions, and how, in thinking more deeply—engaging in reflection—about your dilemma, you explored a number of possible resolutions for your dilemma that led you to make changes to practices, curriculum, learning environment, or classroom culture and supported you in becoming a better teacher . . . the teacher you want to be for your students. In your narrative, you will name a stance and associated practices you want to take up to meet the needs of all your students.

You also want to describe how what you have decided to explore has multiple purposes/foci . . . so discuss how your study will also help you to explore the beliefs/stance(s) you wish to live/enact, address curriculum issues, issues of equity, the power relationships in your classroom, and/or explore how you might create a classroom culture that is collaborative, dialogic, inclusive, culturally relevant and responsive and that supports students in developing identities that embrace dynamic frames, critical literacy . . . among other skills and dispositions.

EXPLORING THE LITERATURE: DISRUPTING THE COMMONPLACES

Then you will discuss how you turned to the literature (knowledge for practice) in order to better understand what you might do to address the needs of your students and the possible implications of particular beliefs/stances, decisions/practices. You will want to cite 8–10 sources and describe/discuss in a narrative format what you learned from the literature (be very specific), as well as how the literature influenced your plans for creating a learning environment; designing instruction, learning tasks, and assessments; making decisions about classroom structures/routines; and designing your inquiry (choice of data sources, analysis methods, etc.). As you end this section, provide a summary of what is known, and what you now know, about your topic, as well as possibilities for how your study will add to the knowledge and conversations we are currently having about teaching and learning.

This section will end with the following sentence (or some appropriate variation): Therefore, I used these questions to study my practice and its consequences for my students. Then list your questions.

OUR JOURNEY

You will begin with a paragraph or two that provide an overview of what happened during the 8 weeks in which you implemented your inquiry. This summary might include stories of how/why you collected data before your study began. You will also want to briefly summarize the differences that occurred from week to week related to your pedagogy, learning tasks, assessment, and grouping strategies. You might end this paragraph by describing how/why you collected data during the last week of your study to explore your students' perceptions of their experiences during your full-time teaching.

Weekly Stories

Each week, for 8 weeks of student teaching, you will tell stories about what happened in your classroom related to the change or practice you implemented. You'll describe how you created the learning environment with your students, planned for teaching and learning, elicited and probed/supported/challenged student thinking. You will also share the consequences of your teaching and learning tasks for your students ... making claims/assertions about what/how students were making sense of the content and revising/elaborating/extending their thinking. You will share how you are engaging in reflection on all that you are learning and using what you learn to make improvements to your teaching day by day, week by week, in order to meet the needs of all students. You might use excerpts from your lesson plans, examples of student work, excerpts from dialogue/your Teacher Researcher Notebook (TRN), or video clips to illustrate your stories and to provide evidence of/support for the claims you make. You will also want to discuss how you are living particular beliefs/stances, how you are creating a more equitable learning environment and sharing power. In order to create narratives each week, it will be important for you to write each day and to engage in ongoing data analysis.

As you tell stories week by week, you'll describe how you are continuing some practices, modifying others, or taking up new practices/creating new learning tasks/assessments. It will be important to discuss what is informing your decisions and to explore/illustrate the consequences of what is happening in the classroom for your students.

OUR LEARNING

In this section, you will describe and discuss the learning/growth/transformation of your students, which may illustrate their intellectual growth, their emotional, social, and/or behavioral growth, as well as their development of growth mindsets, of identities as learners, readers, and writers. You will make use of synthesis statements that encompass the patterns you noticed over the course of your study, and you will describe/discuss how students' learning may have been influenced by your pedagogies, interactions/relationships, learning tasks, and assessments. You will also want to describe/discuss how students made use of various resources (funds of knowledge, cultural/community assets, prior knowledge, etc.) in order to participate in instruction and accomplish the goals you had for their learning . . . in other words what else contributed to their success outside of the changes you made during your study. You might also support the statements/claims about student learning with evidence from the literature. In addition to reporting the positive outcomes of your study, you also want to describe and discuss the outliers: who wasn't as successful with the learning and what factors might have contributed to their struggles.

You also want to describe/discuss your own learning . . . what you have learned from studying teaching. You'll describe/discuss what you've learned about creating an equitable learning environment, about particular pedagogies, about designing curriculum, learning tasks, and assessments, about the content you taught, about particular students, about interacting with your students, about engaging students with dialogue, writer's workshop, and other activities. You will connect the claims you make about your own learning by making connections to specific aspects of your study, possibly by making connections with the literature, possibly by making connections to coursework or previous PDS experiences. You might also identify challenges/barriers you faced, how you attempted to address these challenges, with what success (or not). You might end this section by describing/discussing your development/growth/transformation as a teacher . . . who you are becoming as a result of what you have learned this semester.

A REFLECTIVE PAUSE WITH AN EYE TO THE FUTURE

You might think of this section as describing/discussing the implications of what you have learned for your own future practice and the practice of other educators. Consider what you described/discussed in the previous section related to what you have learned . . . then be very specific about how you will use that learning to create a learning environment with your students, develop curriculum and instruction, design learning tasks and assessments, interact with students, their families, colleagues, and others. How you will use what you learned might mean describing how you will continue particular practices and/or what changes you might make, as well as what additional practices you might take up. Be sure to always discuss why you will do what you do.

You will also describe/discuss how your study was informed by/embraced particular stances and/or beliefs, how you were able to live those stances/beliefs (or not), and how you will continue to do so in the future, describing changes/modifications you will make to your practice. Describe/discuss who you are becoming as a teacher and how you are moving toward the vision you have for teaching and learning in your classroom.

Then you will describe/discuss how you have developed as a reflective practitioner. You will also describe/discuss what you have learned about engaging in inquiry . . . how to identify questions, designate focal students, choose data sources, analyze and interpret data, and disseminate your findings. Your discussion of inquiry might also include how you might make use of PLCs and/or critical friends as a support system for becoming a better teacher.

You will end this section by sharing the questions that have been raised by your study . . . why these questions would be important to pursue, how you might explore these questions . . . as well as how you will continue to learn to teach through studying your teaching.

FINAL THOUGHTS

Hopefully, this experience of designing and engaging in an inquiry, in learning to teach through studying teaching, has led you to identify broader issues in your classroom, school, the professional landscape that need to be addressed . . . individually and/or collectively. Describe/discuss the ways in which you might change the ways we do school (individually and collectively) . . . the ways in which you might begin to advocate for these changes and to put these changes into practice. What will you take away from your study that will have long-lasting effects as you engage in the lifelong learning that is an integral part of learning to teach, of becoming a teacher? You do want to end on a positive note.

APPENDIX D

Destiny's Book Club: *Stamped* by Reynolds & Kendi (2020)

(This is an abbreviated version, amended to include the first meeting only.)

Imagined context: Rural school community in West Virginia

Ground rules (adapted from Equity Literacy Institute & EdChange, http://www.edchange.org/multicultural/activities/groundrules.html):

1. Listen before you speak. Respect others when they are talking and do not interrupt or talk over people.
2. Do not speak for communities you are not a part of (being an ally and supportive is different than this, it is okay!), use your own personal experiences.
3. It is okay to challenge each other's ideas, but personal attacks are NOT okay.
4. A successful book club requires active participation from everyone!
5. You do not have to agree with everyone, but it is the goal to gain a deeper understanding of experiences other than your own.
6. Be conscious of body language and nonverbal responses—they can be as disrespectful as words.

Meeting 1 discussion questions:
1. How does the media/literature influence racism today?
2. While many will consider themselves "antiracists," how do we sometimes fall back into the "assimilationist" title without meaning to?
3. Are there any newer "extreme" theories that influence racism, like the ones mentioned in our book so far?
4. Does Zurara deserve the title, "The World's First Racist?"

Definitions collage activity:
1. After reading the introduction and section one of our book, listen to Brene and Kendi's free podcast to learn more about *How to*

Be an Antiracist and today's systemic policies linked to racial disparities: https://brenebrown.com/podcast/brene-with-ibram-x-kendi-on-how-to-be-an-antiracist/
2. Bring pictures, book covers, newspaper headlines, snippets of text, or any other resources to add to our collage. Try to bring a piece that would fall under each racial position: Segregationists, Assimilationists, and Antiracists. Work together to make a collage for each position, discussing together where each resource should fall and why. Book club members may want to explore https://haggerston.hackney.sch.uk/learning-to-be-an-antiracist-school/anti-racism-artwork/ for inspiration if needed.

Classroom connections:
1. Discuss the grade levels, standards, and other connections that would accompany this book in the classroom.
2. Brainstorm ideas to introduce and discuss segregationist, assimilationist, and antiracist racial positions in the classroom.

Open the floor to discuss general content, concerns, and any missed connections before closing.

References

Abrams, L. (2010). *Oral history theory*. Routledge.

Adair, J. K., & Colegrove, K. S. (2021). *Segregation by experience: Agency, racism, and learning in the early grades*. University of Chicago Press.

Aguilar, E. (2018). *Onward: Cultivating emotional resilience in educators*. John Wiley.

Ahmed, S. (2012). *On being included: Racism and identity in institutional life*. Duke University Press.

Alim, H. S., & Paris, D. (2017). What is culturally sustaining pedagogy and why does it matter? In D. Paris and H. S. Alim (Eds.), *Culturally sustaining pedagogies: Teaching and learning for justice in a changing world* (pp. 1–24). Teachers College Press.

Anderson, S. K. (2017). *Bringing school to life: Place-based education across the curriculum*. Rowman & Littlefield.

Andre-Bechely, L. (2005). *Could it be otherwise? Parents and the inequalities of public school choice*. Routledge.

Anyon, J. (2014). *Radical possibilities: Public policy, urban education, and a new social movement*. Routledge.

Appiah, K. A. (2020, June 18). The case for capitalizing the 'B' in Black. *The Atlantic*. https://www.theatlantic.com/ideas/archive/2020/06/time-to-capitalize-blackand-white/613159/

Apple, M. W. (2006). *Educating the "right" way: Markets, standards, God, and inequality* (2nd ed.). Routledge.

Apple, M. W. (2007). Ideological success, educational failure? On the politics of No Child Left Behind. *Journal of Teacher Education, 58*, 108–116.

Apple, M. W. (2013). Curricular form and the logic of technical control: Commodification returns. In *Knowledge, power, and education: The selected works of Michael W. Apple* (pp. 96–115). Routledge.

Ashton, E. (2015). Troubling settlerness in early childhood curriculum development. In V. Pacini-Ketchabaw and A. Taylor (Eds.), *Unsettling the colonial places and spaces of early childhood education* (pp. 81–97). Routledge.

Bachelard, G. (1964). *The poetics of space*. Orion.

Baker, R. S. (2022). The historical racial regime and racial inequality in poverty in the American South. *American Journal of Sociology, 127*(6), 1721–1781.

Bakhtin, M. M. (1981). *The dialogic imagination: Four essays*. University of Texas Press.

Ball, D. L., & Cohen, D. K. (1999). Developing practice, developing practitioners: Toward a practice-based theory of professional education. In G. Sykes and

L. Darling-Hammond (Eds.), *Teaching as the learning profession: Handbook of policy and practice* (pp. 3–32). Jossey-Bass.

Ball, S. J. (1999). *Global trends in educational reform and the struggle for the soul of a teacher!* [Paper presentation]. British Educational Research Association Annual Conference, University of Sussex at Brighton, England.

Ball, S. J. (2003). The teacher's soul and the terrors of performativity. *Journal of Education Policy, 18*(2), 215–228.

Bang, M., Curley, L., Kessel, A., Marin, A., Suzukovich, E., & Strack, G. (2014). Muskrat theories, tobacco in the streets, and living Chicago as Indigenous land. In K. McCoy, E. Tuck, & M. McKenzie (Eds.), Special issue on land education: Indigenous, postcolonial, and decolonizing perspectives on place and environmental education research. *Environmental Education Research, 20*(1), 37–55.

Banks, A., & Hicks, H. (2016). Fear and implicit racism: Whites' support for voter ID laws. *Political Psychology, 37*(5), 641–658.

Barad, K. (2007). *Meeting the universe halfway: Quantum physics and the entanglement of matter and meaning.* Duke University Press.

Bartolome, L. I. (1994). Beyond the methods fetish: Towards a humanizing pedagogy. *Harvard Educational Review, 64*(2), 173–195.

Barton, A., & Tan, E. (2009). Funds of knowledge and discourses and hybrid space. *Journal of Research in Science Teaching, 46*(1), 50–83.

Basso, K. (1996). *Wisdom sits in places: Landscape and language among the Western Apache.* University of New Mexico Press.

Beane, J. A., & Apple, M. W. (2008). *Democratic education: Lessons in powerful schools* (2nd ed.). Heinemann.

Beech, B. M., Ford, C., Thorpe, R. J. Jr., Bruce, M. A., & Norris, K. C. (2021, September 6). Poverty, racism, and the public health crisis in America. *Frontiers in Public Health.* https://doi.org/10.3389/fpubh.2021.699049

Bennett, C. I., McWhorter, L. M., & Kuykendall, J. A. (2006). Will I ever teach? Latino and African American students' perspectives on PRAXIS I. *American Educational Research Journal, 43*(3), 531–575.

Bhaba, H. K. (2004). *The location of culture* (2nd ed.). Routledge.

Biesta, G. (2009). Education between accountability and responsibility. In M. Simons, M. Olsses, & M. A. Peters (Eds.), *Re-reading education policies: A handbook studying the policy agenda of the 21st century* (pp. 650–666). Sense.

Bird, S. E. (2002). It makes sense to us: Cultural identity in local legends of place. *Journal of Contemporary Ethnography, 31,* 519–547.

Blaise, M., & Ryan, S. (2020). Engaging with critical theories and the early childhood curriculum. In J. J. Mueller and N. File (Eds.), *Curriculum in early childhood education: Re-examined, reclaimed, renewed* (2nd ed., pp. 80–95). Routledge.

Bobick, S. (2018). *Medicine bag: An autoethnographic account of learning to use memory and indigeneity as resources in college student advising* [Unpublished doctoral dissertation]. West Virginia University.

Bobo, L. D. (2001). Racial attitudes and relations at the close of the twentieth century. In National Research Council, *America becoming: Racial trends and their consequences, 1* (pp. 264–310). National Academy Press.

References

Bozalek, V., & Zembylas, M. (2017). Diffraction or reflection? Sketching the contours of two methodologies in educational research. *International Journal of Qualitative Studies in Education, 30*(2), 111–127.

Bradbury, A., & Roberts-Holmes, G. (2018). *The datafication of primary and early years education: Playing with numbers.* Routledge.

Brantlinger, E. (2003). *Dividing classes: How the middle class negotiates and rationalizes school advantage.* Routledge.

Brinkmann, S., & Kvale, S. (2014). *Interviews: Learning the craft of qualitative research interviewing* (3rd ed.). Sage.

Bronfenbrenner, U. (1992). Ecological systems theory. In R. Vasta (Ed.), *Six theories of child development: Revised formulations and current issues* (pp. 187–249). Jessica Kingsley Publishers.

Brookfield, S. (1995). *Becoming a critically reflective teacher.* Jossey-Bass.

Brown, C. P. (2009a). Being accountable for one's own governing: A case study of early educators responding to standards-based early childhood education reform. *Contemporary Issues in Early Childhood, 10*(1), 3–23.

Brown, C. P. (2009b). Confronting the contradictions: A case study of early childhood teacher development in neoliberal times. *Contemporary Issues in Early Childhood, 10*(3), 240–259.

Brown, C. P. (2009c). Pivoting a prekindergarten program off the child or the standard? A case study of integrating the practices of early childhood education into elementary school. *The Elementary School Journal, 110*(2), 202–227.

Brown, C. P. (2015). Conforming to reform: Teaching prekindergarten in a neoliberal early education system. *Journal of Early Childhood Research, 13*(3), 236–251.

Brown, C. P. (2020). Introducing the text and examining the emergence, maintenance, and expansion of gaps, deficits, and risks through early childhood policy. In F. Nxumalo and C. P. Brown (Eds.), *Disrupting and countering deficits in early childhood education* (pp. 1–19). Routledge.

Brown, C. P. (2021). *Resisting the kinder-race: Restoring joy to early learning.* Teachers College Press.

Brown, C. P., & Barry, D. P. (2020). Public policy and early childhood curriculum in the United States. In J. J. Mueller and N. File (Eds.), *Curriculum in early childhood education: Re-examined, reclaimed, renewed* (2nd ed., pp. 17–33). Routledge.

Brown, C. P., Feger, B. S., & Mowry, B. N. (2018). *Rigorous DAP in the early years: From theory to practice.* Redleaf Press.

Brown, C. P., & Mowry, B. (2015). Close early learning gaps with Rigorous DAP. *Phi Delta Kappan, 96*(7), 53–57.

Brown, C. P., Puckett, K., Barry, D. P., & Ku, D. H. (2021). The double-voiced nature of becoming a teacher in the era of neoliberal teaching and teacher education. *Action in Teacher Education, 43*(4), 447–463.

Brown, C. P., & Weber, N. B. (2016). Struggling to overcome the state's prescription for practice: A study of a sample of early educators' professional development and action research projects in a high-stakes testing context. *Journal of Teacher Education, 67*(3), 183–202.

Buber, M. (1958). *Paths in utopia.* Beacon Hill.

Buchanan, R. (2017). *"It's not about that anymore": An ecological examination of the theory-practice divide in contemporary teacher education* [Unpublished doctoral dissertation]. University of California Santa Cruz.

Buchanan, R., Byard, T., Ferguson, G., Billings, K., Dana, M., & Champagne, J. (2019). Navigating standardized spaces in student teaching. *The Educational Forum, 83*(3), 237–250.

Buzzelli, C. A. (2020). Changing the discourse: The capability approach and early childhood education. In J. J. Mueller and N. File (Eds.), *Curriculum in early childhood education: Re-examined, reclaimed, renewed* (2nd ed., pp. 161–176). Routledge.

Caro-Bruce, C., Flessner, R., Klehr, M., & Zeichner, K. (Eds.; 2007). *Creating equitable classrooms through action research*. Corwin Press.

Ceppi, G., & Zini, M. (1998). *Children, spaces, relations: Metaproject for an environment for young children*. Reggio Children.

Charmaz, C. (2014). *Constructing grounded theory* (2nd ed.). Sage.

Clandinin, D. J., & Connelly, F. M. (2004). *Narrative inquiry: Experience and story in qualitative research*. Jossey-Bass.

Clark, J., & Richards, S. (2017). The cherished conceits of research with children: Does seeking the agentic voice of the child through participatory methods deliver what it promises? *Sociological Studies of Children and Youth, 22*(1), 127–147.

Cochran-Smith, M., & Lytle, S. L. (1999). Chapter 8: Relationships of knowledge and practice: Teacher learning in communities. *Review of Research in Education, 24*(1), 249–305.

Cochran-Smith, M., & Lytle, S. L. (2009). *Inquiry as stance: Practitioner research for the next generation*. Teachers College Press.

Cochran-Smith, M., Reagan, E. M., & National Academy of Education (2021, September). "Best practices" for evaluating teacher preparation programs. Evaluating and Improving Teacher Preparation Programs. *National Academy of Education*.

Cochran-Smith, M., Carney, M. C., Keefe, E. S., Burton, S., Chang, W., Fernandez, M. B., Miller, A. F., Sanchez, J. G., & Baker, M. (2018). *Reclaiming accountability in teacher education*. Teachers College Press.

Comber, B. (2016). *Literacy, place, and pedagogies of possibility*. Routledge.

Comber, B., & Kamler, B. (2004). Getting out of deficit: Pedagogies of reconnection. *Teaching Education, 15*(3), 293–310.

Comber, B., Thomson, P., & Wells, M. (2001). Critical literacy finds a "place": Writing and social action in a low-income Australian grade 2/3 classroom. *The Elementary School Journal, 101*(4), 451–464.

Common Core State Standards Initiative. (2022). *English Language Arts Standards/Writing/Kindergarten*. http://www.corestandards.org/ELA-Literacy/W/K/

Connell, R. W. (1995). *Teachers' work*. Allen & Unwin.

Cornelius, J., & Harris, F. (2018, August). Graduate educational leadership students' perceptions of academic readiness of content knowledge on the Praxis test. *Alabama Journal of Educational Leadership, 5*, 19–28.

Costello, K., & Hodson, G. (2014). Explaining dehumanization among children: The interspecies model of prejudice. *British Journal of Social Psychology, 53*(1), 175–197.

References

Cuban, L. (1990). A fundamental puzzle of school reform. In A. Lieberman (Ed.), *Schools as collaborative cultures: Creating the future now* (pp. 71–78). The Falmer Press.

Curry, M. (2008). Critical friends groups: The possibilities and limitations embedded in teacher professional communities aimed at instructional improvement and school reform. *Teachers College Record, 110*(4), 733–774.

Dahlberg, G., & Moss, P. (2005). *Ethics and politics in early childhood education.* Routledge.

Darling-Hammond, L. (2020). Accountability in teacher education. *Action in Teacher Education, 42*(1), 60–71.

Darling-Hammond, L., Bullmaster, M. L., & Cobb, V. L. (1995). Rethinking teacher leadership through professional development schools. *The Elementary School Journal, 96*(1), 87–106.

Davies, B., & Gannon, S. (2013). Collective biography and the entangled enlivening of being. *International Review of Qualitative Research, 5*(4), 357–376.

de Certeau, M. (1984). *The practice of everyday life.* University of California Press.

Deleuze, G., & Guattari, F. (1988). *A thousand plateaus: Capitalism and schizophrenia.* Bloomsbury.

Delpit, L. (2006). *Other people's children: Cultural conflict in the classroom.* The New Press.

Demarest, A. B. (2015). *Place-based curriculum design: Exceeding standards through local investigations.* Routledge.

Denton, D. (2013). Responding to edTPA: Transforming practice or applying shortcuts? *AILACTE Journal, 10*(1), 19–36.

Derman-Sparks, L., LeeKeenan, D., & Nimmo, J. (2015). *Leading anti-bias early childhood programs: A guide for change.* Teachers College Press.

Derman-Sparks, L., & Ramsey, P. (2011). *What if all the kids are White? Anti-bias multicultural education with young children and families* (2nd ed.). Teachers College Press.

Dewey, J. (1902/2000). *The school and society and The child and the curriculum* (combined ed.). University of Chicago Press.

Dewey, J. (1933). *How we think: A restatement of the relation of reflective thinking to the educative process.* Henry Regnery.

Dominguez, M. (2017). Se hace puentas al andar: Decolonial teacher education as a needed bridge to culturally sustaining and revitalizing pedagogies. In D. Paris & H. S. Alim (Eds.), *Culturally sustaining pedagogies: Teaching and learning for justice in a changing world* (pp. 225–246). Teachers College Press.

Donaldson, J. (2006). *The Gruffalo.* Puffin.

Doucet, F., & Adair, J. K. (2013). Preschool through the primary grades: Addressing race and inequity in the classroom. *Young Children, 68*(5), 88–97.

Doucet, F., & Tudge, J. (2007). Co-constructing the transition to school: Reframing the novice versus expert roles of children, parents, and teachers from a cultural perspective. In R. C. Pianta, M. J. Cox, & K. L. Snow (Eds.), *School readiness and the transition to kindergarten in the era of accountability* (pp. 307–328). Paul H. Brookes Publishing.

Douglass, A. L. (2017). *Leading for change in early care and education: Cultivating leadership from within.* Teachers College Press.

Dudley-Marling, C. (2020). Rejecting deficit views of children in poverty in favor of a philosophy of abundance. In F. Nxumalo and C. P. Brown (Eds.), *Disrupting and countering deficits in early childhood education* (pp. 53–66). Routledge.

Duhn, I. (2012a). Places for pedagogies, pedagogies for places. *Contemporary Issues in Early Childhood, 13*(2), 99–107.

Duhn, I. (2012b). Making 'place' for ecological sustainability in early childhood education. *Environmental Education Research, 18*(1), 19–29.

Ellis, C. (1998). Interpretive ethnography: Ethnographic practices for the twenty-first century. *Contemporary Sociology, 27*(4).

Erickson, F. (2007). Some thoughts on "proximal" formative assessment of student learning. In P. A. Moss (Ed.), *Evidence and decision making* (pp. 186–216). Blackwell.

Feiman-Nemser, S. (2012). *Teachers as learners*. Harvard Education Press.

Florida CS/CS/HB 1557 (2022, January 11). Parental Rights in Education bill. General bill by Judiciary Committee and Education and Employment Committee, Representative Harding. Retrieved from www.flsenate.gov

Foucault, M. (2007). *Security, territory, population: Lectures at the College de France 1977–1978* (M. Senellart, Ed., G. Burchell, Trans.). Picador.

Frank, C. (1999). *Ethnographic eyes: A teacher's guide to classroom observations*. Heinemann.

Freire, P. (1970). *Pedagogy of the oppressed*. Herder and Herder.

Furman, G. C., & Gruenewald, D. A. (2004). Expanding the landscape of social justice: A critical ecological analysis. *Educational Administration Quarterly, 40*(1), 47–76.

Fyfe, B. (2012). The relationship between documentation and assessment. In C. Edwards, L. Gandini, & G. Forman (Eds.), *The hundred languages of children: The Reggio Emilia experience in transformation* (pp. 273–291). Praeger.

Gawande, A. (2007). *Better: A surgeon's notes on performance*. Metropolitan.

Gibbs, T. J., & Howley, A. (2000). *World class standards and local pedagogies: Can we do both?* Clearinghouse on Rural Education and Small Schools, Appalachia Educational Laboratory.

Gonzalez, N. E., Moll, L., & Amanti, C. (Eds.). (2005). *Funds of knowledge: Theorizing practices in households, communities, and classrooms*. Erlbaum.

Goodwin, A. L. (2010). Globalization and preparation of quality teachers: Rethinking knowledge domains for teaching. *Teaching Education, 21*(1), 19–32.

Gorski, P. (2013). *Reaching and teaching students in poverty: Strategies for erasing the opportunity gap* (1st ed.). Teachers College Press.

Gorski, P. (2018). *Reaching and teaching students in poverty: Strategies for erasing the opportunity gap* (2nd ed.). Teachers College Press.

Grant, C., & Sleeter, C. (2012). *Doing multicultural education for achievement and equity* (2nd ed.). Routledge.

Greenblatt, D., & O'Hara, K. E. (2015, Summer). Buyer beware: Lessons learned from edTPA implementation in New York State. *Thought & Action*, 57–68.

Greenwood, D. (2013). A critical theory of place-conscious education. In R. Stevenson, M. Brody, J. Dillon, & A. J. Walsh (Eds.), *International handbook of research on environmental education* (pp. 93–100). Routledge.

References

Groenke, S. L., & Hatch, J. A. (Eds.). (2009). *Critical pedagogy and teacher education in the neoliberal era: Small openings.* Springer.

Grossman, P. (2011). Framework for teaching practice: A brief history of an idea. *Teachers College Record, 113*(12), 2836–2843.

Gruenewald, D. (2003a). Foundations of place: A multidisciplinary framework for place-conscious education. *American Educational Research Journal, 40*(3), 619–654.

Gruenewald, D. (2003b). The best of both worlds: A critical pedagogy of place. *Educational Researcher, 32*(4), 3–12.

Gruenewald, D. A. (2005). Accountability and collaboration: Institutional barriers and strategic pathways for place-based education. *Ethics, Place and Environment, 8*(3), 261–283.

Gutierrez, K. (2008). Language and literacies as civil rights. *Counterpoints, 316,* 169–184.

Haraway, D. (1997). *Modest_Witness@Second_Millenium:FemaleMan_Meets_OncoMouse: Feminism and technoscience.* Routledge.

Hargreaves, A. (1994). *Changing teachers, changing times.* Cassell.

Hatch, J. A. (2002). Accountability shovedown: Resisting the standards movement in early childhood education. *Phi Delta Kappan, 83*(6), 457–462.

Hatch, J. A., & Groenke, S. L. (2009). Issues in critical teacher education: Insights from the field. In S. L. Groenke and J. A. Hatch (Eds.), *Critical pedagogy and teacher education in the neoliberal era: Small openings* (pp. 63–84). Springer.

Haug, F. (2000). Memory work: The key to women's anxiety. In S. Radstone (Ed.), *Memory and methodology* (pp. 155–177). Berg.

Hawkman, A. M. (2017). *Swimming through whiteness: Examining nonracism and anti-racism in social studies teacher education* [Unpublished doctoral dissertation]. University of Missouri–Columbia.

Hayes, S. B. (2015). *10 characteristics of the novice teacher–revised* [Unpublished manuscript].

Heckman, J. (2000). Policies to foster human capital. *Research in Economics, 54,* 3–56.

Heimer, L., & Ramminger, A. E. (2020). *Reshaping universal preschool: Critical perspectives on power and policy.* Teachers College Press.

Helm, J. H., & Katz, L. G. (2016). *Young investigators: The project approach in the early years* (3rd ed.). Teachers College Press.

Hicks, D. (2002). *Reading lives: Working-class children and literacy learning.* Teachers College Press.

Hlebowitsh, P. S. (2005). General ideas in curriculum: A historical triangulation. *Curriculum Inquiry, 35*(1), 73–87.

Hoffman, E. (2002). *Play lady/La señora juguetona.* Redleaf Press.

Holland, D., Lachicotte, W., Skinner, D., & Cain, C. (1998). *Identity and agency in cultural worlds.* Harvard University Press.

Holloway, J., & Brass, J. (2018). Making accountable teachers: The terrors and pleasures of performativity. *Journal of Education Policy, 33*(3), 361–382.

Holmes Group (1995). *Tomorrow's schools of education.* Holmes Group.

hooks, b. (2009). *Belonging: a culture of place.* Taylor & Francis.

Housing Assistance Council. (2012). https://ruralhome.org

Howley, C., & Howley, C. (2015). Farming the poor: Cultivating profit at the schoolhouse door. In K. Sturges (Ed.), *Neoliberalizing educational reform* (pp. 21–51). Brill Sense.

Huerta, T. M., & Brittain, C. M. (2010). Effective practices that matter for Latino children. In E. G. Murillo, Jr., S. A. Villenas, R. Trinidad Galvan, J. Sanchez Munoz, C. Martinez, & M. Machado-Casas (Eds.), *Handbook of Latinos and education: Theory, research, and practice* (pp. 382–399). Routledge.

Hursh, D., Henderson, J., & Greenwood, D. (2015). Environmental education in a climate [Editorial]. *Environmental Education Research, 21*(3), 299–318.

Iruka, I. U., Curenton, S. M., Durden, T. R., & Escayg, K. (2020). *Don't look away: Embracing anti-bias classrooms*. Gryphon House.

Johnston, P. H. (2012). *Opening minds*. Stenhouse.

Jones, A. (2003). Primary teacher trainees: Identity formation in the age of anxiety. *Asia-Pacific Journal of Teacher Education, 31*(3), 181–193.

Kanter, J. W., Williams, M. T., Kuczynski, A. M., Manbeck, K. E., Debreaux, M., & Rosen, D. C. (2017). A preliminary report on the relationship between microaggressions against Black people and racism among White college students. *Race and Social Problems, 9*(4), 291–299.

Karabon, A. (2017). They're lovin' it: how preschool children mediated their funds of knowledge into dramatic play. *Early Child Development and Care, 187*(5–6), 896–909.

Karabon, A. (2021, September). Examining how early childhood preservice teacher funds of knowledge shapes pedagogical decision making. *Teaching and Teacher Education, 106*, 1–10.

Karabon, A., & Johnson, K. G. (2020, Summer). Conceptualizing culture: How preservice teachers in the rural Midwest confront subjectivities. *Teacher Education Quarterly*, 32–54.

Kashyap, M. B. (2020, November). U.S. settler colonialism, White supremacy, and the racially disparate impacts of COVID-19. *California Law Review Online, 11*, 517–529.

Keefe, S. E. (2000). *Mountain identity and the global society in a rural Appalachian county*. ERIC no. ED 443 646. https://eric.ed.gov/?id=ED443646

Keisch, D. M., & Scott, T. (2015). U.S. education reform and the maintenance of White supremacy through structural violence. *Landscapes of Violence, 3*, 1–44.

Kendi, I. (2019). *How to be an antiracist*. One World.

Kincheloe, J., Pinar, W. F., & Slattery, P. (1994). A last dying chord? Toward cultural and educational renewal in the South. *Curriculum Inquiry, 24*(4), 407–436.

Kinloch, V. (2018). Necessary disruptions: Examining justice, engagement, and humanizing approaches to teaching and teacher education. *TeachingWorks Working Papers*. University of Michigan.

Kliebard, H. (1970). Reappraisal: The Tyler rationale. *The School Review, 78*(2), 259–272.

Krechevsky, M., Mardell, B., Rivard, M., & Wilson, D. (2013). *Visible learners: Promoting Reggio-inspired approaches in all schools*. Sage.

Kumashiro, K. K. (2008). *The seduction of common sense: How the right has framed the debate on America's schools*. Teachers College Press.

Ladson-Billings, G. (1995). Toward a theory of culturally relevant pedagogy. *American Educational Research Journal, 32*(3), 465–491.

References

Ladson-Billings, G. (2003). New directions in multicultural education: Complexities, boundaries, and critical race theory. In J. A. Banks and C. A. M. Banks (Eds.), *Handbook of research in multicultural education* (2nd ed., pp. 50–65). Jossey-Bass.

Ladson-Billings, G. (2009). *The dreamkeepers: Successful teachers of African American children*. Jossey-Bass.

Ladson-Billings, G., & Dixson, A. (2021). Put some respect on the theory: Confronting distortions in culturally relevant pedagogy. In C. Compton-Lilly, T. L. Ellison, K. H. Perry, & P. Smagorinsky (Eds.), *Whitewashed critical perspectives: Restoring the edge to edgy ideas* (pp. 122–137). Routledge.

Land, N., Hamm, C., Yazbeck, S., Danis, I., Brown, M., & Nelson, N. (2019). Facetiming common worlds: Exchanging digital place stories and crafting pedagogical contact zones. *Children's Geographies*, 1–14. https://doi.org/10.1080/14733285.2019.1574339

Lave, J., & Wenger, E. (1991). *Situated learning: Legitimate peripheral participation*. Cambridge University Press.

Lawrence-Lightfoot, S. (2003). *The essential conversation: What parents and teachers can learn from each other*. Ballantine.

Lawrence-Lightfoot, S., & Davis, J. H. (1997). *The art and science of portraiture*. Jossey-Bass.

Lewis, R. L. (2002). Americanizing immigrant coal miners in northern West Virginia. In K. Fones-Wolf & R. L. Lewis (Eds.), *Transnational West Virginia: Ethnic communities and economic change, 1840–1940* (pp. 261–298). West Virginia University Press.

Lewis, S., & Holloway, J. (2019). Datafying the teaching "profession": Remaking the professional teacher in the image of data. *Cambridge Journal of Education*, 49, 35–51.

Lichter, D. T., & Brown, D. L. (2011). Rural America in an urban society: Changing spatial and social boundaries. *Annual Review of Sociology*, 37, 565–592.

Lipman, P. (2013). *The new political economy of urban education: Neoliberalism, race, and the right to the city*. Taylor & Francis.

Liu, K. (2015). Critical reflection as a framework for transformative learning in teacher education. *Educational Review*, 67(2), 135–157.

Liu, K. (2017). Creating a dialogic space for prospective teacher critical reflection and transformative learning. *Reflective Practice*, 18(6), 805–820.

Luna, S. M. (2016). (Re)defining "good teaching": Teacher performance assessments and critical race theory in early childhood teacher education. *Contemporary Issues in Early Childhood Education*, 17(4), 442–446.

MacCauley, D. (1990). *Black and white*. HMH Books.

Massey, D. (1991). The political place of locality studies. *Environment and Planning A*, 23, 267–281.

Massey, D. (1994). *Space, place, and gender*. University of Minnesota Press.

McCarty, T. L., & Lee, T. S. (2014). Critical culturally sustaining/revitalizing pedagogy and Indigenous education sovereignty. *Harvard Educational Review*, 84(1), 101–136.

McElhinny, B. (2022, June 8). West Virginia charter schools anticipate about 1,500 students this fall. West Virginia MetroNews. https://wvmetronews.com/2022/06/08/west-virginia-charter-schools-anticipate-about-1500-students-this-fall/

McInerney, P., Smyth, J., & Down, B. (2011). "Coming to a 'place' near you?" The politics and possibilities of critical pedagogy and place-based education. *Asia-Pacific Journal of Teacher Education, 39*(1), 3–16.

McLaren, P. (2003). *Life in schools: An introduction to critical pedagogy in the foundations of education* (4th ed.). Allyn and Bacon.

Mendoza, J. A., & Katz, L. (2013). Nature education and the project approach. In D. R. Meier & S. Sisk-Hilton (Eds.), *Nature education with young children: Integrating inquiry and practice* (pp. 153–171). Routledge.

Mercado, C. (2005). Reflections on the study of households in New York City and Long Island: A different route, a common destination. In N. Gonzalez, L. C. Moll, & C. Amanti (Eds.), *Funds of knowledge: Theorizing practices in households, communities, and classrooms* (pp. 233–256). Routledge.

Merriam, S. B., & Tisdell, E. J. (2015). *Qualitative research: A guide to design and implementation* (4th ed.). John Wiley & Sons.

Mezirow, J. (Ed.). (1990). *Fostering critical reflection in adulthood: A guide to transformative and emancipatory learning*. Jossey-Bass.

Mezirow, J. (2000). *Learning as transformation*. Jossey-Bass.

Michael, A., & Conger, M. C. (2009, Spring). Becoming an antiracist White ally: How a White affinity group can help. *Perspectives on Urban Education, 6*(1), 56–60.

Milner, R. H., IV. (2010). What does teacher education have to do with teaching? Implications for diversity studies. *Journal of Teacher Education, 61*(1–2), 118–131.

Moffa, E., & McHenry-Sorber, E. (2018). Learning to be rural: Lessons about being rural in teacher education programs. *The Rural Educator*, 26–40.

Moll, L., Amanti, C., Neff, D., & Gonzalez, N. (2005). Funds of knowledge for teaching: Using a qualitative approach to connect homes and classrooms. In N. Gonzalez, L. C. Moll, & C. Amanti (Eds.), *Funds of knowledge: Theorizing practices in households, communities, and classrooms* (pp. 71–87). Routledge.

Moss, P. (2008). Sociocultural implications for assessment. In P. Moss, D. Pullin, J. P. Gee, E. H. Haertl, & L. J. Young (Eds.), *Assessment, equity and opportunity to learn* (pp. 222–258). Cambridge University Press.

Mueller, J. J., & File, N. (2020). Standards, correlations, and questions: Examining the impact of the accountability regime on early childhood curriculum. In J. J. Mueller & N. File (Eds.), *Curriculum in early childhood education: Re-examined, reclaimed, renewed* (2nd ed., pp. 34–63). Routledge.

Mueller, J. J., & Whyte, K. L. (2020). The curriculum theory lens on early childhood: Moving thought into action. In J. J. Mueller & N. File (Eds.), *Curriculum in early childhood education: Re-examined, reclaimed, renewed* (2nd ed., pp. 64–79). Routledge.

Murray, J. A., Swennen, A., & Shagir, L. (2009). Understanding teacher educators' work and identities. In A. Swennen & M. van der Klink (Eds.), *Becoming a teacher educator: Theory and practice for teacher educators* (pp. 29–43). Springer.

National Commission on Excellence in Education. (1983). *A nation at risk: The imperative for educational reform. An open letter to the American people. A report to the nation and the Secretary of Education*.

Ng, P. T., & Tan, C. (2009). Community of practice for teachers: Sensemaking or critical reflective learning? *Reflective Practice, 10*(1), 37–44.

Nieto, S. (2000). Placing equity front and center: Some thoughts on transforming teacher education for a new century. *Journal of Teacher Education, 31*(3), 180–187.

No Child Left Behind Act of 2001, P.L. 107–110, 20 U.S.C. § 6319 (2002).

Noddings, N. (2003). *Caring: A feminine approach to ethics and moral education.* University of California Press.

Nxumalo, F. (2015). Forest stories: Restorying encounters with "natural" places in early childhood education. In V. Pacini-Ketchabaw & A. Taylor (Eds.), *Unsettling the colonial places and spaces of early childhood education* (pp. 21–42). Routledge.

Nxumalo, F. (2019). *Decolonizing place in early childhood education.* Routledge.

Nxumalo, F. (2020). Disrupting racial capitalist formations in early childhood education. In F. Nxumalo & C. P. Brown (Eds.), *Disrupting and countering deficits in early childhood education* (pp. 164–178). Routledge.

O'Leary, S. (2018, December 17). *Booms and bust: Natural gas update.* https://wvpolicy.org/booms-and-bust-natural-gas-update/

Olssen, M., & Peters, M. A. (2005). Neoliberalism, higher education and the knowledge economy: From the free market to knowledge capitalism. *Journal of Education Policy, 20,* 313–345.

Paris, D., & Alim, H. S. (Eds.). (2017). *Culturally sustaining pedagogies: Teaching and learning for justice in a changing world.* Teachers College Press.

Patel, L. (2015). *Decolonizing educational research: From ownership to answerability.* Routledge.

Patel, L. (2016). Reaching beyond democracy in educational policy analysis. *Educational Policy, 30*(1), 114–127.

Payne, R. (2005). *A framework for understanding poverty* (4th ed.). aha! Process.

Pearson, S. (2013). "The last bastion of colonialism": Appalachian settler colonialism and self-indigenization. *American Indian Culture and Research Journal, 37*(2), 165–184.

Pelojoaquin, K., & Pelo, A. (2006/2007, Winter). Why we banned Legos: Exploring power, ownership, and equity in an early childhood classroom. *Rethinking Schools, 21*(2).

Perry, K. H. (2021). What the FOK? An illustrative case of how Whitewashing occurs in higher education. In C. Compton-Lilly, T. L. Ellison, K. H. Perry, & P. Smagorinsky (Eds.), *Whitewashed critical perspectives: Restoring the edge to edgy ideas* (pp. 41–62). Routledge.

Phillips, D. K., & Carr, K. (2014). *Becoming a teacher through action research* (3rd ed.). Routledge.

Pinar, W. (2004). *What is curriculum theory?* Lawrence Erlbaum.

Poole, A., & Huang, J. (2018). Resituating Funds of Identity within contemporary interpretations of *perzhivanie. Mind, Culture, and Activity, 25*(2), 125–137.

Powell, S. K. (2022). *Reckoning with privilege in Appalachia and higher education: A project of critical consciousness* [Unpublished doctoral dissertation]. West Virginia University.

Power, K. (2011). Getting lost in Logan. In M. Somerville, B. Davies, K. Power, S. Gannon, & P. de Carteret (Eds.), *Place, pedagogy, change* (pp. 51–62). Sense.

Power-Carter, S., & Bloome, D. (2021). Dialoguing and personhood. In C. Compton-Lilly, T. L. Ellison, K. H. Perry, & P. Smagorinsky (Eds.), *Whitewashed critical perspectives: Restoring the edge to edgy ideas* (pp. 138–163). Routledge.

Pratt, M. L. (1991). Arts of the contact zone. *Profession*, 33–40.

Price, T. A. (2014). Teacher education under audit: value-added measures, TVAAs, EdTPA and evidence-based theory. *Citizenship, Social and Economics Education*, 13(3), 211–225.

Purcell-Gates, V. (1997). *Other people's words: The cycle of low literacy*. Harvard University Press.

Pyle, R. (2001). The rise and fall of natural history: How a science grew that eclipsed direct experience. *Orion*, 20, 16–23.

Quintero, E. P. (2020). A story about story: The promise of multilingual children and teachers and a framework for integrated curriculum. In J. J. Mueller & N. File (Eds.), *Curriculum in early childhood education: Re-examined, reclaimed, renewed* (2nd ed., pp. 144–160). Routledge.

Recchia, S. L., & McDevitt, S. E. (2018). Unraveling universalist perspectives on teaching and caring for infants and toddlers: Finding authenticity in diverse funds of knowledge. *Journal of Research in Childhood Education*, 32(1), 14–31.

Reynolds, J., & Kendi, I. X. (2020). *Stamped: Racism, antiracism, and you*. Little, Brown.

Reynolds, A. J., Temple, J. A., Robertson, D. L., & Mann, E. A. (2002). Age 21 cost-benefit analysis of the Title I Chicago child-parent centers. *Educational Evaluation and Policy Analysis*, 24, 267–303.

Reznitskaya, A. (2012). Dialogic teaching: Rethinking language use during literature discussions. *The Reading Teacher*, 65(7), 446–456.

Riessman, C. K. (2007). *Narrative methods for the human sciences*. Sage.

Richmond, G., Salazar, M., & Jones, N. (2019). Assessment and the future of teacher education. *Journal of Teacher Education*, 70(2), 86–89.

Rinaldi, C. (2001, Fall). The pedagogy of listening: The listening perspective from Reggio Emilia. *Innovations in Early Education: The Reggio Emilia Exchange*, 8(4).

Rinaldi, C. (2012). The pedagogy of listening: The listening perspective from Reggio Emilia. In C. Edwards, L. Gandini, & G. Forman (Eds.), *The hundred languages of children: The Reggio Emilia experience in transformation* (pp. 233–246). Praeger.

Rogoff, B. (1990). *Apprenticeship in thinking: Cognitive development in social context*. Oxford University Press.

Sachs, J. (2001). Teacher professional identity: Competing discourses, competing outcomes. *Journal of Education Policy*, 16(2), 149–161.

Sachs, J. (2022, January 24). Steep rise in gag orders, many sloppily drafted. *PEN America: The Freedom to Write*. https://pen.org/steep-rise-gag-orders-many-sloppily-drafted/

Sachs, J., & Friedman, J. (2022, February 15). Educational gag orders target speech about LGBTQ+ identities with new prohibitions and punishments. *PEN America: The Freedom to Write*. https://pen.org/educational-gag-orders-target-speech-about-lgbtq-identities-with-new-prohibitions-and-punishments/

Saldana, J. (2015). *The coding manual for qualitative researchers* (3rd ed.). Sage.

References

Sapon-Shevin, M. (2010). *Because we can change the world* (2nd ed.). Corwin.

Schindel, A., & Tolbert, S. (2017). Critical caring for people and place. *The Journal of Environmental Education, 48*(1), 26–34.

Schneider, B. (2016, September 13). Why so many red states are turning blue. *Reuters*. https://www.reuters.com/article/us-usa-election-commentary/commentary-why-so-many-red-states-are-turning-blue-idINKCN11I1DN

Schonfeld, D., Kawashima-Gunsberg, K., Greenwalt, K., McAvoy, P., Stitzlein, S., & Patterson, T. M. (2021, January 11). *How should schools teach kids about what happened at the US Capitol on Jan. 6? We asked 6 education experts.* The Conversation. https://theconversation.com/how-should-schools-teach-kids-about-what-happened-at-the-us-capitol-on-jan-6-we-asked-6-education-experts-152884

Schon, D. A. (1983). *The reflective practitioner*. Basic Books.

Schultz, K. (2010). After the blackbird whistles: Listening to silence in classrooms. *Teachers College Record, 112*(11), 2833–2849.

Schultz, K., Jones-Walker, C. E., & Chikkatur, A. P. (2008). Listening to students, negotiating beliefs: Preparing teachers for urban classrooms. *Curriculum Inquiry, 38*(2), 155–187.

Schweinhart, L. J., & Weikart, D. P. (1980). Young children grow up: The effects of the Perry Preschool Program on youths through age 15. *Monographs of the High/Scope Educational Research Foundation, 7*. High Scope Education Research Foundation.

Scott, R. R. (2009). Appalachia and the construction of Whiteness in the United States. *Sociology Compass, 3*(5), 803–810.

Seemiller, C., & Grace, M. (2019). *Generation Z: A century in the making*. Routledge.

Semali, L., & Kincheloe, J. (1999). *What is indigenous knowledge? Voices from the academy*. Falmer Press.

Sherfinski, M. (2017). Becoming critical communities of practice in pre-kindergarten. *Journal of Family Diversity in Education, 2*(3), 71–93.

Sherfinski, M. (2020, December). "Confidence" problems in literacy coaching: How a suburban kindergarten divided "good" and "bad" teachers in the accountability shovedown. *Journal of Early Childhood Literacy*. https://doi.org/10.1177/1468798420980085

Sherfinski, M. (2021, July). Spaces for coping with change: Kindergarten educators' emotional refuges. *International Journal of Early Years Education*. https://doi.org/10.1080/09669760.2021.1956438

Sherfinski, M. (2022, September). Relational aspects of writer's workshop in kindergarten: Learning from Black boys who used their creativity and strength to speak back to the scripted curriculum. *Journal of Early Childhood Teacher Education*. https://doi.org/10.1080/10901027.2022.2125463

Sherfinski, M., Hayes, S., Zhang, J., & Jalalifard, M. (2019). "Do it all but don't kill us": (Re)positioning teacher educators and preservice teachers amidst edTPA and the teacher strike in West Virginia. *Education Policy Analysis Archives, 27*(151), 1–44.

Sherfinski, M., Hayes, S., Zhang, J., & Jalalifard, M. (2021). Grappling with funds of knowledge in rural Appalachia and beyond: The shifting contexts of preservice teachers. *Action in Teacher Education, 43*(2), 106–127.

Sherfinski, M., Jalalifard, M., Zhang, J., & Hayes, S. (2019). Narrative portfolios as culturally responsive resistance to neoliberal early childhood teacher education: A case study. *Journal of Research in Childhood Education, 33*(3), 490–519.

Sherfinski, M., & Slocum, A. (2018). Playing the festival queen in Appalachia: Exploring the influences of local culture on classroom play. *Journal of Research in Childhood Education, 32*(4), 455–471.

Sherfinski, M., Slocum, A., & Lough, J. (2022). How might place be pedagogical in Appalachia? New possibilities for early childhood classrooms in the Anthropocene. *Pedagogy, Culture & Society, 30*(5), 617–637.

Sherfinski, M., Weekley, B. S., & Slocum, A. (2016). After Arthurdale: Place-based education and early childhood in West Virginia. *Journal of Curriculum and Pedagogy, 13*(2), 164–183.

Simon, N. S., & Johnson, S. M. (2015). Teacher turnover in high-poverty schools: What we know and can do. *Teachers College Record, 117*(3), 1–36.

Sinclair, S., Kendrick, A., & Jacoby-Senghor, D. (2014). Whites' interpersonal interactions shape, and are shaped by, implicit prejudice. *Policy Insights from the Behavioral and Brain Sciences, 1*(1), 81–87.

Sisk-Hilton, S., & Meier, D. R. (2016). *Narrative inquiry in early childhood and elementary school*. Routledge.

Sleeter, C. (2017). Critical race theory and the Whiteness of teacher education. *Urban Education, 52*(2), 155–169.

Slocum, A., Hathaway, R., & Bernstein, M. (2018). Striking signs: The diverse discourse of the 2018 West Virginia teachers' strike. *English Education, 50*(4), 365–374.

Smagorinsky, P. (2021). Third and hybrid spaces in literacy scholarship and practice: They are different and their differences matter. In C. Compton-Lilly, T. L. Ellison, K. K. Perry, & P. Smagorinsky (Eds.), *Whitewashed critical perspectives: Restoring the edge to edgy ideas* (pp. 18–40). Routledge.

Smith, G. A., & Williams, D. R. (1999). Re-engaging culture and ecology. In G. A. Smith & D. R. Williams (Eds.), *Ecological education in action: On weaving education, culture, and the environment* (pp. 1–18). State University of New York Press.

Sobel, D. (2013). *Place-based education: Connecting classrooms and communities* (2nd ed.). Orion.

Soja, E. W. (1989). *Postmodern geographies: The reassertion of space in critical social theory*. Verso.

Somerville, M. J. (2010). A place pedagogy for 'global contemporaneity'. *Educational Philosophy and Theory, 42*(3), 326–344.

Somerville, M. J. (2011). Becoming frog: Learning place in primary school. In M. Somerville, B. Davies, K. Power, S. Ganon, & P. de Carteret, *Place pedagogy change* (pp. 65–79). Sense.

Sommer, D. (2021, May-June). Democracy requests the pleasure of your company. *Harvard Magazine*. https://www.harvardmagazine.com/2021/05/features-democracy-requests-company

Sparkes, A. C., & Smith, B. (2008). Narrative constructionist inquiry. In J. A. Holstein & J. F. Gubrium (Eds.), *Handbook of constructionist research* (pp. 295–314). Guilford Press.

References

Stack, S. F. (2008). Implementing Brown v. Board of Education in West Virginia: The Southern Schools news report. *West Virginia History*, 2(1).

Stack, S. F. (2016). *The Arthurdale community school: Education and reform in Depression-Era Appalachia*. University of Kentucky Press.

Stremmel, A. J., Burns, J. P., Nganga, C., & Bertolini, K. (2020). Countering the essentialized discourse of curriculum: Opening spaces for complicated conversations. In J. J. Mueller & N. File (Eds.), *Curriculum in early childhood education: Re-examined, reclaimed, renewed* (2nd ed., pp. 177–192). Routledge.

TallBear, K. (2019). Caretaking relations, not American dreaming. *Kalfou*, 6(1), 24–41.

Terman, A. R. (2020). Social identities, place, mobility and belonging: Intersectional experiences of college-educated youth. *Journal of Rural Studies*, 77, 21–32.

Thomas, M., & Liu, K. (2012). The performance of reflection: A grounded analysis of prospective teachers' ePortfolios. *Journal of Technology and Teacher Education*, 20, 305–330.

Tuck, E. (2009). Suspending damage: A letter to communities. *Harvard Educational Review*, 79(3), 409–427.

Tuck, E., & Gorlewski, J. (2016). Racist ordering, settler colonialism, and edTPA: A participatory policy analysis. *Educational Policy*, 30(1), 197–217.

Tuck, E., & McKenzie, M. (2015). *Place in research: Theory, methodology, and methods*. Routledge.

U.S. Census (2020). State profile. *West Virginia 2020 Census*. https://www.census.gov/library/stories/state-by-state/west-virginia-population-change-between-census-decade.html

U.S. Census Bureau (2018). Poverty status in last 12 months—2017, *American Community Survey*. https://data.census.gov/cedsci/table?q=poverty%20wv%202017&tid=ACSST1Y2017.S1701

Valenzuela, A. (1999). *Subtractive schooling: U.S.-Mexican youth and the politics of caring*. SUNY Press.

van Manen, M. (1977). Linking ways of knowing with ways of being practical. *Curriculum Inquiry*, 6(3), 205–228.

van Manen, M. (1991). *The tact of teaching: The meaning of pedagogical thoughtfulness*. Althouse Press.

Vascellaro, S. (2011). *Out of the classroom and into the world*. The New Press.

Vasquez, V. M. (2014). *Negotiating critical literacies with young children* (2nd ed.). Routledge.

Veracini, L. (2011). Introducing settler colonial studies. *Settler Colonial Studies*, 1(1), 1–12.

Vygotsky, L. S. (1978). *Mind in society: The development of higher psychological processes*. Harvard University Press.

Weinstein, M. (2007). We are already owned: What are the resulting implications if we continue to treat curriculum/teaching theory and practice as separate domains of academic research? *Journal of Curriculum & Pedagogy*, 4(1), 54–60.

Wenger, E. (2002). *Cultivating communities of practice: A guide to managing knowledge*. Harvard Business School Press.

West Virginia Department of Education. (2016). *West Virginia alternative certification frequently asked questions*. Alternative-Certification-FAQs-final-9_2016.pdf (wvde.us)

West Virginia Department of Education. (2022). *Kindergarten content objectives and standards for science.* https://wvde.us/tree/early-learning-p-5/kindergarten/science-kindergarten/

West Virginia SB 498 (2022, February 28). West Virginia Legislature, 2022 Regular Session, Committee Substitute for Senate Bill 498 by Senators Rucker, Azinger, Sypolt, Karnes, and Maynard (Originating in Committee on Education). https://www.wvlegislature.gov/Bill_Status/bills_text.cfm?billdoc=SB498%20SUB1.htm&yr=2022&sesstype=RS&i=498

Wetzel, M. M., Hoffman, J. V., & Maloch, B. (2017). *Mentoring preservice teachers through practice: A framework for coaching with care.* Routledge.

Whyte, K. L., & Karabon, A. (2016). Transforming teacher–family relationships: Shifting roles and perceptions of home visits through the Funds of Knowledge approach. *Early Years, 36*(2), 207–221.

Wiggins, G., & McTighe, J. (2005). *Understanding by design* (2nd ed.). ASCD.

Wynter, S. (2006). On how we mistook the map for a territory, and reimprisoned ourselves in our unbearable wrongness of being, of *Desêtre*: Black Studies toward the human project. In L. R. Gordon & J. A. Gordon (Eds.), *Not only the master's tools: African American Studies in theory and practice* (pp. 121–184). Routledge.

Yazbeck, S., & Danis, I. (2015). Entangled frictions with place as assemblage. *Canadian Children, 40*(2), 22–31.

Yendol-Hoppey, D., Hoppey, D., Morewood, A., Hayes, S. B., & Graham, M. S. (2013). Micropolitical and identity challenges influencing new faculty participation in teacher education reform: When will we learn? *Teachers College Record, 115,* 1–31.

Yin, R. K. (2009). *Case study research: Design and methods* (4th ed.). Sage.

Young, J. C., & Friedman, J. (2022, February 1). In higher education, new educational gag orders would exert unprecedented control over college teaching. *PEN America: The Freedom to Write.* https://pen.org/in-higher-education-new-educational-gag-orders/

Young, M. D., & Diem, S. (2014). Putting critical educational perspectives to work in educational policy. *International Journal of Qualitative Studies in Education, 27*(9), 1063–1067.

Zeichner, K. (2020). Preparing teachers as democratic professionals. *Action in Teacher Education, 42*(1), 38–48.

Zeichner, K. M., & Liston, D. (1996). *Reflective teaching: An introduction.* Lawrence Erlbaum.

Zhao, Y. (2010). Preparing globally competent teachers: A new imperative for teacher education. *Journal of Teacher Education, 61*(5), 422–431.

Zipin, L. (2009). Dark funds of knowledge, deep funds of pedagogy: Exploring boundaries between lifeworlds and schools. *Discourse: Studies in the Cultural Politics of Education, 30*(3), 317–331.

Index

Abrams, L., 130
Accountability, x
  accountabiity "shove-down" of neoliberal standards, 14
  alternative approaches to teacher certification, 16, 17, 54–55, 59, 82
  democracy and, 16, 18, 21–22, 44–45
  Educative Teacher Performance Assessment (edTPA), 5, 16–20, 34, 41–42, 46, 54, 75, 82, 88, 105, 108
  Funds of Knowledge (FoK) and, 18–20. *See also* Funds of Knowledge (FoK)
  nature of, 3–4
  portfolios in. *See* Narrative portfolio project
  Praxis tests, 17–18, 19, 41, 42, 46, 59, 82, 105
  reclaiming, 16–20
  role of assessment in the education process, 107–108, 115
  standards-based, 5, 8–10, 14–17, 25–27, 38–41, 44, 70, 82, 83, 88–89, 108–109, 115
  teacher education assessment systems, 16–18, 41–42, 54–55, 108–118, 119. *See also* Narrative portfolio project
Action research. *See* Place-based teacher education
Adair, J. K., 82, 83, 96, 102, 108
Agency
  accountability and, 109
  nature of, 109

Aguilar, E., 92–93
Ahmed, S., 96
Alim, H. S., 25, 26, 30, 47, 133
Amanti, C., 18, 47–49, 117, 133
Amy (preservice teacher), 42, 61–65, 67, 69–70, 75–77, 128
Anderson, S. K., 25
Andre-Bechely, L., 9
Antiracist education, 54, 83–99. *See also* People of Color (POC); Racial justice; Whites/Whiteness
  Black Lives Matter (BLM) movement and, 6, 83, 88, 92
  COVID-19 pandemic and, 87–88
  "line of flight" (Deleuze & Guattari) and, 84–85
  nature of antiracist work, 83
  policymakers' reinforcements in, 86–87
  sample lessons, 92–99
  strengthening, 85–86
  teaching that makes students "feel bad" vs., 86–87
  texts supporting, 83–84, 92–93, 95–99, 145–146
Anyon, J., 118
Appiah, K. A., 1
Apple, M. W., 4, 9, 14, 19, 39, 45, 47, 54, 55, 133
Ashton, E., 96
Asians. *See* People of Color (POC)
Assessment systems. *See* Accountability
Audit culture, 6, 13–16, 18, 131, 132

Bachelard, G., 130
Baker, M., 16, 18, 55, 113, 120
Baker, R. S., 11

Bakhtin, M. M., 34, 43, 65, 131
Ball, D. L., 21
Ball, S. J., 9, 15, 41, 94–95, 107
Bang, M., 29
Banking model of education (Freire), 72, 114
Banks, A., 10
Barad, K., 32, 36
Barry, D. P., ix, 9, 10, 31, 34, 38–39, 43, 66, 83
Bartolome, L. I., 24, 110
Barton, A., 44
Basso, K., 100
Beane, J. A., 45, 47, 54, 55, 133
Beech, B. M., 11
Bennett, C. L., 17–18
Bernstein, M., 8
Berry, Wendell, 25
Bertolini, K., 39, 107
Bhaba, H. K., 53
Biesta, G., 9
Billings, K., 18
Bird, S. E., 53
Black and White (MacCauley), 97–98
Black Lives Matter (BLM) movement, 6, 83, 88, 92
Blacks. *See* People of Color (POC)
Blaise, M., 70
Bloome, D., 35
Bloom's taxonomy, 69–70
Bobick, S., 131
Bobo, L. D., 10
Bozalek, V., 36
Bradbury, A., 41, 47
Brantlinger, E., 2, 41, 66
Brass, J., 15, 33
Brinkmann, S., 127
Brittain, C. M., 99
Broadhagen, Barbara, 54
Bronfenbrenner, U., 22
Brookfield, S., 33
Brown, Christopher P., ix–xi, 3, 9, 10, 14, 19, 21, 31, 34, 38–39, 41, 43, 59, 65, 66, 83, 101, 108, 109, 112, 117–119
Brown, D. L., 23
Brown, M., 118

Bruce, M. A., 11
Buber, M., 35
Buchanan, R., 18, 19
Bullmaster, M. L., 95
Burns, J. P., 39, 107
Burton, S., 16, 18, 55, 113, 120
Bush, George W., 8
Buzzelli, C. A., 15, 35
Byard, T., 18

Cain, C., 109
California, 17
Caring relationships
    Indigenous knowledge and, 24, 28–30, 111–112
    in narrative portfolio project vignette, 71–75
    nature of, 23, 35
    as strategy for sensing and resisting neoliberal policies, 22, 23, 35–36, 46, 57, 82, 96
Carney, M. C., 16, 18, 55, 113, 120
Caro-Bruce, C., 49
Carr, K., 49, 54, 125
Ceppi, G., 61
Champagne, J., 18
Chang, W., 16, 18, 55, 113, 120
Change process in teacher education, 114–118
    avoiding dis-placement, 116–117
    how we teach, 115
    positive deviance in, 117–118
    what we teach, 115–116
    who we teach, 116
    why we teach, 116
Charmaz, C., 21
Chikkatur, A. P., 48–49, 60, 66, 68
Clandinin, D. J., 126, 129–130
Clark, J., 108, 109
Cobb, V. L., 95
Cochran-Smith, M., ix, 14, 16, 18, 31, 45, 48, 55, 60, 109–113, 117, 120, 131
Cohen, D. K., 21
Colegrove, K. S., 96, 102, 108
Colorblind approach, 11, 12, 26, 83–84, 96, 110
Comber, B., 7, 29, 99, 101, 103, 122

Common Core State Standards
    Initiative, 27, 38–39
Communities of practice, 30–32, 120
Conger, M. C., 29
Connell, R. W., 101
Connelly, F. M., 126, 129–130
Content knowledge, 135
Conversation, The (Schonfeld et al.), 93
Cora (preservice teacher), 73–75, 128
Cornelius, J., 17
Costello, K., 10
Council for the Accreditation of
    Educator Preparation (CAEP), 15,
    16–17, 109
COVID-19 pandemic, 5, 55, 62–63,
    71–77, 87–99, 101, 115, 126–130
Critical and family literacy (Vasquez),
    47, 82, 133
Critical friends groups, 30, 32, 43, 60,
    100–105, 120
Critical place-based teacher education.
    See Place-based teacher education
Critical place inquiry/Indigenous
    knowledge, 24, 28–30, 111–112
Critical Race Theory (CRT), 82, 86,
    105
Cuban, L., 121
Culturally relevant, responsive, and
    sustaining teaching (Ladson-
    Billings; Paris & Alim), 18, 21,
    25–28, 30, 47, 51, 82, 84, 85, 118,
    133, 140
Culture of power (Delpit), 18
Curenton, S. M., 10, 94–97, 99
Curley, L., 29
Curry, M., 32

Dahlberg, G., 29, 32
Dana, M., 18
Danis, I., 28, 73, 118
Dark Funds of Knowledge, 88–92, 97,
    122
  COVID-19 pandemic and, 89–92,
    94–95
  extractive economy and, 7–8, 25, 60,
    66, 89, 101, 111
  failure to access student, 89
  Whitewashing and, 88–89

Darling-Hammond, L., 3–4, 95, 108
Davies, B., 33
Davis, J. H., 129
Debreaux, M., 10
De Certeau, M., 53
Deficit-based perspectives, 11, 12, 14,
    30, 42–43, 48–49, 66–67, 72–73,
    75, 96, 109, 120, 126
Deleuze, G., 23, 84–85
Delpit, L., 18
Demarest, A. B., 11, 26–28
Democracy
  accountability and, 16, 18, 21–22,
    44–45. *See also* Narrative
    portfolio project
  January 6, 2021 insurrection and, 86,
    93, 116
  neoliberalism and, 9. *See also*
    Neoliberal model of education
  placed-based education and, 11–12,
    16, 18, 21–22. *See also* Place-
    based teacher education
  political parties in, 7–8
Democratic education (Beane & Apple),
    45, 47, 54–55, 133
Denton, D., 41
Derman-Sparks, L., 11, 54, 83–84, 89,
    95, 117, 118
Derrida, Jacques, 96
Destiny (preservice teacher), 98, 105,
    128, 145–146
Dewey, John, 25, 28, 32–33
Dialogic teaching (Reznitskaya), 47,
    82, 133
Dialogism
  in narrative portfolio project vignette,
    65–71
  nature of, 23, 34, 66
  as strategy for sensing and resisting
    neoliberal policies, 22, 23,
    34–35, 46, 57, 82
Diem, S., 109
Differentiated Instruction class, 69,
    79–80
Diffraction
  in narrative portfolio project
    vignettes, 75–80, 89–92
  nature of, 23, 36

Diffraction (*continued*)
  as strategy for sensing and resisting neoliberal policies, 22, 23, 36–37, 46, 57, 82
Diverse communities, in approach to place-based education, 24, 25–28
Dixson, A., 89
Documentation
  vignettes in narrative portfolios, 51–53, 61–80, 89–92
  as "visible listening" (Rinaldi), 51–52
Dominguez, M., 118
Donaldson, J., 74
Don't Look Away (Iruka et al.), 95, 96–97, 99
Doucet, F., 43, 82, 83
Douglass, A. L., 113
Down, B., 26
Dudley-Marling, C., 19, 43, 116–117
Duhn, I., 2, 3, 22, 23, 28, 36, 43, 74, 93, 105
Dunn, A. H., ix
Durden, T. R., 10, 94–97, 99

Ecological Framework for Teacher Education, An, 13
EdChange, 145–146
Educative Teacher Performance Assessment (edTPA), 5, 16–20, 34, 41–42, 46, 54, 75, 82, 88, 105, 108
Elementary and Secondary Education Act (ESEA, 1965), 9–10
Elementary Education Special Professional Association (SPA), 16–17, 109, 131
Ellis, C., 131
ePortfolios, 46–47
Equity Literacy Institute, 145–146
Erickson, F., 117
Escayg, K., 10, 94–97, 99
Every Student Succeeds Act (ESSA), 38–39

Farver, S., ix
Feger, B. S., 119
Feiman-Nemser, S., 19
Ferguson, G., 18

Fernandez, M. B., 16, 18, 55, 113, 120
File, N., 14
5-Year Teacher Education Program, 5–6, 12–13, 57, 87–88, 125–132
Fixed and dynamic frames (Johnston), 47, 82, 133
Flessner, R., 49
Florida CS/CS/HB 1577, 87
Ford, C., 11
Foucault, M., 39, 44
Frank, C., 49, 131
Frankie (preservice teacher), 98–99, 129
Freire, P., 24, 72, 112, 114, 115
Friedman, J., 87
Funds of Knowledge (FoK), 18–20, 21
  in countering the deficit perspective, 48–49
  Dark Funds of Knowledge. *See* Dark Funds of Knowledge
  engaging students and families through, 43–44, 62–65, 73–80
  learning in "third spaces" (Quintero), 53
  theoretical basis (Moll et al.), 18, 47, 48–49, 82, 133
Furman, G. C., 3
Fyfe, B., 29, 52

Gannon, S., 33
Gawande, A., 117
"Getting Lost in Logan" (Power), 58, 62, 138
Gibbs, T. J., 28
Globalization trend, 2–4, 5, 14, 28, 30, 83, 103, 111
Gonzalez, N. E., 18, 47–49, 117, 133
Goodwin, A. L., 5
Google Classroom, 88
Gore, Al, 8
Gorlewski, J., 110–112
Gorski, P., 21, 47, 48, 65, 84, 133
Grace, M., 40
Graham, M. S., 19
Grant, C., 89
Greenblatt, D., 17
Greenwalt, K., 93
Greenwood, D., 10, 26

Groenke, S. L., 14, 54
Grossman, P., 31, 115
Gruenewald, D. A., 3–5, 10, 26, 41, 54, 60, 61, 66, 71, 74, 107, 112, 114, 130
Guattari, F., 23, 84–85
Guenther, A., ix
Gutierrez, K., 26

Hamm, C., 118
Haraway, D., 36
Hargreaves, A., 15
Harris, F., 17
Harris, Kamala, 86
Hatch, J. A., 14, 54
Hathaway, R., 8
Haug, F., 131
Hawkman, A. M., 87
Hayes, Sharon B., 1, 5, 8, 15, 17, 19, 34, 42–44, 89, 104–105, 108, 109, 127, 134–135, 137–143
Head Start, 10
Heckman, J., 10
Heidi (preservice teacher), 54–55
Heimer, L., 101
Helm, J. H., 54
Henderson, J., 10, 26
Hicks, D., 75
Hicks, H., 10
Higher Education Act (HEA, 1998), 16, 113
Hlebowitsh, P. S., 39
Hodson, G., 10
Hoffman, F., 26
Hoffman, J. V., 52, 114
Holland, D., 109
Holloway, J., 15, 33, 109
Holmes Group, 39, 40
Home visits, 44, 59, 100, 101–102
hooks, b., 101
Hoppey, D., 19
Housing Assistance Council, 7
Howley, A., 28
Howley, Caitlin, 26
Howley, Craig., 26
How to Be an Antiracist (Kendi), 95, 98, 145–146
Huang, J., 94, 97

Huerta, T. M., 99
Human capital theory, 2, 3, 10, 28, 108–109
Hursh, D., 10, 26

Imogene (preservice teacher), 42, 100, 102, 103–105, 128
Improving America's Schools Act (IASA), 38–39
Inclusive education (Sapon-Shevin), 47, 82, 111–112, 133, 140
Indigenous knowledge, 24, 28–30, 111–112
Inquiry-based practices, 47–49, 82–83, 133–134. See also Place-based teacher education
  critical and family literacy (Vasquez), 47, 82, 133
  culturally relevant, responsive, and sustaining teaching (Ladson-Billings; Paris & Alim), 18, 21, 25–28, 30, 47, 51, 82, 84, 85, 118, 133, 140
  democratic education (Beane & Apple), 45, 47, 54–55, 82, 133
  dialogic teaching (Reznitskaya), 47, 82, 133
  fixed and dynamic frames (Johnston), 47, 82, 133
  funds of knowledge (Moll et al.), 18, 47, 48–49, 82, 133. See also Funds of Knowledge (FoK)
  inclusive education (Sapon-Shevin), 47, 82, 111–112, 133, 140
  inquiry as stance, 31, 47, 135
  opportunity gap elimination (Gorski), 21, 47, 48, 65, 82, 84, 133
Intersectionality, 11, 97, 105, 110
Iruka, I. U., 10, 94–97, 99
I-You vs. I-It relationships
  Indigenous knowledge and, 24, 28–30, 111–112
  in narrative portfolio project vignette, 71–75
  nature of, 23, 35
  as strategy for sensing and resisting neoliberal policies, 22, 23, 35–36, 46, 57, 82, 96

Jacoby-Senghor, D., 10
Jalalifard, M., 8, 15, 17, 19, 34, 42–43, 89, 104–105, 108, 109
Joanna (preservice teacher), 42, 55, 60, 66–71, 77–78, 128
Johnson, K. G., 30, 83, 89
Johnson, Lyndon B., 9
Johnson, S. M., 105
Johnston, P. H., 47, 133
Jones, A., 3
Jones, May, 85
Jones, N., 41
Jones-Walker, C. F., 48–49, 60, 66, 68

Kamler, B., 29
Kanter, J. W., 10
Karabon, A., 29, 30, 44, 72, 83, 89
Kashyap, M. B., 23, 111
Katz, L. G., 25, 54
Keefe, E. S., 16, 18, 55, 113, 120
Keefe, S. E., 8
Keisch, D. M., 10
Kendi, I. X., 10, 83, 95, 98, 145–146
Kendrick, A., 10
Kessel, A., 29
Kincheloe, J., 33, 111
Kinloch, V., 107–108, 115
Klehr, M., 49
Kliebard, H., 47
Krechevsky, M., 61
Ku, D. H., ix, 34, 43, 66
Kuczynski, A. M., 10
Kumashiro, K. K., 39
Kuykendall, J. A., 17–18
Kvale, S., 127

Lachicotte, W., 109
Ladson-Billings, G., 18, 21, 28, 47, 82, 83, 89, 133
Land, N., 118
Land rights of Indigenous communities, in approach to place-based education, 24, 28–30, 111–112
Latinx. *See* People of Color (POC)
Lave, J., 30–31
Lawashima-Gunsberg, K., 93
Lawrence-Lightfoot, S., 72, 129
Lee, T. S., 28

LeeKeenan, D., 54, 117, 118
Lewis, R. L., 7
Lewis, S., 109
Lexie (preservice teacher), 100, 102–105, 129
Lichter, D. T., 23
Lipman, P., 110
Listening stance, 57, 60, 61, 68, 70–71. *See also* Dialogism
Liston, D., 33, 61
Liu, K., 33, 46, 61
Lough, J., 8, 89, 109
Luna, S. M., 82
Lytle, S. L., 14, 31, 45, 48, 60, 110–113, 117, 131

MacCauley, D., 97–98
Maloch, B., 52, 114
Manbeck, K. E., 10
Mann, E. A., 10
Mardell, B., 61
Marin, A., 29
Marketization, 15
Maryland, 8
Massey, D., 22, 90
Maya (preservice teacher), 42, 51, 94, 96–98, 110–112, 128
Mayville University (pseudonym), 2
    author self-study of teaching practices, 130–131
    5-Year Teacher Education Program, 5–6, 12–13, 57, 87–88, 125–132
    narrative portfolio project. *See* Narrative portfolio project
    place-based teacher education and. *See* Place-based teacher education
McAvoy, P., 93
McCarty, T. L., 28
McDevitt, S. E., 100
McElhinny, B., 8
McHenry-Sorber, E., 30
McInerney, P., 26
McKenzie, M., 23, 28–29, 107, 112
McLaren, P., 12
McTighe, J., 39
McWhorter, L. M., 17–18

Meier, D. R., 61
Memory, 130–131
Mendoza, J. A., 25
Mentor teachers, 42–44, 53, 67, 68–69, 79, 85
Mercado, C., 18
Meritocracy, 4, 11, 12, 87, 104, 105, 131
Merriam, S. B., 126, 131, 132
Mezirow, J., 4, 33
Michael, A., 29
Miller, A. F., 16, 18, 55, 113, 120
Miller, L., 19
Millicent (preservice teacher), 71–73, 129
Milner, R. H., IV, 12
Moffa, E., 30
Moll, L., 18, 47–49, 117, 133
Morewood, A., 19
Moss, P., 15, 29, 32
Mowry, B. N., 21, 109, 119
Mueller, J. J., 5, 9, 14, 48, 53
Murray, J. A., 19

Narrative portfolio project, x, 38–81, 120
  as bridge between parts of community of practice, 31–32
  communities and, 54–55
  contents of portfolios, 46–47
  in context of teacher education program, 38–44
  coursework overview, 49–51
  COVID-19 pandemic and, 55, 62–63, 71–72, 73–77, 126–130
  democratic accountability elements in, 45
  documentation as "visible listening" and, 51–53
  inquiry-based practices and. See Inquiry-based practices
  narrative portfolio as counter-narrative to failure, 44–55
  nature of, 12–13, 21–22
  origins and development of, 5, 13, 44, 46–47
  Phase 1: pre-pandemic, 126
  Phase 2: during the pandemic, 126–130

Portfolio Night, 55
Portrait of Becoming a Teacher, 49, 137–143
  strengths and weaknesses of, 85–86
  transforming ePortfolio into a narrative portfolio, 46–47
  vignettes in, 51–53, 61–80, 89–92
National Association for the Education of Young Children (NAEYC), 93
National Council for Accreditation of Teacher Educators (NCATE), 15, 16–17, 49, 109
National Council for Teacher Quality (NCTQ), 16
National Council for Teachers of English (NCTE), 93
Nation at Risk, A, 38–39
Native Americans. *See also* People of Color (POC)
  Indigenous knowledge, 24, 28–30, 111–112
Natural environment, in approach to place-based education, 24–25
Neff, D., 18, 47, 49, 133
Nelson, N., 118
Neoliberal model of education
  accountability and, 14, 108–109. *See also* Accountability
  audit culture in, 6, 13–16, 18, 131, 132
  "bubble" in education process and, ix, 2–4, 5, 24–25, 29–30, 32, 58, 80, 88, 99, 107, 109
  consumerism and, 9, 11
  globalization trend and, 2–4, 5, 14, 28, 30, 83, 103, 111
  human capital theory and, 2, 3, 10, 28, 108–109
  meritocracy and, 4, 11, 12, 87, 104, 105, 131
  narrative portfolio project vs. *See* Narrative portfolio project
  nature and impact of neoliberalism, ix, x, 2–4, 9–10, 38, 60
  place-based education vs., 4, 11, 13–16, 32–37. *See also* Place-based teacher education

Neoliberal model
of education (*continued*)
  privatization and corporatization in, 8–9
  sample lessons in challenging, 92–99
  silencing of poverty and, 10–11. *See also* Poverty
  standards-based approach in, 5, 8–10, 14–17, 25–27, 38–41, 44, 70, 82, 83, 88–89, 108–109, 115
  strategies for sensing and resisting neoliberal policies, 21–22, 23, 32–37, 46, 48–49, 57, 82, 96. *See also* Place-based teacher education
  as structural problem of education, 9–10
  teachers as "cognitive experts" in, 120–121
  White supremacy and, 10, 11. *See also* Whites/Whiteness
New Jersey, 8, 9
Ng, P. T., 33
Nganga, C., 39, 107
Nieto, S., 13
Nimmo, J., 54, 117, 118
No Child Left Behind (NCLB, 2002), 14, 16, 38–39, 40–41, 94
Noddings, N., 35, 36
Norris, K. C., 11
North Carolina, 8, 9
Nxumalo, F., ix, 3, 60, 101–102, 111

Obama, Barack, 16
O'Hara, K. E., 17
O'Leary, S., 8, 111
Olssen, M., 109
Onward (Aguilar), 92–93
Opportunity gap elimination (Gorski), 21, 47, 48, 65, 82, 84, 133

Paris, D., 25, 26, 30, 47, 133
Patel, L., 104, 116
Patterson, T. M., 93
Payne, Ruby, 43, 84
Pearson Learning, Inc., 17, 29, 30, 111
Pedagogy knowledge, 134–135
Pedagogy of place
  nature of, 25
  principles of, 25
Pelo, A., 85
Pelojoaquin, K., 85
Pence, Mike, 86
People of Color (POC). *See also* Antiracist education
  Black Lives Matter (BLM) movement, 6, 83, 88, 92
  colorblind approach and, 11, 12, 26, 83–84, 96, 110
  Indigenous knowledge, 24, 28–30, 111–112
  White supremacy and, 3, 10, 11, 13, 42–44, 51, 60, 95, 96, 111
Perry, K. H., 49, 74–75
Peters, M. A., 109
Phillips, D. K., 49, 54, 125
Pinar, W. F., 33, 48
Place-based teacher education
  action research in, 49, 53–54, 89–92. *See also* Narrative portfolio project
  approaches to, 22–29
  assessment and accountability in. *See* Accountability
  author positionalities and, 1–2
  author self-study of teaching practices, 130–131
  background for study, 125
  barriers to, 75–80. *See also* Neoliberal model of education
  case study methodology, 125–132
  challenges of connecting places in study, 9–11
  challenges of the teacher education program, 38–44
  change process and, 114–118
  communities of practice in, 30–32, 120
  contexts of, 5, 7–9, 38–44
  critical approach to place in, 29–32, 111–112
  critical friends groups in, 30, 32, 43, 60, 100–105, 120
  decolonizing approach to, 28–29, 60, 102, 110–112, 116, 117–118
  documentation in, 51–53. *See also* Narrative portfolio project

globalization trend and, 2–4, 5, 14, 28, 30, 83, 103, 111
humanizing place-based education in school classrooms, 23–29
lenses for critically reflective practice in, 47–49, 82–83, 133–134. *See also* Inquiry-based practices
listening stance in, 57, 60, 61, 68, 70–71
meaning-making and, 21–22, 29, 34
nature of, ix, 3–4, 11–12
need for, 11–13
neoliberal approach vs., 4, 11, 13–16. *See also* Neoliberal model of education
participant list (pseudonyms), 128–129
place as taken for granted, 105–106
post-graduation, 99–104
potential of, 4–5
practice and policy implications, 107–123
preservice teachers "getting lost" in PDS communities, 58–60, 62, 66, 67, 138
racial justice and. *See* Racial justice
relationships and trustworthiness in, 132
research study years (2015–2021), 5–6, 13, 40–41
school classrooms and mentor teachers in, 42–44, 53, 67, 68–69, 79, 85
social and cultural contexts in, 4–5
standardization vs., 5, 8–10, 14–17, 25–27, 38–41, 44, 70, 82, 83, 88–89, 108–109, 115
strategies for, 21–22, 23, 32–37, 46, 48–49, 57, 82, 96
suggestions for practice, 118–123
teaching as political act and, ix
"10 Characteristics of the Novice Teacher," 12–13, 39, 48, 53, 55, 134–135
transforming teacher education assessment in, 4, 112–118
Play Lady/La Señora Juguetona (Hoffman), 26

Poetics of Space, The (Bachelard), 130
Poole, A., 94, 97
Portfolio project. *See* Narrative portfolio project
Positive deviance, 117–118
Postmodern perspective, 70
Post-positivist evaluation approach, 109–111
Poverty
 deficit perspective and, 42–43, 66–67
 neoliberalism and "at risk" children, 9–10
 in rural West Virginia, 7–8, 60
 silencing of, 10–11
 as structural problem within education, 10–11
Powell, S. K., 105
Power, K., 58, 67, 138
Power-Carter, S., 35
Pragmatic evaluation approach, 109–111
Pratt, M. L., 58
Praxis Performance Assessment of Teachers (PPAT), 17–18, 19, 41, 42, 46, 59, 82, 105
Price, T. A., 14
Privatization, 8
Problem posing/problem solving (Freire), 115
Professional development schools (PDS). *See also* Place-based teacher education
 critical friends and, 30, 32, 43, 60, 100–105, 120
 democratic classroom practices and, 54–55
 establishing, 40
 mentorship and collaboration through, 42–44, 53, 67, 68–69, 79, 85
 nature of, 32
 Teacher Education Coordinators (TECs), 40, 42, 53
Project approach (Helm & Katz), 54
Puckett, K., ix, 34, 66
Purcell-Gates, V., 22, 100
Pyle, R., 60

Quintero, E. P., 53, 100

Race to the Top (RTTT), 16
Racial justice, 82–106. *See also*
    Antiracist education
    Black Lives Matter (BLM)
        movement, 6, 83, 88, 92
    Critical Race Theory (CRT), 82, 86,
        105
    Dark Funds of Knowledge and,
        88–92. *See also* Dark Funds of
        Knowledge
    reverse racism and, 84
    Whitewashing process and, 30, 83,
        88–89, 131
Ramminger, A. E., 101
Ramsey, P., 11, 83–84, 89, 95
*Reaching and Teaching Students in
    Poverty* (Gorski), 21, 48, 84
Reading First, 38–39
Reagan, E. M., 109
Recchia, S. L., 100
*Reclaiming Accountability in Teacher
    Education* (Cochran-Smith et al.),
    16–20, 55, 113, 120
Reece (preservice teacher), 42,
    100–103, 105, 128
Reflection/critical reflection,
    32–34
    in author self-study of teaching
        practices, 130–131
    in narrative portfolio project vignette,
        61–65
    nature of, 23, 32–33
    in A Portrait of Becoming
        assignment, 49, 142–143
    reflection-in-action/reflection-on-
        action, 33
    as strategy for sensing and resisting
        neoliberal policies, 22, 23,
        32–34, 46, 57, 82
Reggio Emilia approach, 32, 54, 61
Reynolds, A. J., 10
Reynolds, J., 95, 98, 145–146
Reznitskaya, A., 47, 133
Richards, S., 108, 109
Richmond, G., 41
Riessman, C. K., 129, 130

Rinaldi, C., 51–52, 54, 61
Rivard, M., 61
Roberts-Holmes, G., 41, 47
Robertson, D. L., 10
Rogoff, B., 4
Roosevelt, Franklin D., 7–8
Rosen, D. C., 10
Ryan, S., 70

Sachs, J., 15, 86, 87
Salazar, M., 41
Saldana, J., 126, 130
Sanchez, J. G., 16, 18, 55, 113, 120
Sandra (teacher educator), 67, 79
Sapon-Shevin, M., 47, 133
Schindel, A., 11, 29
Schneider, B., 8
Schon, D. A., 32, 33, 61
Schonfeld, D., 93
School and Society, The (Dewey), 25
Schoology, 88
School-university partnerships, 19
Schultz, K., 48–49, 60, 66, 68, 69
Schweinhart, L. J., 10
Scott, R. R., 105
Scott, T., 10
Seemiller, C., 40
SeeSaw app, 55, 88
Semali, L., 111
Shagir, L., 19
Sherfinski, Melissa, 2–3, 8, 14, 15, 17,
    19, 24, 34, 38, 42–45, 50, 54, 75,
    86, 89, 104–105, 108, 109, 111,
    118
Simon, N. S., 105
Sinclair, S., 10
Sisk-Hilton, S., 61
Skinner, D., 109
Slattery, P., 33
Sleeter, C., 9, 15, 89, 102–103
Slocum, A., 2–3, 8, 44, 54, 75, 89, 109
Smagorinsky, P., 30
Smith, B., 137
Smith, G. A., 25
Smyth, J., 26
Sobel, D., 2, 24, 25, 68–69
Social constructionism/social
    constructivism, 21, 31, 37

Index

Soja, E. W., 101
Somerville, M. J., 60, 103–104, 117
Sommer, D., 116
Sophie (preservice teacher), 88, 89–92, 101, 129
Sparkes, A. C., 137
Stack, S.F., 8, 59
Stamped: Remix (Reynolds & Kendi), 95, 98, 145–146
Standards-based accountability, 5, 8–10, 14–17, 25–27, 38–41, 44, 70, 82, 83, 88–89, 108–109, 115
Stanford Center for the Assessment of Learning and Equity (SCALE), 17
Stitzlein, S., 93
Stories and storytelling, 26, 28, 31, 117
 A Portrait of Becoming assignment, 49, 137–143
 vignettes in narrative portfolios, 51–53, 61–80, 89–92. *See also* Narrative portfolio project
Strack, G., 29
Stremmel, A. J., 39, 107
Surveillance, 3, 15
Suzukovich, E., 29
Swennen, A., 19

Taguchi, Lenz, 48
TallBear, K., 29
Tammy (teacher), 1–2, 100
Tan, C., 33
Tan, E., 44
Temple, J. A., 10
"10 Characteristics of the Novice Teacher," 12–13, 39, 48, 53, 55, 134–135
Terman, A. R., 103, 105
Thomas, M., 46
Thomson, P., 29
Thorpe, R. J., Jr., 11
Tisdell, E. J., 126, 131, 132
Tolbert, S., 11, 29
Tomorrow's Schools of Education (TSE), 39–40
Transformative learning, 4
Tuck, E., ix, 23, 28–29, 107, 110–112
Tudge, J., 43

Tyler, Ralph, 39, 47
Tyler rationale, 39, 47, 56, 115

U.S. Census Bureau, 7, 8
University of Wisconsin–Madison, 1–2
Urbanormativity trend (Terman), 103, 105

Valenzuela, A., 105
Van Manen, M., 33, 52
Vascellaro, S., 89, 95
Vasquez, V. M., 47, 133
Veracini, L., 130–131
Vygotsky, L. S., 4, 21

War on Poverty, 9–10
Weber, N. B., 19, 118
Weekley, B. S., 2–3, 44, 54, 75
Weikart, D. P., 10
Weinstein, M., 33
Wells, M., 29
Wenger, E., 30–31
West Virginia
 Dark Funds of Knowledge of students and, 89–92
 Mayville University. *See* Mayville University (pseudonym)
 political parties in, 7–8
 rural communities as context for study, ix–x, 1–2, 5–9
West Virginia Department of Education, 17, 27
West Virginia SB 498 ("Creating Anti-racism Act of 2022 Bill"), 87
Wetzel, M. M., 52, 114
Wexler, L. J., ix
What If All the Kids Are White? (Derman-Sparks & Ramsey), 83–84
Whites/Whiteness. *See also* Antiracist education; Racial justice
 "bubble" in education process and, ix, 2–4, 5, 24–25, 29–30, 32, 58, 80, 88, 99, 107, 109
 colorblind approach and, 11, 12, 26, 83–84, 96, 110
Critical Whiteness, 105

Whites/Whiteness (*continued*)
   deficit perspective and, 66–67
   implicit bias and, 2, 10
   neoliberal model of education and, 3, 10, 11–13. *See also* Neoliberal model of education
   pushing back against. *See* Place-based teacher education
   as racial terms, 1
   standardized exam performance and, 18, 41
   of teachers and teacher educators, 7, 29, 30, 82, 83–84, 86, 88–89, 93, 105, 121, 122, 126
   White supremacy and, 3, 10, 11, 13, 42–44, 51, 60, 95, 96, 111
   Whitewashing process, 30, 83, 88–89, 131
Whyte, K. L., 5, 9, 48, 53, 72
Wiggins, G., 39
Williams, D. R., 25
Williams, M. T., 10
Wilson, D., 61
Wisconsin, 1–2, 41, 54, 75, 86
Wren (preservice teacher), 49, 78–80, 95–96, 98, 129
Wynter, S., 96

Yang, K. W., ix
Yazbeck, S., 28, 73, 118
Yendol-Hoppey, D., 19
Yin, R. K., 125
Young, J. C., 87
Young, M. D., 109

Zeichner, K. M., 11, 19, 33, 49, 61
Zembylas, M., 36
Zhang, J., 8, 15, 17, 19, 34, 42–43, 89, 104–105, 108, 109
Zhao, Y., 2
Zini, M., 61
Zipin, L., 88, 122

About the Authors

The author, **Melissa Sherfinski,** has been an educator for more than 30 years, first engaging with place-based education in the pond and woods near Crestwood Elementary School in Madison, Wisconsin, as a preservice teacher, and later as a 4th and 5th grade teacher, kindergarten teacher, and home-based childcare provider. Melissa is currently Associate Professor of Early Childhood and Elementary Education at West Virginia University, where she worked in the 5-Year Teacher Education Program for a decade. She collaborated to infuse social justice education and a praxis orientation into program structures to support preservice teachers' understandings and uses of multiple forms of teacher leadership for social justice aims and to spread "positive deviance" in order to locally disrupt aspects of the neoliberal system that contribute to exclusion, marginalization, and inequalities.

Contributor **Sharon Hayes** has been an educator for more than 30 years in elementary, middle, and university classrooms. Her work in public schools provided experiences in a number of places and she learned, firsthand, how our historical, social, and political conditions contribute to the disparities many of our students and their families experience in our educational system. Her current work, as an Associate Professor of Elementary Education at WVU and former program coordinator for the 5-Year Teacher Education program, have created opportunities for her to work with prospective and practicing teachers to interrogate the status quo and create more equitable and authentic curriculum and instruction. She is particularly interested in how we become educators over the course of our professional careers and how we embrace opportunities to disrupt and transform who we are and the places/spaces in which we live and learn.